ARCHAEOLOGY AND FOLKLORE

THEORETICAL ARCHAEOLOGY GROUP (TAG)

In this series:

ARCHAEOLOGY AND FOLKLORE

edited by
Amy Gazin-Schwartz
and Cornelius Holtorf

London and New York

First published 1999
by Routledge
11 New Fetter Lane, London EC4P 4EE

Simultaneously published in the USA and Canada
by Routledge
29 West 35th Street, New York, NY 10001

Routledge is an imprint of the Taylor & Francis Group

© 1999 Selection and editorial matter,
Amy Gazin-Schwartz and Cornelius J. Holtorf;
individual chapters, the contributors

Typeset in Bembo by The Florence Group, Stoodleigh, Devon
Printed and bound in Great Britain by Biddles Ltd,
Guildford and King's Lynn

British Library Cataloguing in Publication Data
A catalogue record for this book is available from the British Library.

Library of Congress Cataloging in Publication Data
A catalogue record for this book has been requested

ISBN 0-415-20144-6

A reputed Roman road at Henley in West Sussex has recently been proved by excavation to be medieval. A lady living in the locality had occasion to inform her maid of this fact, only to hear – 'Well, miss, it has been a Roman road as long as ever I've known it!'

Cecil Curwen in *Antiquity* 11 (1937): 86

Niels Milan Pedersen, 1990

CONTENTS

ILLUSTRATIONS

CONTRIBUTORS

Emma Blake has recently completed her PhD in archaeology at Cambridge University, studying the spatial arrangement of domestic and funerary architecture in the Sardinian Bronze Age. Her research interests include western Mediterranean prehistory, new approaches to spatial analysis, and the application of social theory to archaeology. Her interest in folklore derives from her encounters with Sardinia's rich local traditions.

Martin Brown is Assistant County Archaeologist for East Sussex. His interests include manifestations of archaeology in popular culture and the role of the historic environment in contemporary society. His involvement in traditional practice includes membership of a Lewes Bonfire society.

Pat Bowen is a professional storyteller and Workshop Leader who tells traditional, personal and original tales – with humour, hope and humanity. Nature inspires her and she brings imagination, research and reflection to her tales on and of the land.

Mats Burström is Associate Professor in Archaeology at Stockholm University. His research interests include general theory, research history, the symbolic dimension of material culture, and archaeology as a socio-political practice in the present. In Burström's studies on the cultural construction of archaeological objects folklore is considered to be essential.

Sara Champion has particular research interests in social and economic organisation in the central European iron age, and in feminist perspectives on the historiography of archaeology. However, her first academic post was at University College, Galway, and it is from that time that her interest in Irish prehistory and early history stems. She now teaches archaeology at the University of Southampton, UK.

John Collis is Professor of European Archaeology in the Department of Archaeology and Prehistory, University of Sheffield, England. His main speciality is in the Iron Age of western Europe, and he has been working in recent years in France and Spain. This has led him into research on the origin of the concept of the Celts, and how this has affected our interpretations of archaeological data, especially in Britain.

Gabriel Cooney teaches at the Department of Archaeology, University College, Dublin.

Kathryn Denning will be completing her PhD at the University of Sheffield's Department of Archaeology and Prehistory in mid-1999. Her research in the history, philosophy, and sociology of archaeology focuses on the problems of archaeology and alterity, particularly questions about popular narratives involving the past.

Amy Gazin-Schwartz completed her PhD in Anthropology at the University of Massachusetts, specializing in folklore and archaeology in Scotland and New England. Her thesis explores how people use folklore and archaeology to create meaningful pasts in Scotland. She is currently Visiting Instructor in Anthropology at Assumption College in Massachusetts.

Miranda Green, Professor of Archaeology and Director of SCARAB Research Centre, University of Wales College, Newport. Research interests are mainly in Iron Age and Roman studies. Particular interests include the archaeology of ritual practice, the metaphoric significance of iconography, and folklore issues such as resonances of the past in storytelling.

Uta Halle holds a Doctorate in Archaeology and has been a fellow of the Deutsche Forschungsgemeinschaft (1991–1992) and the Ministry for Research and Science in Nordrhein-Westfalen, Germany (1993–1996). Her research is concerned with pottery of the seventeenth–nineteenth centuries, and with the role of archaeology during the Third Reich.

Ingunn Holm, Hedmark County Administration, Hamar, Norway. Main research interest is Iron Age and medieval farming practices and land use, especially the use of forest areas. Folklore interest is the study of eighteenth-century traditions concerning various beings connected to the forest and the ancient monuments found there.

Cornelius Holtorf is currently a STINT Visiting Scholar at the Institute of Archaeology, University of Gothenburg, Sweden. Among his main research interests are the various meanings of archaeological finds and sites for different people at different times, including those reflected in popular culture and traditions.

Robert Layton, Professor, Department of Anthropology, University of Durham. Research interests include social change and social evolution, art, indigenous rights. Regional interests are France (rural communities) and Australia (indigenous communities). In folklore he is interested in oral tradition, especially in Australia.

Lynn Meskell is Assistant Professor in the Department of Anthropology at Columbia University. She was previously Research Fellow at New College,

Oxford University. Her recent volumes include *Archaeology Under Fire* (1998, Routledge) and *Archaeologies of Social Life: Age, Sex, Class, etc. In Ancient Egypt* (1999, Blackwell).

Julia Murphy is currently based in Oxford, training to be an English teacher, and simultaneously completing an MPhil in the Department of Archaeology at the University of Wales, Lampeter on 'Writing Prehistory – Archaeology, Discourse, Evidence'. She hopes to keep alive her dual interests in literature and archaeology.

Martin Schmidt has directed the Archaeological Open-air Museum at Oerling-hausen, Germany, since 1993. His research interests include experimental archaeology, in particular the reconstruction of prehistoric houses, also the fields of archaeology and the public, and archaeology and education.

David Shankland is trained as a Social Anthropologist and has conducted extensive fieldwork in rural Turkey. His interest in archaeology derives from a three-year spell as Assistant and Acting Director at the British Institute of Archaeology at Ankara. Now he lectures in the Anthropology Department of the University of Wales Lampeter and continues to research at Çatalhöyük.

James Symonds is an Historical Archaeologist and Executive Director of Archaeological Research and Consultancy at the University of Sheffield. He is currently undertaking research in the Outer Hebrides of Scotland and Nova Scotia investigating the nineteenth century Highland Clearances and the social impact of the Scottish diaspora.

John Staeck is Assistant Professor of Anthropology at College of DuPage in Illinois. His research interests focus on the later prehistory of the mid-western United States. His interests in folklore centre around the way in which it functions to help define and negotiate identity, and how these are manifest in material culture.

Diura Thoden van Velzen explored Etruscan funerary ritual in a PhD (1995) at Cambridge University, leading her to discover the polemics of Etruscan myths, past and present. A fellowship at the Warburg Institute (1996) provided further research opportunities. She currently focuses on Cambridgeshire's archaeology as Scheduling Officer for English Heritage.

PART I

ARCHAEOLOGY AND FOLKLORE STUDIES

CHAPTER ONE

'AS LONG AS EVER I'VE KNOWN IT . . .'

On folklore and archaeology

AMY GAZIN-SCHWARTZ AND CORNELIUS HOLTORF

ABSTRACT

In this introductory chapter, we will consider questions of history, historical accuracy and meaning in formulating new relationships between archaeology and folklore. How do archaeology and folklore, in their broadest senses, differ in constructing ideas about the past? How have these differences arisen historically in different places, and how have archaeologists used or referred to folklore in previous studies? What roles might folklore play in an interpretive archaeology, which focuses on the meanings of the past in the past and in the present?

CONSTRUCTING THE PAST IN FOLKLORE AND ARCHAEOLOGY

Everyone concerned with the past – archaeologist, historian, politician, storyteller, priest, parent – constructs ideas and images of the past from materials available in the present. Through these ideas and images, we invest meaning in past events; but these meanings may differ according to our perspectives. We view the past through the lenses of the present; indeed, people have probably always done so. Archaeology and folklore are two of the many lenses through which the past is given meaning, and it is the aim of this volume to explore and understand differences and similarities in how archaeology and folklore create, and are created through, ideas about the past. In the intersections between these similarities and differences, we hope to find new lenses, through which we can begin to create alternative images of people's histories. The papers that follow will explore the meanings people attach to the past, or to artefacts associated with the past. They will demonstrate the value of developing a dialogue between different systems of meaning. What aspects of the past, time, material culture are remembered, retold in folklore, and made meaningful in popular culture? How may such memories, stories and practices inform archaeological interpretations?

We do not seek to define a new field, folklore and archaeology (comparable to zooarchaeology or ethnoarchaeology); rather, we have set out to explore the possibilities of developing an interdisciplinary dialogue, and making this dialogue fruitful to the future development of both disciplines. In contrast to a common archaeological practice of borrowing methods, models or data from another field, we want to open a discourse between the fields, believing that a conversation about the many methods, models and sets of data that already exist in the two disciplines will enrich both, by creating new approaches to thinking about common questions, and indeed by raising new questions. The wide range of authors and approaches in our volume gives an indication of the diverse realms this dialogue may address. The multiple ways in which the connections between archaeology and folklore may serve, stimulate or trouble archaeology reveal the potential for a dialogue at the interface of the two fields.

In our introduction, we will briefly review some of the historical background for a study of folklore and archaeology, outlining the origins of both fields of study in a common antiquarian background and tracing the divergence of the two fields over the past century. We will then outline several lines of inquiry through which a study of folklore can enrich and broaden archaeological constructions of the past. First, we will deal with questions about historical accuracy, which lie at the heart of archaeologists' worries about the reliability of folklore as evidence or data for archaeological interpretation. We will argue that this concern is based on limited views of both folklore evidence and more conventional archaeological evidence. Next we will address the value of folklore for understanding the history of monuments and the multiple meanings those monuments carry throughout their histories. Finally, we will give a brief overview of other areas where attention to folklore can inform archaeological interpretation and practice: issues of time, of identity, of the politics and sociology of archaeology as a discipline, and of the relationships between academic archaeology and the public. These issues do not define the limits of the dialogue between archaeology and folklore; we merely set them out as first steps in demonstrating the value of these connections.

Our thinking is grounded in four key convictions about archaeology, folklore and the creation of history, which we share with most of the authors of subsequent chapters.

First, our arguments are not based in the belief that folklore contains accurate and reliable representations of past behaviour, beliefs or events. The reliability of folklore for historical information has been, as we will discuss further below, the subject of often contentious argument. Our approach seeks to move beyond this problem. Folklore is not the only field where a concern with historical accuracy is problematic; archaeology too gives us the past as perceived and interpreted by present people. Neither field can be relied upon to tell us about the actual past. Folklore does give us a broader understanding of the past as perceived, remembered, and made significant by both past and present people.

Second, we are interested in what monuments and other archaeological objects meant (and mean) to people in their respective lifeworlds and how they were (and are) used in the formation of collective identities. In this context, the antiquity of a particular element of folklore is less important than its significance for interpreting meaning. As interpretive archaeologies have come to understand, the past is a creation of everyone who interprets material remains or fragments of tradition from past people's lives, whether in the form of folklore or archaeological study. This past can be crucial for people's understanding of the cultural landscape and their identities therein. Where these identities and different approaches to the past conflict, it is important to develop ways of establishing a dialogue among them.

These problems of accuracy and meaning are fundamental to the history of archaeological uses of folklore. Previously, when archaeologists attempted to apply folklore to archaeological materials, they often found that folk tradition and archaeological remains did not match. Rather than simply rejecting folklore as unreliable and inaccurate, several authors in the book deal with these problems and find that, when folklore is analysed (as archaeological materials have to be analysed), it sometimes does provide plausible interpretation for those materials, whether or not they can prove unbroken continuity of transmission.

Finally, archaeological approaches to sites and monuments most frequently focus on the time of their construction and intensive use. However, visible monuments have life histories as well, extending from their construction up until the present. Folklore reflects some of the later interpretations of prehistoric sites, and contemporary folklore constitutes one important part of present-day understandings of monuments. It thus supplements recent concerns about the role and interpretation of the past in the present, which have mainly focused on various aspects of 'managed' heritage.

It will be argued throughout this book that folklore is valuable to archaeologists because it offers us alternative ideas about the past that counter our tendency to portray everyone in all time as versions of ourselves, and because it provides knowledge about the continued importance and therefore the later history of archaeological monuments.

DEFINITIONS

To begin, we should introduce definitions – not because the terms we are using are difficult to understand, but because they are subject to public and academic assumptions. We need to make clear what we will be concerned with in this book.

The term 'folklore' usually encompasses both a field of study and the subject matter of that study. In the past, folklore was commonly understood as the traditions and beliefs of a people below the level of 'high culture' (after Newall 1980: xv). This limited definition encompassed things like fairy and other folk tales, place names, and regular ceremonies and rituals. However, we wish our definition to be as broad as possible, to include not only traditional oral literature and rituals, but also all material culture, social customs and artistic performances associated with a group of people. This broad definition follows the ideas of contemporary folklorists who recognise that all groups of people maintain many different kinds of traditions, and define themselves through these traditional practices (see also Newall 1980: xv).

This definition is close to the current German understanding of *Volkskunde*, including whatever is significant in popular culture and people's everyday lives, with open boundaries to both sociology and (European) ethnology (see Bausinger *et al.* 1978; Brednich 1988). In Germany, folklore studies (*Volkskunde*) have a long tradition; since the 1960s, they have focused on the empirical study of culture as a whole, both contemporary and historical. Culture is understood in a very wide sense, including virtually everything that was part of the way people lived (and live) their everyday lives. *Volkskundler*, like social/cultural anthropologists, are concerned with how people use material culture, how they act and treat each other, what they believe and think, what they say, how they speak, and what they do, at home, at work or in their spare time, among other things. The past (as tradition, remains or understanding) is then seen not as something which has simply survived and lives on somehow in the present, but as a meaningful and functioning part of a given culture. Ancient elements of a culture may or may not be of great age, but this does not affect their social and cultural significance.

For us, archaeology encompasses the academic study of the past through interpretation of its material remains. Because individuals living in the past had multiple perceptions, understandings and experiences, and because the same can be said for people in the present, we view archaeology as an endeavour open to multiple approaches and perspectives (as outlined by Shanks and Hodder 1995). The goal of archaeology is not to reconstruct the one true past, but to develop rich and sensitive interpretations, in order to make the past intelligible in the present. Many such interpretations and understandings of the past are possible.

HISTORICAL PERSPECTIVES

Both archaeologists and folklorists trace the origins of their disciplines to the works of antiquarians in the sixteenth to nineteenth centuries, but they view antiquarians through different lenses (for detailed accounts of the history of archaeology and of folklore studies respectively, see Bahn 1996; Daniel 1980, 1981; Dorson 1968b; Newall 1980; Trigger 1989). Archaeologists focus on antiquarian recording of archaeological monuments – Stukeley's detailed drawings of Avebury, or Inigo Jones' and Stukeley's plans of Stonehenge before some of the stones had fallen – as examples of antiquarian concern with material culture and monuments of prehistoric Britain. They see this concern prefiguring archaeological interests in these same aspects of the past (Ucko *et al.* 1991).

Folklorists, on the other hand, are more likely to note the same antiquarians' descriptions of 'popular antiquities', which included traditions, legends, tales, sayings, proverbs, songs and activities. Antiquarians themselves rarely distinguished between observing ancient material relics and recording 'relics' of ancient practices or beliefs in the form of folk rituals and tales. They viewed the latter as 'sharing with material remains the same character of misshapen fragments surviving from a bygone day' (Fenton 1993: 7).

These fragments, both material and oral, are viewed by antiquarians, folklorists and archaeologists alike as fast disappearing relics of the past (see, for example, Bruford and Macdonald 1994; A. Carmichael 1928; Henderson [1879] 1967; Macpherson 1768; Thoms [1846] 1965; preservation legislation). This tradition of the threat to heritage materials follows on antiquarians' convictions that they were preserving information about the nature of the 'vulgar' people, reflecting the original cultures, character and histories of their nations (Wright [1846] 1968: 41). Whenever relics of the past have been recorded, they have been thought to be in imminent danger of being lost for all time. With regard to folklore, however, we agree with those who have argued that this concern is largely based on a misunderstanding of its character:

> Folklore is not a phenomenon that is dying out or decaying or showing any signs of being in a decline . . . Certainly it ages, and one part of it and then another may die off. But it is also capable of breeding; it grows, it spreads, it feeds on other matter, and it has the greatest ability to adapt to changing circumstances.
>
> (Opie and Opie 1980: 68)

Archaeological sites, too, were threatened by destruction, through development and agricultural intensification. Antiquarians, and later archaeologists, therefore recorded them as comprehensively as they could, in some cases knowing that their records were likely to be all that future generations of archaeologists would have. For example, on the island of Rügen in Germany only 54 megalithic monuments are preserved today; archaeological research makes the most of Friedrich von Hagenow's map and description from 1829, when 236 megaliths were still known (Schuldt 1972: 10, 16–18). Archaeological concern with preservation and recording continues today, through the practices of cultural resource (heritage) management (CRM) and through other surveys like those conducted by the Association of Certificated Field Archaeologists on the island of Raasay, Scotland (see for example Macdonald and Wood 1997).

Defining new fields: folklore and archaeology in the nineteenth century

In the nineteenth century, the fields of archaeology and folklore began to define themselves as separate academic disciplines, in contrast to each other and to the antiquarianism from which they evolved. In 1846 William Thoms proposed the term folklore to replace what had been termed popular antiquities or popular literature (Thoms [1846] 1965: 4–5). Wilhelm H. Riehl, professor for cultural history in Munich, argued as early as 1859 that *Volkskunde* should be considered an independent discipline. When the British Folk-Lore Society was founded in 1878, it defined its objectives as 'the preservation and publication of Popular Traditions, Legendary ballads, Local Proverbial Sayings, Superstitions, and Old Customs . . . and all subjects relating to them' (Folk-Lore Society 1878: viii). On the archaeological side, a chair of archaeology was created in Leiden in 1818, and John Disney founded a professorship of archaeology at Cambridge University in 1851. Both positions were devoted to classical or Egyptian archaeology, antiquities and fine arts.

In the process of this self-definition, archaeology became the realm of physical monuments and material remains of the past, while folklore focused on verbal performances and customary activities, including the uses of material culture. There remained institutional similarities in the early development of the two fields. In many regions of Europe, both archaeology and folklore studies began with questionnaires sent by a national institution to the provinces, asking for information about locally known monuments or folk tales. In this way, national inventories were established that laid the basis for much future research and are still important today. One example of an inventory of this kind, which deals with the interface between archaeology and folklore, is the *Corpus du Folklore Préhistorique en France et dans les Colonies Françaises*, compiled by Paul Saintyves (pseudonym of Émile Nouvre) for the *Societé du Folklore Français* in three volumes, 1934–1936.

Outside Europe, the situation was slightly different. In the Americas, European settlers encountered indigenous peoples who maintained oral traditions about their origins and histories (Trigger 1989: 120–126). From the time of European settlement, the study of American prehistory was closely connected with ethnology, conducted under the Bureau of Ethnology, and charged with recording customs and remains of peoples who were seen to be disappearing. Any observable expressions of complexity, as in the mounds of the Ohio River valley or Mexican temples, were attributed to migrations from more civilised areas, even from Egypt or Mesopotamia. When population movements were not evident, ethnologists and archaeologists believed that the activities, material culture and social organisation observed in the nineteenth century were identical with those that existed in the past (Trigger 1989; Zumwalt 1988). Native peoples thus had no history (Wolf 1992), and for the most part were expected to have only a very short future.

In the context of a belief that there was no great antiquity to Native presence in America, folklore, oral history, and information about traditional religion and ritual were not regarded as significant for Native American history: people who do not change don't have a history. Folklore and other ethnological data were rather the expression of timeless and universal behaviours, and could be relevant, not for Native American history, but as sources for the kinds of beliefs and practices followed by prehistoric people everywhere.

Folklore and archaeology in the twentieth century

The history of archaeological practice in this century has led to increasing distancing of the field from folklore (see also Burström, this volume, chapter 3). As archaeology acquired techniques for excavation, dating, sampling and materials analysis from other sciences, archaeologists developed theoretical approaches that sought to follow the empirical practices of those sciences. Folklore studies, on the other hand, moved from treating folklore as a historical artefact, to classifying and describing folk genres and behaviours, and then to analytical approaches which drew from anthropological, psychological and literary studies to understand the cultural, behavioural and literary significance of the creation and transmission of folk material (see, for example, Dorson 1961; Dundes 1965; Georges and Jones 1995; Zumwalt 1988 for discussions of the development of folklore studies).

As divorced as the two fields of folklore studies and archaeology have become, there have always been individuals who maintained an interest in both. Scholars such as Paul Saintyves (1934–6), Horst Ohlhaver (1937), Karel C. Peeters (1969) and Leslie Grinsell (1976) collected and discussed the folklore of prehistoric sites in different countries. They built on the work of many others who had previously recorded and published popular customs and beliefs associated with prehistoric monuments such as chambered tombs, stone circles and standing stones in regional journals such as the British journal *Folk-Lore* (later *Folklore*) or in monographs.

The general connections between archaeology and folklore studies have also been discussed. In 1969, the Dutch folklorist Karel C. Peeters published in the first part of his study on *Volkskunde en Archeologie* an overview of the existing contacts between the fields and their intellectual background within the history of folklore studies. Among important earlier theoretical papers are, in particular, two lectures by Herbert J. Fleure, entitled 'Archaeology and Folk Tradition' (1931) and 'Archaeology and Folklore' (1948). They share an outlook which we will discuss in the next section, that of focusing on folklore as the product of a long unbroken tradition and thus an important source of knowledge about prehistory. In Germany in 1933, F. Boehm gave a lecture on *Archäologie und Volkskunde* in which he even argued (pp. 388–389) that the aim of *Volkskunde* was to infer from folklore a people's natural and intuitive way of thinking and acting, which would allow archaeologists to interpret ancient artefacts of the same people.

In 1951 Clark argued that a study of folklore could provide information on how artefacts were made and utilized, and he used information about peasant technologies in writing *Prehistoric Europe: The Economic Basis* (1954). Estyn Evans in Ireland (1957) and Grant in Scotland (1961) similarly connected ancient and recent technologies, assuming, with Clark, that contemporary peasant subsistence practices and technology provided suitable analogies for prehistoric activities in the same regions. American folklorists and historical archaeologists have also considered material culture as important points of connection between folklore and archaeology (see Glassie 1977; and Symonds, chapter 8).

A third topic at the interface between folklore and archaeology which attracted some interest in both fields was the folklore of prehistoric stone tools. The monographs by Emile Cartailhac on *L'age de Pierre dans les Souvenirs et Superstitions Populaires* (1877) and by Christian Blinkenberg on *The Thunderweapon in Religion and Folklore. A Study in Comparative Archaeology* (1911) are probably still the best studies of folk views of these ancient artefacts.

More recent studies of the connections between folklore and archaeology, however, have been notably different and asked a different set of questions. In her doctoral dissertation in *Volkskunde*, entitled *Neolithische Megalithgräber in Volksglauben und Volksleben* (1986), Claudia Liebers studied the role of megaliths in popular beliefs and everyday life in its own right, including effects on the preservation of monuments and their significance in the contemporary tourism industry. Jerome Voss (1987) dealt with changing cultural values in archaeological folklore. Like Voss, Wolfgang Seidenspinner (1988, 1989, 1993) also looked at the folklore of archaeological sites from new angles and emphasised the common features of folklore and archaeology in their respective interpretations. Most recently, Burström, Winberg and Zachrisson published in 1996 an account of the prehistoric monuments in the landscape of Österrekarne in Sweden, their folklore and present meanings, and the history of antiquarian and archaeological studies of these monuments. They argued that the changing meanings of monuments through the ages together give them their 'cultural value'. Archaeologists and folklorists can work together by incorporating local folk tales into public interpretation of archaeological sites, both gaining perspective and eliciting local interest in preserving these sites (see Brown and Bowen, chapter 17; Champion and Cooney, chapter 13).

FOLKLORE AS A SOURCE FOR THE STUDY OF (PRE-)HISTORY: PROBLEMS OF RELIABILITY

In considering the relationships between folklore and history, both folklorists and historians have long debated questions about the historical accuracy of traditional accounts. Do traditional stories encompass 'true' histories of past events, or do they represent survivals of ancient rituals? Are they, instead, unreliable as sources of history because they have been subject to influence of succeeding events and changes; or are they simply recent inventions? (See, for example, Bausinger and Brückner 1969; Dorson 1968a, 1976; Hobsbawm and Ranger 1983; Joyner 1989; Shils 1981). However, Joyner argued that a discussion of whether folklore arises from actual historical events involves

> a persistent delusion that if folklore did not arise from actual historical situations then clearly folklore was unreliable for the study of history and history was irrelevant to the study of folklore.
>
> (Joyner 1989: 11)

He contends that history and folklore are necessarily joined, that historical events cannot be fully understood without understanding the 'attitudes and actions of real men and women' that are found in folklore, and that folklore can't be fully understood without understanding the historical circumstances of its creation and transmission (Joyner 1989: 18).

Contemporary folklorists recognise that folklore is the active and creative aspect of tradition, and that change is important in the creation of folklore (Bronner 1992: 4). It could be added that folklore itself can become a powerful historical force (Davidson 1974). We will return to this question of the relationships between folklore and history later, after we review some research that assumed folklore did contain historical truths.

Folklore as relic

If oral narratives, fairy tales or rituals were based on some actual historical event or activity, their study opened a whole new avenue for gaining knowledge about the prehistoric human past. This admittedly exciting prospect proved very seductive. It has led scholars over the years to some amazing claims, especially after Heinrich Schliemann proved correct his (naive) belief in the accuracy of Homer's account of the Trojan War, even though the story had not been written down for almost half a millennium. If that was the case in the *Iliad* then why not elsewhere? Stuart Piggott, among others, argued that memories from the building of the stone circle at Stonehenge during the third millennium BC survived in Geoffrey of Monmouth's account *Historia Regum Britanniae*, written about AD 1136 (Piggott 1941: 319). Herbert Fleure and others speculated that the Christian cult at Santiago de Compostela in Spain owes much 'to traditions of the megalithic culture' (Fleure 1931: 17). Both refer to the *Iliad*! Likewise, Canon MacCulloch came to the conclusion that the fairy tradition 'may go back to the hostile relations existing between Paleolithic and Neolithic groups' (*c.* 1932: 375). Otto Huth (1950) and August Nitschke (1978) shared the view that some of Grimm's fairy tales actually reflect 'pre-indoeuropean megalithic culture' (Huth 1950: 13). Similarly, Hans Trümpy (1968) discussed the possible memory of the Roman cult of the goddess Isis in Swiss folklore and concluded that, if not Isis, the Roman occupation as such is almost certainly remembered in place names. Deena Bandhu Pandey recently announced (1989) that an Indian source of the eleventh century AD contains information about life in the Neolithic. Kurt Ranke, the famous German folklorist, reminded us of various cases in which archaeological excavations of prehistoric monuments seem to have confirmed astonishing details of legends associated with these sites (Ranke 1969: 106–110). A list of similar cases could be continued almost endlessly.

Here is not the place for a detailed review of the validity of such individual hypotheses. It is worth noting that, although the assumption that folklore contains relics of past activities is still strong in much popular literature (for example, Bord and Bord 1990), these hypotheses are hardly of much concern in recent folklore research or in fact archaeology (see Davidson 1963; Opie and Opie 1980; Seidenspinner 1988, 1993). There are many reasons for this professional scepticism.

Folklore as invention

On the level of source criticism, is it a genuine folk tradition if you can find a story told printed in a novel by Sir Walter Scott? Scott certainly claimed his sources were authentic folk traditions; but contemporary folklorists usually are disappointed to find that their informants only know stories from Scott, or another antiquarian novelist. Among German folklorists, this phenomenon is known as folklorism, a term used to describe 'the presentation of folk culture at second-hand' (Hans Moser, cited after Newall 1980: xxv). Folkloristic phenomena do not exist as remnants of the innermost core of a people's culture; they are adopted for a particular reason: economic interests in tourism, entertainment, or a particular political agenda (see also Thoden van Velzen, chapter 12).

Similarly, some folklore can be proved to be of relatively recent origin. The Christmas tree as we know it is not older than the second half of the sixteenth century, at best (Bausinger 1994: 112). Other folk practices, like Up-Helly-A, or traditions like clan tartans have been shown to be recent 'inventions', or at least recent recreations of older traditions (Davidson 1969: 177–178; Trevor-Roper 1983).

As far as time depth is concerned, it is one thing for archaeologists, historians and folklorists to accept that stories about nineteenth-century Scottish Highland clearances or Native American encounters with European-Americans moving west may represent historically accurate oral tradition. Such stories may give archaeologists clues about the locations of deserted settlements, for example, or the names of the people who once lived in these settlements. They may even serve to enliven our understanding of the daily lives of these people. In these ways, stories about the relatively recent past serve for archaeologists as historical documents, filling the same role that literature or deeds or diaries may fill (Symonds, chapter 8; see also Mackay 1990; Spector 1993). For most archaeologists, it is another thing altogether to consider a continuous tradition from the much more distant past of prehistory, which would allow us to use folklore as a (pre-)historical source.

In the instances when archaeologists could investigate the historical accuracy of folklore evidence, they were often disappointed. For example, in the early days of archaeological and ethnographic interest in the Pueblo peoples of the American Southwest, people attempted to correlate contemporary Pueblo origin myths with the locations and physical evidence of older Anasazi sites on the Colorado Plateau (for example, Fewkes 1893). The myths didn't always – or even often – match very well, and the attempts at correlation were later considered a waste of time.

Accuracy and interpretation

As Bendix (1997) has argued, this concern with authenticity and accuracy should itself be historically situated. The issue of whether folklore is 'authentic' – in terms of being actual oral tradition, or historically accurate in what it records, or even in terms of the accuracy of its recording and transmission – is intimately tied to the development of the academic disciplines of folklore and anthropology. Concerns with authenticity were strongly influenced both by desires to legitimate the disciplines, and by the nationalist aims of much early research in these fields.

Beyond these issues, the ongoing concern with accuracy and the expectation that folk tradition should agree with archaeological observations betray a rather naive use of those stories. Stories are not necessarily meant to be taken literally. Origin myths are told in mythological language, which is symbolic and interpretive. They reveal not so much facts about the past, as the significance of the past. It is thus more appropriate to look to the stories for meaning than for facts. It is this meaningfulness of the story which ensures its transmission, not its historical accuracy (Thompson 1988: 113). And, when meaning is taken as the most significant aspect of folklore, the question of its authenticity becomes moot: if it has become part of the folk tradition about the past, it is part of that tradition whether or not its origins are in literature or commercial invention.

Further, because meaningful stories are likely to be transmitted more accurately, we may, in exceptional circumstances, find within them accurate information about very old practices – information about the uses of material culture, about the conduct of daily activities, and about the meaning of features on the landscape. Our problem today is that we cannot be sure which particular feature in a given folklore may indeed be 'old'. But why does this matter? What matters more socially is what people *understand* to be old and hence give the meaning of being 'ancient'. As with material culture and historical documents, we should seek to understand the significance of folklore for constructing the past (Seidenspinner 1993).

Folklore cannot be accepted on face value as portraying factual truths about the past. But neither can it be rejected as false. Like other items of culture, folklore speaks with many voices, and accrues over its history aspects of each phase of that history (Bronner 1992: 3–4). Acknowledging the historical dimensions of items of folklore can allow us to develop analytical approaches to their use as historical sources. As many problems as there are with assuming the antiquity of folklore, it is well established that oral traditions can be very conservative and indeed preserve the memory of certain events or practices over very long time periods (see Blench and Spriggs 1997: part IV; Vansina 1985) The value of such traditions in understanding African and Polynesian history has been demonstrated by Vansina (1985), Tonkin (1992), Friedman (1992) and others. Even in Europe, traditions may preserve memory or knowledge of past events. So, the folk tradition that a stone wall on the island of Skye covers the bodies of those killed in one of the last clan battles in the seventeenth century is confirmed by the archaeological discovery of skeletal remains eroding from under the wall (M. Wildgoose, personal communication, 1997).

Folklorists and oral historians have developed methodological standards which elements of folklore have to fulfil in order to justify any claim that they are indeed ancient (Davidson 1963; Gerndt 1981: 160–167; Thompson 1988; Trümpy 1968; Vansina 1985). Under certain circumstances, modern archaeologists too have referred to folklore as an independent source for knowledge about the past (see Holm, chapter 14; Staeck, chapter 5). Furthermore, archaeologists may feel justified in employing oral tradition and folklore as a factor in the past which helps explain certain peculiarities of the archaeological and/or historical record (Green, chapter 4; see also Fleming 1988: 118–120).

The junctures between folklore and history – and between folklore and prehistory – are located in the experiences of people. If we are interested in understanding not only what happened and when, but how events were experienced by people participating in them and remembered by their descendants, folklore may prove a valuable source indeed. Folk-lore may also be valuable if we want to know how these memories influenced the creation, preservation and destruction of monuments in landscapes.

FOLKLORE AS ANOTHER WAY OF UNDERSTANDING TIME AND ANCIENT MONUMENTS

Once we understand that folklore, like other cultural materials, tells us about culture only after we have analysed and interpreted its meaning, we can explore the realms of meaning folklore opens to archaeologists. When folklore is widely defined and encompasses popular culture as a whole, it can make a valuable contribution to an archaeology that is truly interpretive and interested in understanding the meanings of the past and its remains (not only) in our age. Instead of looking at the folklore of prehistoric sites only to understand their original significance in prehis-tory, folklore also gives us the opportunity to study the meanings of these monuments in later societies and in the present. A study of folklore will raise questions about the particular character of the past in general, and of ancient artefacts in particular; about their roles in a given social context; and about social practices that are carried out in relation to such monu-ments (see also Layton, chapter 2).

Archaeology is mightily concerned with time, as is shown by the enor-mous significance of both absolute and relative dating in the discipline (see also Burström, chapter 3). Folklore is not unconcerned with time, and doesn't deny the passage of time. Indeed, accounts are often prefaced by the assertion that 'it used to be like this, but it isn't anymore'. Yet, time within folk stories is often very different from time within archae-ological stories.

Fairy stories offer the best examples of one kind of time we may find in folklore. Typically in fairy stories, especially stories centred on features of the landscape such as mounds or circles, a human is enticed into the world of the fairies by fine music, appetising food, beautiful sights. The human spends what seems to be a short time with the fairies, dancing, singing or playing music, enjoying himself (more rarely herself) immensely. Meanwhile, back in his own part of the world (space is another problem to be dealt with), his friends are searching high and low for him. At long last, he is discovered, either just inside the fairy mound, or sleeping or wandering around the hills. He thinks he's been out all night at a party; everyone else thinks he's been away for years. Time in folklore moves differently from time in our world: it can stand still, or move faster, or even move forward and backward.

On the other hand, Nicolaisen (1980) points out that there are different levels of time in folklore. There is this timeless or outside-of-normal time which frames stories: 'once upon a time'. But within stories, events are often sequential, and expressed in very human terms; things happen over the course of a day or a week. Nicolaisen argues that this enfolding of everyday time within eternal time both connects the audience with the intimate and accessible events of the story, and makes accessible the timelessness of eternity (Nicolaisen 1980: 317).

What does this mean for archaeologists? It means that there is more than one way to think of time. It also means that some of our monuments are the exact places where time is different. Burial mounds, to archaeologists, belong to the period in which they were constructed and used. They are Neolithic, or Bronze Age. Sometimes, they were re-used by later peoples as shown in secondary burials. For archaeologists, the mounds usually have one function – burial – and one or maybe two finite time periods. In folklore, these mounds are outside of time. They belong to no one time, but to alternative time, where life goes on at a different pace. Further, as the focus of folk stories, mounds become places where that alternative time becomes accessible to ordinary people, although such sites remain distant and removed from the everyday (see also Brown and Bowen, chapter 17). By this means, they maintain their significance in the landscape whether or not they are used for burial, whether or not anyone knows that they were once used for burial. The fact that cairns are often the location of entrances to the Otherworld may also argue for continued local knowledge of their original function. Indeed, we might dare ask whether the mounds exist in the form they do, not as burial places, but as entrances to the Otherworld, which are certainly appropriate places to lay the dead.

Attention to folklore allows archaeologists to consider these ideas, not as truths about continuity of practice over thousands of years, but as entrances to interpretations we might not otherwise consider. It offers us ways to understand how people, both in the past and in the present experience historical landscapes. It makes it possible for us to imagine in new ways, to see how meaning is actively created, maintained and re-created. And it forces us to recognise the ongoing significance of monuments.

As folklore belongs to all the times through which it has passed, so too archaeological sites and artefacts belong to all the times following their building or manufacture. If we are interested in what monuments mean, it is our task as archaeologists to study the complete history of monuments rather than restrict our interest to the motivations that led to their first construction (Holtorf 1998). Prehistoric monuments such as megaliths have been interpreted and dealt with in many different ways after they were built in prehistory. These interpretations and uses can be reflected in the folklore of archaeological sites (see Burström *et al.* 1996; Roymans 1995).

Ancient monuments have in many cases led to the emergence of folk tales and legends which would explain why they existed by creating a narrative context in which they had meaning. The enduring monuments themselves later became seen as the physical proof of such aetiological stories. This phenomenon has been described as 'feedback' of a monument to the local body of folklore (Vansina 1985: 157). In the twentieth century too, novel popular interpretations of ancient monuments have emerged under labels such as 'archaeoastronomy', explaining them in the light of modern astronomy and computer technology (Schmidt and Halle, chapter 11; Seidenspinner 1989: 36–39; Voss 1987: 86–87).

Yet this continuing importance of monuments as points of reference in the cultural landscape is often a neglected part of archaeological research. 'Intrusive' elements of later (or earlier) periods may be ignored, or mentioned in passing without playing a part in the interpretation of an excavated monument. Folklore illuminates this ongoing cultural construction of the meanings of monuments and the landscape.

FOLKLORE AND THE POLITICS OF ARCHAEOLOGY

Collective identity

It has often been shown that traditions are very important in defining and maintaining the collective identities of human communities. Such communities can be either geographical (e.g. village, region, nation) or social (e.g. age, profession, company), but in each case people would share a set of particular traditions such as a language or dialect, place names, nicknames, skills, customs, beliefs, and symbols such as a coat of arms or a particular building (see Symonds, chapter 8). The regional sense of belonging in particular (the German *Heimat*) has been discussed in connection with regional folklore and folk life (Köstlin and Bausinger 1980; Widdowson 1980).

Such collective identities are often connected with the folklore of archaeological sites (Voss 1987: 85). This is very evident at the level of villages, where the inhabitants are proud of 'their' monuments. But the whole heritage industry too, which often has strong national connotations, can be seen as an example of the significance of ancient sites in modern communities (Lowenthal 1985). This issue becomes particularly important when the issues of ownership and control over the use, presentation and management of ancient sites are contested, as is the case with Native American sites in North America, or sites in Palestine. In such cases, it is imperative for archaeologists to be knowledgeable about local cultural traditions, and to be able to incorporate such traditions at the most fundamental stages of their research. Understanding the significance for collective identity of folklore about archaeological sites is necessary for undertaking research in which archaeologists collaborate with indigenous owners of the sites they study (D. Carmichael *et al.* 1994). In many cases this may become the only kind of research possible.

Multiple pasts

Folklore and modern science aim to gain different forms of truths. Remains of the past are interpreted in different ways by academic and non-academic people but both make the past in their own way meaningful in the present (see Blake, chapter 15; Shankland, chapter 10; see also Burström *et al.* 1996; Solli 1996; Voss 1987).

Discussions about the reliability of folklore as a (pre-)historical source have implications for archaeologists' professional legitimacy: 'Folk archaeology represents a challenge to archaeology's monopoly on interpretation of the past, and it is to this threat that archaeologists are responding' (Michlovic 1990: 103).

In a way, academic interpretation is akin to popular interpretations of the past also in as much as both are firmly based on standards of their own (sub-)cultural context. Popular views may often not be valid if judged against scientific criteria, but such a judgement in itself would mean to apply values that are not appropriate. It cannot be justifiably claimed that academic knowledge is necessarily superior to all other forms of knowledge (contra Feder 1984). This raises questions about our scientific and ethical responsibilities *vis-à-vis* the public (Feder 1990; Michlovic 1990). As Bob Layton put it (1989: 14): 'What is it exactly that archaeologists have to offer to a cultural group already in possession of a sufficient and valid version of their own history?'

Is it our duty to point to the scientific truth, or do we have the obligation to allow people to have their own accounts of the past (cf. Schmidt and Halle, chapter 11, Collis, chapter 9)? In any case, as Michlovic argues, we should not denounce folk archaeology out of hand, in order to maintain our own position and level of funding, but try to 'understand both the cultural context from which [folk beliefs] emerge and the cultural needs to which they respond' (1990: 104). It could even be said that science is the form folklore takes in our present (Seidenspinner 1988: 103–4, 1989). Does that mean that you can say anything you like about the past and it will all be equally valid? Most definitely not, but we cannot repeat here an argument made elsewhere at length (Lampeter Archaeology Workshop 1997).

It has been argued in the context of the first World Archaeological Congress, and in several of its publications (e.g. D. Carmichael *et al.* 1994; Layton 1989), that in non-Western cultures indigenous traditions of knowing the past ought to be fully respected and must not be eradicated on behalf of Western-style science and enlightenment. Archaeologists are not the only people with a legitimate and genuine interest in the past. This point affects the politics of the past. It has often been repeated and its justification exemplified in an abundance of case studies from around the globe. In this book we extend the argument to include also non-academic understandings of the past within the Western world itself. They too deserve to have a voice, for the same reasons (see also Solli 1996).

There is a political dimension of folklore also in another sense. Folklore, not unlike archaeology, has often been used by politicians (and advertisers) to give their message the flavour of being 'natural', traditional and, of course, popular. Hermann Bausinger argued recently (1994) that the assumption of long-term continuities in folklore has been so dominant in the history of folklore studies because it has had the important ideological significance of supporting national mythologies. It was not surprising that Jacob Grimm published in 1835 a book called *German Mythology*. One century later the Nazis continued to exploit folklore for their own interests, but so did other governments as well (Newall 1980: xxiv ff.).

The folklore of archaeology

Archaeology has in many ways been influenced by changes and fashions in popular culture (see Denning, chapter 7; Meskell, chapter 6). But at the same time archaeology has also made an impact on popular culture. The cliché of the archaeologist has become common in many novels and films.

Moreover, archaeologists have developed their own folklore. Norbert Elias (1988) described what he called 'scientific folklore':

> an intra-disciplinary ancestor worship, special beliefs about selected 'great men and women' belonging to this discipline and to no other, or beliefs about the unique value of one's own field of work, compared with that of others – a folklore which, though perhaps of little cognitive value, does add to the sense of belongingness, to the pride in their own work of members of a discipline which, within reason, people may need.
>
> (Elias 1988: 26)

In this sense, archaeologists can be seen as a sub-culture in our society with its own folklore: traditions and rituals, a distinct repertoire of jokes and anecdotes, and an understanding of a shared past (see Murphy, chapter 16; Moser 1995).

CONCLUSION

Because we are writing as archaeologists, our approaches to these issues are necessarily incomplete. We view the problems of relating folklore and archaeology from an archaeological perspective; further work will have to consider what a study of the two fields can contribute to folklore studies. This book is the first (at least in a long time) to deal explicitly with the relationships between folklore and archaeology. As such, its contents cannot be comprehensive, and its conclusions cannot be final. Of course, both folklore and archaeology are practised worldwide; it is beyond the scope of this introductory chapter and the book, and well beyond our expertise, to discuss all aspects of the two fields. It has been our intention here to raise important issues for archaeologists to consider, and to outline how the dialogues we create inform archaeology. Different chapters will provide case studies and further elaboration on these issues. The result should prompt further thinking, exploration and analysis.

As far as the history of this volume is concerned, we are happy to state explicitly (rather than leave it to the creators of academic legends and oral tradition) that the book is a result of a session organised by us at the Theoretical Archaeology Group (TAG) Conference in Liverpool in December 1996. Although all contributors were enlisted to speak at this session, Symonds and Murphy could not make it for the conference but were able to submit their papers for the book, while other commitments prevented Philip Segadika from preparing a chapter from the paper he gave. Miranda Green published her paper elsewhere and wrote a new paper for this book. We also remember well that the idea for the session (and the book) was born after the TAG Conference two years earlier, in Bradford, when the timetable prevented us from listening to each other's papers. Afterwards, e-mail allowed us to get in touch across the Atlantic, and we decided to explore in more detail what we were both interested in: folklore and archaeology.

ACKNOWLEDGEMENTS

We are grateful to all our contributors for writing such interesting papers, and to Vicky Peters and two enthusiastic referees for their support of this book project. Ymke Mulder has earned our undying gratitude by offering to compile the index. Cornelius Holtorf would also like to acknowledge the practical support he received during the editing process from the Department of Archaeology, University of Wales, Lampeter. Amy Gazin-Schwartz acknowledges the support of the University of Massachusetts for a graduate student travel grant which made it possible for her to attend the TAG meeting in Bradford, and Assumption College for practical support during the last stages of editing. Amy is also grateful to members of the University of Massachusetts Department of Anthropology for general support through the writing and editing process; and to her family for numerous cups of tea and all other varieties of aid.

REFERENCES

Bahn, P. (1996) *The Cambridge Illustrated History of Archaeology*. Cambridge: Cambridge University Press.

Bausinger, H. (1994) 'Zwischen mythos und alltag. Volkskunde und geschichte.' In I.-S. Kowalczuk (ed.) *Paradigmen Deutscher Geschichtswissenschaft*, pp. 106–119. Berlin: GSFP.

Bausinger, H. and Brückner W. (eds) (1969) *Kontinuität? Geschichtlichkeit und Dauer als Volkskundliches Problem. Festschrift Hans Moser.* Berlin: E. Schmidt.

Bausinger, H., Jeggle, U., Korff, G. and Scharfe, M. (1978) *Grundzüge der Volkskunde.* Darmstadt: Wissenschaftliche Buchgesellschaft.

Bendix, R. (1997) *In Search of Authenticity: The Formation of Folklore Studies.* Madison, WI: University of Wisconsin Press.

Blench, R. and Spriggs, M. (1997) *Archaeology and Language I: Theoretical and Methodological Orientations.* One World Archaeology, vol. 27. London and New York: Routledge.

Blinkenberg, C. (1911) *The Thunderweapon in Religion and Folklore. A Study in Comparative Archaeology.* Cambridge: Cambridge University Press.

Boehm, J. (1933) *Archäologie und Volkskunde.* Berlin.

Bord, J. and Bord, C. (1990) *Atlas of Magical Britain.* London: Sidgwick & Jackson.

Brednich, R.W. (ed.) (1988) *Grundriss der Volkskunde. Einführung in die Forschungsfelder der Europäischen Ethnologie.* Berlin: Reimer.

Bronner, S. J. (1992) 'Introduction.' In S.J. Bronner (ed.) *Creativity and Tradition in Folklore: New Directions,* pp. 1–38. Logan, UT: Utah State University Press.

Bruford, A. and Macdonald, D.A. (eds) (1994) *Scottish Traditional Tales.* Edinburgh: Polygon.

Burström, M., Winberg, B. and Zachrisson, T. (eds) (1996) *Fornlämningar och Folkminnen.* Stockholm: Riksantikvarieämbetet.

Carmichael, A. (1928) *Carmina Gadelica: Hymns and Incantations. Vol. 1.* Edinburgh: Oliver and Boyd.

Carmichael, D.L., Hubert, J., Reeves, B. and Schanche, A. (eds) (1994) *Sacred Sites, Sacred Places.* One World Archaeology 23. London: Routledge.

Cartailhac, E. (1877) *L'age de Pierre dans les Souvenirs et Superstitions Populaires.* Paris: Reinwald and Libraires-Editeurs.

Clark, J.G.D. (1951) 'Folk culture and the study of European prehistory.' In W.F. Grimes (ed.) *Aspects of Archaeology in Britain and Beyond,* pp. 39–48. London: Edwardo.

Clark, J.G.D. (1954) *Prehistoric Europe: The Economic Basis.* Stanford, CA: Stanford University Press.

Daniel, G. (1980) *A Short History of Archaeology.* London: Thames and Hudson.

Daniel, G. (ed.) (1981) *Towards a History of Archaeology.* London: Thames and Hudson.

Davidson, H.E. (1963) 'Folklore and man's past.' *Folklore* 74: 527–544.

Davidson, H.E. (1969) 'The chariot of the sun.' *Folklore* 80: 174–180.

Davidson, H.E. (1974) 'Folklore and history.' *Folklore* 85: 73–92.

Dorson, R.M. (ed.) (1961) *Folklore Research Around the World: A North American Point of View.* Bloomington, IN: Indiana University Press.

Dorson, R.M. (1968a) 'The debate over the trustworthiness of oral traditional history.' In F. Harkort, K.C. Peeters and R. Wildhaber (eds) *Volksüberlieferung. Festschrift Kurt Ranke 60. Lebensjahr,* pp. 19–35. Göttingen: Schwartz and Co.

Dorson, R.M. (1968b) *The British Folklorists, A History.* Chicago: University of Chicago Press; London: Routledge and Kegan Paul.

Dorson, R.M. (1976) *Folklore and Fakelore.* Cambridge, MA: Harvard University Press.

Dundes, A. (ed.) (1965) *The Study of Folklore.* Englewood Cliffs, NJ: Prentice-Hall.

Elias, N. (1988) 'Scientific establishment.' In N. Elias, H. Martins and R. Whitley (eds) *Scientific Establishments and Hierarchies*, Sociology of the Sciences Yearbook 6, pp. 3–69. Dordrecht: Reidel.

Evans, E.E. (1957) *Irish Folk Ways*. London: Routledge and Paul.

Feder, K.L. (1984) 'Irrationality and popular archaeology.' *American Antiquity* 49: 525–541.

Feder, K.L. (1990) 'Comment on folk archaeology in anthropological perspective.' *Current Anthropology* 31: 390–391.

Fenton, A. (1993) 'Folklore and ethnology: past, present and future in British universities.' *Folklore* 104: 4–12.

Fewkes, J.W. (1893) 'A-Wa'-tobi: an archaeological verification of a Tusayan legend.' *American Anthropologist* 6: 363–375.

Fleming, A. (1988) *The Dartmoor Reaves. Investigating Prehistoric Land Divisions*. London: Batsford.

Fleure, H.J. (1931) *Archaeology and Folk Tradition*. The Sir John Rhys Memorial Lecture. London: The British Academy.

Fleure, H.J. (1948) 'Archaeology and folklore.' *Folklore* 59: 69–74.

Folk-Lore Society (1878) 'Rules.' *The Folk-Lore Society* publication no. 1: vii–ix.

Friedman, J. (1992) 'The past in the future: history and the politics of identity.' *American Anthropologist* 94(4): 837–859.

Georges, R.A. and M.O. Jones (1995) *Folkloristics: An Introduction*. Bloomington, IN: Indiana University Press.

Gerndt, H. (1981) *Kultur als Forschungsfeld*. München: Beck.

Glassie, H. (1977) 'Archaeology and folklore: common anxieties, common hopes.' In L. Ferguson (ed.) *Historical Archaeology and the Importance of Material Things*, pp. 23–35. Special Publications 2. Columbia, SC: Society for Historical Archaeology.

Grant, I.F. (1961) *Highland Folkways*. London: Routledge and Paul.

Grinsell, L.V. (1976) *The Folklore of Prehistoric Sites in Britain*. London: David and Charles.

Henderson, W. [1879] (1967) *Folklore of the Northern Counties of England and the Borders*. Second edition. Reprinted by permission of the Folk-Lore Society by Kraus Reprint Limited, Nendeln/Liechtenstein.

Hobsbawm, E. and Ranger, T. (eds) (1983) *The Invention of Tradition*. Cambridge: Cambridge University Press.

Holtorf, C.J. (1998) 'The life-histories of megaliths in Mecklenburg-Vorpommern (Germany).' *World Archaeology* 30: 23–38.

Huth, O. (1950) 'Märchen und Megalithreligion.' *Paideuma* 5 (1/2): 12–22.

Joyner, C. (1989) 'A tale of two disciplines: folklore and history.' In D. Rohtman-Augustin and M. Povrzanovic (eds) *Folklore and Historical Process*, pp. 9–22. Zagreb: Institute of Folklore Research.

Kirchner, H. (1955) 'Die Menhire in Mitteleuropa und der Menhirgedanke.' *Akademie der Wissenschaften und der Literatur Mainz. Abhandlungen der Geistes- und Sozialwissenschaftlichen Klasse* 1955, no. 9: 609–817.

Köstlin, K. and Bausinger, H. (eds) (1980) *Heimat und Identität. Probleme Regionaler Kultur. Volkskunde-Kongreß in Kiel 1979*. Neumünster: Wachholtz.

Lampeter Archaeology Workshop (1997) 'Relativism, objectivity and the politics of the past' (with comments). *Archaeological Dialogues* 4: 164–198.

Layton, R. (1989) 'Introduction: Who needs the past?' In R. Layton (ed.) *Who Needs the Past? Indigenous Values and Archaeology*, pp. 1–20. London: Unwin Hyman.

Liebers, C. (1986) *Neolithische Megalithgräber in Volksglauben und Volksleben.* Frankfurt am Main: Lang.

Lowenthal, D. (1985) *The Past is a Foreign Country.* Cambridge: Cambridge University Press.

MacCulloch, Canon J.A. (*c.*1932) 'Were fairies an earlier race of men?' *Folklore* 43: 362–375.

Macdonald, J. and Wood, S. (eds) (1997) *An Archaeological Survey of the Townships of Glame, Manish More, Brochel and the Farmsteads of Doire Domhain, with a Survey of the Surrounding Area, on Raasay, Skye and Lochalsh District, Highland Region.* Association of Certificated Field Archaeologists (Glasgow University) Occasional Paper no. 26, Glasgow.

Mackay, D. (1990) 'Images in a landscape: Bonnie Prince Charlie and the Highland clearances.' In F. Baker, S. Taylor and J. Thomas (eds) *Writing the Past in the Present*, pp. 192–203. Lampeter: St Davids University College.

Macpherson, J. (1768) *Critical Dissertations on the Origin, Antiquities, Language, Manners and Relation of the Ancient Caledonians, their Posterity, the Picts, the British and Irish Scots.* London: printed for T. Becket and P.A. De Hondt.

Michlovic, M.G. (1990) 'Folk archaeology in anthropological perspective.' *Current Anthropology* 31: 103–107.

Moser, S. (1995) 'Archaeology and its disciplinary culture: the professionalisation of Australian prehistoric archaeology.' Unpublished doctoral thesis, University of Sydney.

Newall, V.J. (1980) 'Introduction.' In V.J. Newall (ed.) *Folklore Studies in the Twentieth Century. Proceedings of the Centenary Conference of the Folklore Society*, pp. xv–xxxii. Woodbridge: Brewer; Totowa, NJ: Rowman and Littlefield.

Nicolaisen, W.F.H. (1980) 'Time in folk-narrative.' In V.J. Newall (ed.) *Folklore Studies in the Twentieth Century. Proceedings of the Centenary Conference of the Folklore Society*, pp. 314–319. Woodbridge: Brewer; Totowa, NJ: Rowman and Littlefield.

Nitschke, A. (1978) 'Märchen als Zeugen der Vor- und Frühgeschichte.' *Die Freundesgabe. Jahrbuch der Gesellschaft zur Pflege des Märchens der Europäischen Völker e.V.* 1978: 22–32.

Ohlhaver, H. (1937) 'Großsteingräber und Grabhügel in Glauben und Brauch.' *Mannus* 29: 192–255.

Opie, I. and Opie, P. (1980) 'Certain laws of folklore.' In V.J. Newall (ed.) *Folklore Studies in the Twentieth Century. Proceedings of the Centenary Conference of the Folklore Society*, pp. 64–75. Woodbridge: Brewer: Totowa, NJ: Rowman and Littlefield.

Pandey, D.B. (1989) 'An 11th century literary reference to prehistoric times in India.' In R. Layton (ed.) *Who Needs the Past?*, pp. 57–58. London: Unwin Hyman.

Peeters, K.C. (1969) *Volkskunde en Archeologie.* Bijdragen tot de studie van het Brabantse heem, deel XI. Oisterwijk: Stichting Brabants Heem.

Piggott, S. (1941) 'The sources of Geoffrey of Monmouth. II. The Stonehenge story.' *Antiquity* 15(60): 305–319.

Ranke, K. (1969) 'Oral und literale Kontinuität.' In H. Bausinger and W. Brückner (eds) *Kontinuität? Geschichtlichkeit und Dauer als volkskundliches Problem. Festschrift Hans Moser*, pp. 102–116. Berlin: E. Schmidt.

Reinach, S. (1893) 'Les monuments de pierre brute dans le langage et les croyances populaires.' *Revue Archéologique* (3rd series), 21: 329–366.

Roymans, N. (1995) 'The cultural biography of urnfields and the long-term
history of a mythical landscape' (with comments and reply). *Archaeological
Dialogues* 2: 2–38.

Saintyves, P. (1934–1936) *Corpus du Folklore Préhistorique en France et dans les
Colonies Françaises*. 3 vols. Paris: Librairie E. Nourry.

Schuldt, E. (1972) *Die mecklenburgischen Megalithgräber. Untersuchungen zu ihrer
Architektur und Funktion*. Beiträge zur Ur- und Frühgeschichte der Bezirke
Rostock, Schwerin und Neubrandenburg, vol. 6. Berlin: Deutscher Verlag
der Wissenschaften.

Seidenspinner, W. (1988) 'Mythen von historischen Sagen. Materialien und
Notizen zum Problemfeld zwischen Sage, Archäologie und Geschichte.'
Jahrbuch für Volkskunde N.F. 11: 83–104.

Seidenspinner, W. (1989) 'Germanische Sternwarten und prähistorische Astro-
nauten. Von der wissenschaftlichen Spekulation zur Sage.' *Fabula* 30: 26–42.

Seidenspinner, W. (1993) 'Archäologie, Volksüberlieferung, Denkmalideologie.
Anmerkungen zum Denkmalverständnis der Öffentlichkeit in Vergangenheit
und Gegenwart.' *Fundberichte aus Baden-Württemberg* 18: 1–15.

Shanks, M. and Hodder, I. (1995) 'Processual, postprocessual and interpretive
archaeologies.' In I. Hodder, M. Shanks, A. Alexandri, V. Buchli, J. Carman,
J. Last and G. Lucas (eds) *Interpreting Archaeology. Finding Meaning in the Past*,
pp. 3–29. London: Routledge.

Shils, E. (1981) *Tradition*. London: Faber and Faber.

Solli, B. (1996) 'Narratives of Veøy. On the poetics and scientifics of archaeology.'
In P. Graves-Brown, S. Jones and C. Gamble (eds) *Cultural Identity and Archaeology. The Construction of European Identities*, pp. 209–227. London: Routledge.

Spector, J.D. (1993) *What This Awl Means: Feminist Archaeology at a Wahpeton
Dakota Village*. St Paul MN: Minnesosta Historical Society Press.

Thompson, P. (1988) *The Voice of the Past: Oral History*. Second edition. Oxford:
Oxford University Press.

Thoms, W. [1846] (1965) 'Folklore.' *The Athenaeum* 983: 862–863. Reprinted
in A. Dundes (ed.) (1965) *The Study of Folklore*, pp. 4–6. Englewood Cliffs,
NJ: Prentice-Hall.

Tonkin, E. (1992) *Narrating Our Pasts: The Social Construction of Oral History*.
Cambridge: Cambridge University Press.

Trevor-Roper, H. (1983) 'The invention of tradition: the highland tradition of
Scotland.' In E. Hobsbawm and T. Ranger (eds) *The Invention of Tradition*,
pp.15–41. Cambridge: Cambridge University Press.

Trigger, B.G. (1989) *A History of Archaeological Thought*. Cambridge: Cambridge
University Press.

Trümpy, H. (1968) 'Die Göttin Isis in schweizerischen Sagen.' In E. Schmidt
(ed.) *Provincialia. Festschrift für Rudolf Laur-Belart,* pp. 470–486. Basel and
Stuttgart: Siftung Pro Augusta Raurica.

Ucko, P.J., Hunter, M., Clark, A.J. and David, A. (1991) *Avebury Reconsidered:
From the 1660s to the 1990s*. London: Unwin Hyman.

Vansina, J. (1985) *Oral Tradition as History*. London: Currey.

Voss, J.A. (1987) 'Antiquity imagined: cultural values in archaeological folklore.'
Folklore 98: 80–90.

Widdowson, J. (1980) 'Folklore and regional identity.' In V.J. Newall (ed.) *Folklore Studies in the Twentieth Century. Proceedings of the Centenary Conference of the Folklore Society*, pp. 443–453. Woodbridge: Brewer; Totowa, NJ: Rowman and Littlefield.

Wolf, E. (1992) *Europe and the People Without History*. Berkeley: University of California Press.

Wright, T. [1846] (1968) 'On Dr. Grimm's German mythology.' In *Essays on Subjects connected with the Literature, Popular Superstitions, and History of England in the Middle Ages*. London: John Russell Smith. Reprinted in R. Dorson (ed.) (1968) *Peasant Customs and Savage Myths*, vol. 1, pp. 41–51. London: Routledge and Kegan Paul.

Zumwalt, R.L. (1988) *American Folklore Scholarship: A Dialogue of Dissent*. Bloomington, IN: Indiana University Press.

CHAPTER TWO

FOLKLORE AND WORLD VIEW

ROBERT LAYTON

ABSTRACT

Folklore can be regarded as the expression of a vernacular world view amenable to anthropological study. As a world view, any folklore tradition embodies particular ways of representing space and temporal processes which are likely to differ from those of the academic archaeological tradition. They determine what, and how, events are remembered or reconstructed, and which objects are considered significant. Folklore also expresses a value system that guides the way in which the remains of the past are treated. Anthropological techniques can be applied both to elucidating and translating folkloric conceptions, and to rendering a more reflexive outlook upon the academic vision. These points will be exemplified through a critical discussion of chapters in this book.

INTRODUCTION

Looked at from the perspective of anthropology, the striking feature of folklore is the distinctive way in which it represents space and time, and the way in which it portrays being in the world. Rather than treat these aspects in isolation, it seems preferable to look for consistencies. Folklore can then be seen not as a disorganised collection of fragments, but as the expressions of a world view characterised by a different interpretative orientation to archaeology. Oral traditions are constructed according to definite styles and rely upon complex techniques (Finnegan 1973: 127). As Amy Gazin-Schwartz and Cornelius Holtorf remark in their introduction, a dialogue between archaeology and folklore must be a dialogue between different systems of meaning.

Oral traditions represent the past through a characteristic 'lens' which determines what is capable of representation. Space is characteristically appropriated through conspicuous features in the landscape that provide tangible points of reference to which legends can be anchored. Research in the heavily colonised regions of eastern Australia, for example, suggests that the more conspicuous the feature, the more often it is talked about and therefore the more readily it continues to function as a mnemonic for indigenous tradition (Creamer 1984: 9.2). In a similar way, the Irish monuments, Anatolian tells and Sardinian towers described in this book become the focus for legends. I have argued elsewhere that, even in the regions of northern and central Australia where oral traditions remain strong, places in the landscape provide a vital set of reference points which facilitate translation between indigenous and Western discourses (Layton 1995, 1997).

Oral traditions typically represent time in a different way to written traditions and the lists of dates, kings and thinkers that writing codifies. Shankland's chapter in this volume notes the compression of historical phases in Anatolian oral history but, as Amy Gazin-Schwartz and Cornelius Holtorf observe, this tendency does not imply indigenous traditions have no time depth (see also Layton 1989: 8–10). It is hard for us to empathise with visions of history that have not experienced the nineteenth-century geological revolution. An Alawa legend, from the Gulf Country of northern Australia, records how during the Creation Period a group of dogs attacked and killed a goanna at the edge of a lagoon. I was forcibly reminded of the different time scales of other cultures when a senior Alawa man, telling me the legend, pointed to the gum trees fringing the lagoon and explained, 'Those trees are the dogs waiting for the goanna,' adding, 'not the young trees, the really old ones'. The scale of the transformation in European thought brought about by the nineteenth-century revolution in archaeological knowledge is well expressed by Trautmann: 'very suddenly, the bottom dropped out of history and its beginnings disappeared in an abyss of time' (Trautmann 1992: 380).

TIME AND 'THE OTHER'

Archaeology usually represents the past through a linear chronology which identifies moments when traits originated and then traces their subsequent development. Folklore, on the other hand, tends to represent the past in terms of prototypes and their subsequent re-embodiments. Oral narratives generally cluster around particularly important events and people. Time is telescoped to bring key events into direct association. The original protagonists may be displaced by characters who are locally more prominent, or more relevant to the present (Allen and Montell 1981: 32–7). Sara Champion and Gabriel Cooney, for example, describe how King Charles I replaces the legendary hero Diarmaid in part of Ireland. Archaeology constantly pushes the origin of customs further into the past, while folklore constantly draws the prototypes forward toward their most recent manifestations. Mats Burström's chapter describes how the long-range chronological lens was introduced to Swedish archaeology, and notes how its introduction led archaeology to diverge from folklore studies.

Folklore tends to record the deeds of great men and women which, while they may encapsulate profound social change, are unlikely to leave archaeological traces. The sacking of a city or the construction of a tomb may do so, but the discrepancy in representations of time between folklore and archaeology makes correlations difficult, as Champion and Cooney's chapter shows. It is when folklore reveals beliefs whose customary practice continued long enough to accumulate sufficient material residue that legend and archaeology are likely to be able to refer their discourse to the same objects. The chapters by Miranda Green and John Staeck give examples of how this might be achieved.

No general rules have yet been established for predicting the duration of oral traditions (cf. Layton 1989: 13–15). The tempting supposition that Irish traditions concerning the fairies have their roots in the representation of Bronze Age peoples by incoming Celts remains unproven. On the other hand, Norwegian folklore concerning a previous tradition of hoe farming, rediscovered by Ingunn Holm, appears to provide an accurate record of a settlement pattern which had disappeared by 1650. Oral traditions are, moreover, open to new elements taken from written ones. Collis points out the naivety of supposing 'the uneducated classes . . . unwittingly preserve in their oral traditions some truths . . . uncontaminated by the effects of education'.

The way in which folklore represents the opposition between an everyday mode of being and manifestations of 'the other' reveals a theory of being with distinctive notions of causality. The translation of theories of being is the most difficult part of rendering other discourses rational. Norwegian cairn folk with animal tails, Irish fairies in tombs and hill forts, Welsh soldiers brought back from the Otherworld who lack the power of speech all embody a theory of being with its own criteria for plausibility. Marriage with the Huldra underground folk of Norway will produce children bearing cows' tails, Irish fairies plait the flax of those who damage sacred trees, Welsh cauldrons bring the dead back to life, deprived of the power of speech. The ontology underlying folklore is not an obscuring fantasy ('primitive superstition') but fundamental in determining what is deemed convincing in the construction of a narrative. 'What people believe happened is often as important as what actually happened, for people think, act and react in accordance with what they believe to be true' (Allen and Montell 1981: 89).

The academic can often only approach alternative rationalities by considering their apparent motivation. Like written accounts of history, folklores have for example their own political agendas which, while widely varying, frequently embody local resistance against a centralising authority. An understanding of these agendas may assist in conservation, as the chapter by Emma Blake exemplifies. The value system embedded in folklore enables us to understand why the past's remains are evaluated in specific ways, and thus how they are treated, whether that be to loot and destroy, or to defend against excavation by archaeologists. The tomb robber Luigi Perticarari, who claims the spirits of ancient Etruscans befriended him when he was most desperate for money and led him to tombs, as cited by Diura van Velzen, seems to be offering a thinly veiled excuse tinged with guilt. The villagers living near Çatalhöyük suffer similar qualms. Sara Champion and Gabriel Cooney quote several cases of physical disability which befell peasant farmers who damaged ancient monuments – a withered arm or transformation into a dwarf – but go on to note such sanctions are no use against capitalist-minded landlords or young modernising farmers. Other Irish monuments have been wantonly destroyed, while yet others have, like the Sardinian nuraghe, slipped into domestic use. Kathryn Denning's chapter is particularly interesting in its argument that respect for the ancient traditions of other civilisations is promulgated through popular writings which suggest (at a time of approaching millennium) that, if only we could decode them, ancient civilisations have messages which can help us avert catastrophe. Denning shows how archaeologists have harnessed these competing world views to their own manifesto, but Collis questions whether they can safely be tolerated.

TRANSLATING FOLKLORE

Given the distinctive ways in which oral tradition represents time, space and causality, it is preferable not to dismantle the narratives of folklore, in order to sift vestiges of truth from various kinds of fantasy but, as Emma Blake argues in her chapter on ancient towers in Sardinia, to treat oral traditions holistically. If folklore is an unfamiliar way of representing the past, is it possible to identify, translate or match what it represents into an archaeological discourse? Ingunn Holm argues that Norwegian farmers can recognise evidence of past agricultural activity better than archaeologists who have grown up in towns. Local folklore, recorded in the 1930s, provided a more accurate explanation for abandoned fields than archaeologists had provided in the 1980s. A number of methodological issues nonetheless arise from translating the unfamiliar discourse of folklore into the familiar one of archaeology, of which the most difficult is to reveal the rationality behind competing theories of being. The scale of the difficulties translation might present is illustrated by the legend of Walgundu, a rock shelter in the Gulf Country of northern Australia. According to the legend, a band of people out hunting and gathering killed a large snake, not realising it was a legendary being of the Creation Period. In revenge, the snake's friend lightning pursued them to the shelter and killed them there. There are several reasons for thinking this tradition may recall an attempt to represent the wholly unprecedented event of a colonial massacre, not least the fact that the shelter is said to contain skeletons displaying bullet wounds (Holmes 1965: 11).

Diura van Velzen links the robbing of ancient Etruscan tombs to the legend of the unexpected fortune told among the 'popular classes' of the region. Legends of finding treasure are widely used in the peasant communities of Europe to explain why one family becomes richer than the rest (in the French village of Pellaport, where I did my doctoral research, one family's rise to prosperity was said to have begun when they found treasure hidden in the house of an old man which they had bought to convert after his death). Put into the context of an egalitarian, interdependent peasant community, the legend can be seen as an explanation for social differentiation. Our response depends on how we interpret the impact of a market economy on communities dominated by reciprocity. Banfield once used the unkind metaphor of 'peasant pie' to explain jealousy towards those who are most successful in market enterprises (Banfield 1958). If all deserve equal slices of a limited resource, only luck or dishonesty could explain how one household becomes wealthier than others. It is noteworthy that it was because Banfield was himself a proponent of the transformation of peasant society into rural capitalism that he had difficulty representing the egalitarianism which protects individual peasant households against risk. Scott portrayed this more sympathetically as 'the moral economy of the peasant' (Scott 1976).

John Staeck attempts to disentangle roles in Ho-Chunk society at the time the legends were transcribed by Radin, from the roles described in the legends themselves. Whereas Radin described the Ho-Chunk as egalitarian and patricentred, Staeck contends there are numerous portrayals of hierarchy and matricentred behaviour in the legends, in particular cases of lowly men marrying chiefs' daughters and succeeding to the position of chief. Two of the classic anthropological objections to treating legends as historical documents should be noted in response to Staeck's analysis. The first, the Functionalist objection, is that legends must make sense to the narrator and audience. They must, that is, appeal to contemporary issues and take place in recognisable settings, as when the marriage at Cana or raising of Lazarus take place in fifteenth-century Dutch settings (Fuchs 1978: 13, 19; cf. Malinowski 1954: 125–126). Before inferring a historical content, consideration should be given to ways in which the plot of a legend appeals to members of the contemporary society. The second, or Structuralist, objection is that myths may invert as well as reproduce everyday structures. The men who marry Ho-Chunk chiefs' daughters may represent a real possibility, or they may be male Cinderellas. Legends can create an imagined past which reverses the present in order to account for the origin of the social order (Lévi-Strauss 1973: 153). Staeck responds to these objections in his chapter. Miranda Green's chapter is noteworthy for the method it adopts in order to distinguish evidence for the uses of cauldrons at the period when the legends were written down, from the uses attributed to cauldrons in myth and evidenced in pre-medieval archaeology. Finding these to be different, Green argues the legends can throw light on the culture whose beliefs caused the distinctive archaeological trace left by cauldron disposal over preceding centuries. The narratives are not simply transpositions of classical 'commonplaces' into tenth-century ethnography.

ARCHAEOLOGY AND FOLKLORE

The fallacy of treating folklore as an independent system, the miraculous survival of a pre-Enlightenment tradition, is noted by Amy Gazin-Schwartz and Cornelius Holtorf in their introduction. There is, on the contrary, considerable evidence that what Redfield called the 'Great' and 'Little' traditions have interacted (Redfield 1960). Contributors provide several examples of flow from the National or 'Great' tradition into the 'Little' one of folklore. Gazin-Schwartz and Holtorf, and Collis note that historical novels can enter local oral tradition and become recalled as fact. Diura van Velzen shows how wealthy families such as the Medici, drawing on classical Roman legend, used the ancient Etruscans to validate claims to Tuscan independence. Their claim conferred a significance on Etruscan artefacts that not only stimulated tomb robbing, but allowed the robbers themselves to claim an affinity with the ancients. Other papers document a flow in the reverse direction in support of Nazism and nineteenth-century Irish nationalism. The latter drew on legends and beliefs first written down in the eleventh or twelfth centuries which have been tapped again in the late twentieth century to promote the tourist potential of Ireland. Lynn Meskell gives examples of the interaction between academic and popular archaeology. Kathryn Denning examines the interaction between archaeological writing and the alternative apocalyptic discourse of the imminent second Millennium. She challenges the idea of a dominant academic discourse oppressing an anarchic fringe, arguing that competing discourses have quite enough power to promote their own interpretations of the past.

The problem of how folklore can be used by archaeologists then becomes not a question of treating it as a partial, fragmentary record of the past with 'true' elements that can be rescued from a clouding fantasy, but rather of how two, sometimes interacting modes of representing the past provide different accounts of the same events and objects. As a world view, any tradition of folklore embodies distinctive ways of representing space, time and cause which are likely to differ from the representations deployed in the academic tradition of archaeology. To translate folklore, the researcher must identify what 'objects' oral tradition refers to; or what it is objectifying.

The mediating processes of folkloric representation determine which events are remembered or reconstructed, and how; which objects are considered significant and why. Anthropological techniques can be applied both to elucidating and translating folkloric conceptions, and to rendering a more reflexive outlook upon the alternative, academic vision. It should not be forgotten, however, that anthropology has its own theoretical axes to grind, one of which is the tendency of Functionalist and Structuralist theory to discount the historical content of oral tradition (see Layton 1989: 2). No analysis is transparent. The analyst's theory may itself determine what are taken to be the objects referred to in an alternative discourse (Layton 1997: 129–130). The problem, as Emma Blake and Lynn Meskell argue in their respective chapters, is to discard the modernist notion of academic truth battling against local superstition, without falling into the 'postmodernist' trap of a complete relativity which denies that discourse can make reference to objects external to it, or refuses to accept that translations of meaning between discourses can be approximated.

Three approaches to these dilemmas can be identified among contributors. The first is the revival of an earlier approach, namely to sift oral tradition for information about the material residues of the past. The 'muted' traditions of the provincial or powerless may contain historical information which the powerful have suppressed or neglected (cf. Allen and Montell 1981: 98). This is Ingunn Holm's method for reconstructing a vanished Norwegian agricultural system.

A second use of folklore is as a mirror within which to see archaeological subjectivities, a cause for reflection on the politics of academic knowledge. Martin Brown and Pat Bowen suggest that the closer one goes to a monument, the more evocative folkloric interpretations seem, while Emma Blake points out that local knowledge embraces aesthetic and ethical values which professional archaeology disdains. Collis, Brown and Bowen, and Murphy point out that archaeology has its own received wisdoms, uncritically transmitted from writer to writer. Mats Burström shows how Swedish archaeology was itself disciplined, in Foucault's sense, during the late nineteenth century. The control of time conferred power. Just as workers were subjected to the surveillance of their supervisor with his pocket watch, so the discipline of time was imposed on the remains of the past (cf. Foucault 1977). While to us, the folkloric representation of time and process may seem fatally blurred over the crucial question of chronology, reflection upon the chronological strain within archaeology can make us aware of how that too is a subjective lens. In another session of the 1996 TAG conference, Phil Sidebottom argued persuasively that, in their desire to create a chronology, archaeologists had misused stylistic traits to construct a chronology for Derbyshire crosses which were in fact, he argued, all created at the same time. A well-known example of false chronology is the tendency of an earlier generation of researchers working on the art of the Upper Palaeolithic in Europe to label any simple or ambiguous representation as 'early' or 'degenerate', whereas finely detailed and readily recognisable figures of horses, bison, etc. were deemed the product of the high point in a cycle of artistic development (see discussions in Ucko 1987 and Layton 1991). The local response to excavation also helps encourage a reflexive gaze upon the purpose of archaeology. The archaeologist is cast as an obstructive conservator in Tuscany and nineteenth-century Ireland, a wanton destroyer at Çatalhöyük, or an apologist for extremism in the case of the Externsteine described in Martin Schmidt and Uta Halle's chapter. Emma Blake draws on the philosophic tradition of Pragmatism to argue that ethical judgements cannot be applied to abstract ideas; ideas can only be judged by their effects, when they are translated into action.

A third use for folklore in the present volume is to provide an ethnographic parallel for prehistoric thought upon the past and its monuments. Julia Murphy adopts this approach in her study of Welsh megaliths, as do Emma Blake and Mats Burström. This approach can be developed to hint at the malleability of meanings attributed to monuments, despite the apparent durability of folklore. Emma Blake argues that the concept of 'rereading' commonly supposes that later readings are related to earlier ones. But, she objects, ruptures occur which prevent any progressive evolution: 'the monuments are just there'. Sara Champion and Gabriel Cooney cite the translation of 'pagan' monuments into Christian sites by marking them with a cross, renaming and reshaping their significance as examples of a presumably recurrent process. The stone on an Irish hill known as the White Horse seems to have been subjected to various readings over a longer period of time.

A hundred years ago archaeology struggled to separate itself from the study of folklore and gain credibility as an objective science. In the current, postmodern mood, the move to decentre archaeology and re-establish a dialogue with folklore presents some interesting challenges which contributors meet in a variety of ways.

REFERENCES

Allen, B. and Montell, L. (1981) *From Memory to History: Using Oral Sources in Local Historical Research.* Nashville: American Association for State and Local History.

Banfield, E.C. (1958) *The Moral Basis of a Backward Society.* New York: Free Press.

Creamer, H. (1984) *A Gift and a Dreaming: The New South Wales Survey of Aboriginal Sacred and Significant Sites 1973–1983.* Report to the New South Wales National Parks and Wildlife Service, Sydney.

Finnegan, R. (1973) 'Literacy versus non-literacy: the great divide? Some comments on the significance of "literature" in non-literate cultures.' In R. Finnegan and R. Horton (eds) *Modes of Thought: Essays on Thinking in Western and Non-Western Societies*, pp. 112–144. London: Faber.

Foucault, M. (1977) *Discipline and Punish: The Birth of the Prison.* London: Penguin.

Fuchs, R.H. (1978) *Dutch Painting.* London: Thames and Hudson.

Holmes, S. (1965) 'The Nagarren Yubidarawa.' *Milla Wamilla, The Australian Bulletin of Comparative Religion* 5: 8–17.

Layton, R. (1989) 'Introduction: who needs the past?' In R. Layton (ed.) *Who Needs the Past? Indigenous Values and Archaeology*, pp. 1–20. London: Unwin.

Layton, R. (1991) 'Figure, motif and symbol in the hunter-gatherer rock art of Europe and Australia.' In P. Bahn and A. Rosenfeld (eds) *Rock Art and Prehistory*, pp. 28–38. Oxford: Oxbow.

Layton, R. (1995) 'Relating to the country in the Western Desert.' In E. Hirsch and M. O'Hanlon (eds) *The Anthropology of Landscape: Perspectives on Place and Space*, pp. 210–231. Oxford: Clarendon.

Layton, R. (1997) 'Representing and translating people's place in the landscape of northern Australia.' In A. James, J. Hockey and A. Dawson (eds) *After Writing Culture: Epistemology and Praxis in Contemporary Anthropology*, pp. 122–143. London: Routledge.

Lévi-Strauss, C. (1973) *From Honey to Ashes: Introduction to a Science of Mythology*, vol. 2, trans. J. and D. Weightman. New York: Harper.

Malinowski, B. (1954) 'Myth in primitive psychology.' In *Magic, Science and Religion*. New York: Doubleday.

Redfield, R. (1960) *The Little Community* [and] *Peasant Society and Culture*. Chicago: University of Chicago Press.

Scott, J.C. (1976) *The Moral Economy of the Peasant: Rebellion and Subsistence in Southeast Asia*. New Haven: Yale University Press.

Trautmann, T. (1992) 'The revolution in ethnological time.' *Man* (N.S.) 27: 379–397.

Ucko, P. (1987) 'Débuts illusoires dans l'étude de la tradition artistique.' *Bulletin de la Société Préhistorique Ariège-Pyrenées* 42: 15–81.

CHAPTER THREE

FOCUSING ON TIME

Disciplining archaeology in Sweden

MATS BURSTRÖM

ABSTRACT

In Sweden the establishment of archaeology as a separate discipline during the second half of the nineteenth century was closely connected with the introduction of the typological method and the construction of large-scale chronological schemes. The disciplining of the past coincided with a general disciplining of the citizens in the centralised and industrialised nation that was taking shape. The scholarly status and ambition of archaeology grew considerably with the more solid chronological framework. With this as a foundation the antiquarians established a kind of interpretative supremacy and they started to consider the popular conceptions of ancient monuments as unlearned speculation. This created a split between antiquarian authorities and the general public, which still exists. Today, however, there is gradual recognition that all meanings that have been ascribed to ancient monuments contribute to their cultural value. This realisation motivates a renewed archaeological interest in folklore.

INTRODUCTION

There is an important difference between archaeology and folklore concerning the attitude towards time. While dating and chronology are essential in archaeology, they are of minor importance in folklore tradition. There it is not generally the date that matters, but the place and the meaning of an object such as an ancient monument. To understand the archaeological focus on time it is necessary to adopt a historical perspective. At the period of the establishment of archaeology as a modern science, time was used as a means of disciplining in society in general as well as in archaeology. Professionals within the newly formed archaeological discipline focused on chronological systematisation and considered folklore to be superstition without scientific value. This attitude prevailed for more than a century. Today, however, due to postmodern influences archaeologists are interested in the multitude of meanings that may be invested in the past, including those found in folklore traditions.

PRE-MODERN ARCHAEOLOGY

Before the establishment of archaeology as a modern science and a separate discipline antiquarians made no distinction, in their interest, between archaeology and folklore. This is evident from the instructions for the first nationwide inventory of ancient monuments that was made in Sweden. This great inquiry (*Rannsakningar efter antikviteter*) was initiated under royal decree in 1667 and was continued with variable intervals until the early 1690s. The origins of the inquiries lay both in the political objective of the period to emphasise Sweden's glorious past and in the scholarly aim to study the country's ancestors (cf. Baudou and Moen 1995). In the instructions it is explicitly stated that those carrying out the inventory should not only record ancient monuments but also carefully inquire about their names and the traditions and stories told about them (cf. Ståhle 1960: xii–xxii).

During the seventeenth and eighteenth centuries antiquarian interest focused on monuments that were particularly visible in the landscape. Naturally, these monuments also had attracted the attention of people living in their vicinity and consequently many stories were told about them. This folklore was recorded by the antiquarians. For example, a large number of monuments were associated with ancient giants.

Most kinds of ancient monuments have been interpreted as remains from giants. This applies in particular to monuments with an especially striking size, that is, the same kind of monument that was a focus for early antiquarian interest. In Scandinavia, as in many other parts of the world, giants were supposed to have been the first inhabitants of the land. In folklore tradition the giants differ from other elemental beings by being regarded as long since extinct. How long ago they were living is not specified. Sometimes, however, it is told that the giants were driven away by the sound of the first Christian church bells. Many ancient monuments were given names, both general and particular, that refer to giants, who appear both in folklore tradition and in learned speculations about the past. It was not until the 1760s that the Antiquities Archive officially dissociated itself from the belief (Baudou 1995: 166). In folklore tradition ancient giants remained a very common explanation for different kinds of ancient monuments throughout the nineteenth century and into the beginning of the twentieth. In most districts there was some sort of 'giant's grave'.

Not only ancient monuments but also what we today consider to be natural phenomena were associated with giants. Formations in the landscape that were related to ancient giants were, for example, ridges, ridge hollows ('giant's bowls'), erratic boulders ('giant's throws') and hollows in the rock face ('giant's kettles') (Figure 3.1). This shows that the distinction an archaeologist makes between ancient monuments and natural phenomena is not relevant in another conceptual framework. When people interpret the world around them and ascribe it meaning, all elements are made cultural. The early antiquarians recorded all kinds of cultural interpretations.

Antiquarian interest in folklore continued well into the nineteenth century. This is evident from the antiquarian travel reports initiated and financed by the Royal Academy of Letters, History and Antiquities (*Kngl. Vitterhets Historie och Antikvitets Akademien*). They contain an abundance of traditions and stories collected from local people. All this radically changed, however, with the establishment of archaeology as a modern science and a separate discipline.

DISCIPLINING ARCHAEOLOGY

In Sweden the transformation of archaeology into a recognised discipline took place during the 1870s. From then on there were archaeologists with academic titles, annual archaeological meetings and extensive publication of archaeological literature including journals (cf. Welinder 1994: 197–203).

The establishment of archaeology as a modern science in Scandinavia was closely connected with the introduction of the typological method and the construction of large-scale chronological schemes (cf. Gräslund 1987). The early archaeologists considered the creation of a reliable chronological division of the archaeological sources to be the most important task. They felt that if chronological order was not brought into the chaotic sources, it would not be possible to draw correct historical conclusions.

The most successful of the Swedish chronology-constructors and the most famous of all nineteenth-century typologists was Oscar Montelius (1843–1921). By examining material from closed finds, such as graves and hoards, he determined what types of artefacts occur and do not occur together. On the basis of typological variations in form and decoration in different classes of artefacts, Montelius worked out and correlated a series of regional chronologies throughout Europe. He laid the groundwork for the typological approach that still dominates archaeological research in many parts of the world. Montelius' most lasting contribution to European prehistory was the division of the northern Bronze Age into a series of six periods (Montelius [1885] 1986; cf. Gräslund 1987: 70–85; Klindt-Jensen 1975: 84–96; Trigger 1989: 155–161) (Figure 3.2).

To understand why Swedish archaeology developed the way it did during the 1870s, it is necessary to consider both the internal archaeological logic and the contemporary context in general. The internal factors have often been emphasised and are comparatively well known (see e.g. Gräslund 1987; Klindt-Jensen 1975; Trigger 1989: 73–86). In short, chronological research is seen as a continuation and refinement of the work that started with the Three-Age System of the Dane C.J. Thomsen (1788–1865) in the 1820–30s. Also of importance were the rapidly

Figure 3.1 Farmer Anders Axel Petersson (1870–1930) shows an offering kettle to an antiquarian surveyor in 1927 in Sorunda parish, Södermanland, Sweden. The kettle is a so-called 'giant's kettle'. In folk tradition this geological phenomenon was supposed to be a kettle used by the giants that originally inhabited the land

Source: The Antiquarian-Topographical Archive, Stockholm

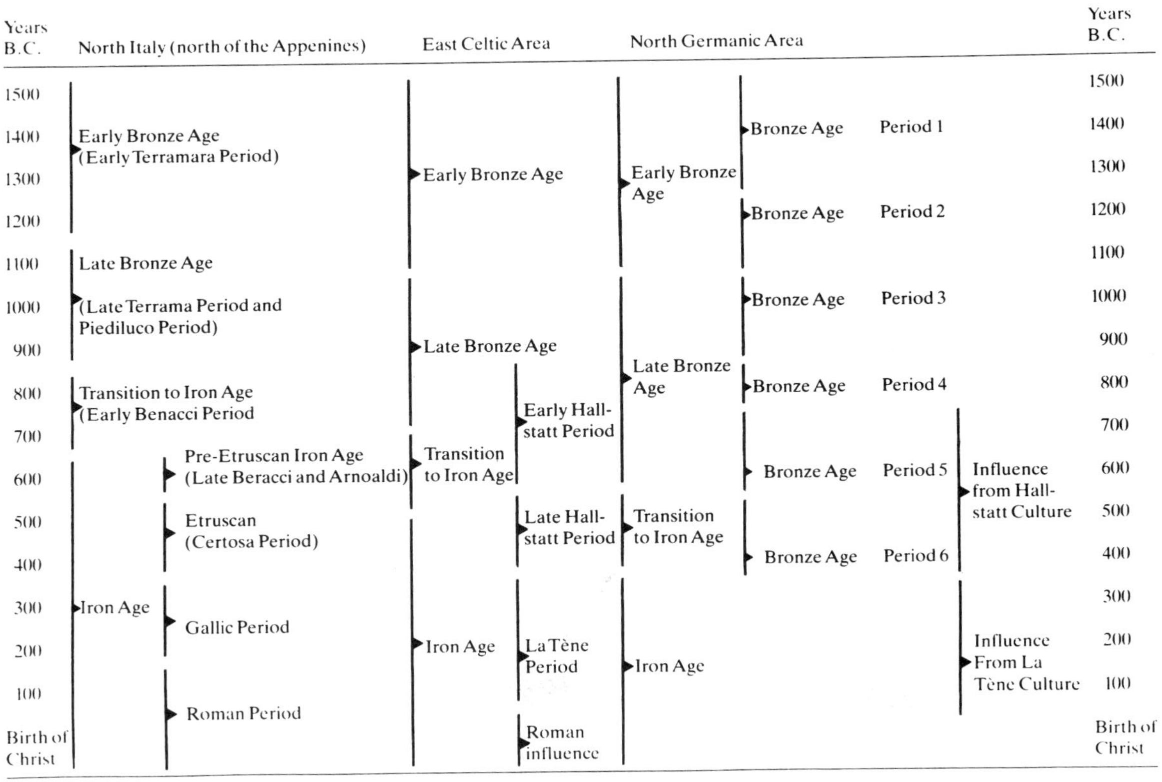

Figure 3.2 — chronological table (Montelius 1885)

Years B.C.	North Italy (north of the Appenines)	East Celtic Area	North Germanic Area		Years B.C.
1500					1500
1400	Early Bronze Age (Early Terramara Period)			Bronze Age — Period 1	1400
1300		Early Bronze Age	Early Bronze Age		1300
1200				Bronze Age — Period 2	1200
1100	Late Bronze Age				1100
1000	(Late Terrama Period and Piediluco Period)			Bronze Age — Period 3	1000
900		Late Bronze Age	Late Bronze Age		900
800	Transition to Iron Age (Early Benacci Period)	Early Hall-statt Period		Bronze Age — Period 4	800
700		Transition to Iron Age			700
600	Pre-Etruscan Iron Age (Late Beracci and Arnoaldi)			Bronze Age — Period 5 — Influence from Hall-statt Culture	600
500	Etruscan (Certosa Period)	Late Hall-statt Period	Transition to Iron Age		500
400				Bronze Age — Period 6	400
300	Iron Age	Iron Age			300
200	Gallic Period	La Tène Period	Iron Age	Influence From La Tène Culture	200
100	Roman Period	Roman influence			100
Birth of Christ					Birth of Christ

Figure 3.2 In 1885 Montelius summarised his chronological division of the northern Bronze Age into six main periods. Like a railway timetable, the table shows different routes connected in time and space
Source: After Montelius (1885): 196–197 (cf. Montelius 1986: 124)

growing collections of artefacts at the Museum of National Antiquities (*Statens Historiska Museum*) in Stockholm, which made it possible to construct increasingly fine chronological schemes. What has not attracted much attention, however, is the fact that archaeological preoccupation with dating coincided with a general interest in contemporary society with regard to handling time and making it uniform.

FOCUSING ON TIME

The 1870s was a period of exceptional economical and industrial expansion in Sweden (Lundmark 1989: 54). During this development a great deal of interest was focused on time as a phenomenon and on people's attitude towards it. New means of communication, telegraphy and railways, demanded a uniform time throughout the nation. This was made clear especially by the problems caused to railway timetables by different regional times. Therefore a nationwide standard time was introduced in Sweden in 1879. This is supposed to have been the first official, national standard time ever to have been introduced (ibid.: 56).

The building of railways was also an important reason for the rapidly growing collections of archaeological artefacts. The new railways made it possible for Montelius to travel and study museum collections throughout Europe. This was essential for his work on establishing and correlating different regional chronologies. Considering this and the decisive role of the railway in the introduction of a national standard time, it seems suitable that Montelius used the development of the railway carriage to illustrate the typological series (Figure 3.3).

Time was central also for other reasons. Industrial mass production demanded a new kind of discipline with regard to time, which had not been necessary in the previously agrarian society. The adjustment to an abstract clock-time was problematic and led to different measures from the authorities (Löfgren 1987). An important external sign of the new attitude towards time was the personal pocket-watch, which during the 1870s increasingly found a place among men's personal possessions (Medelius 1989: 77). The pocket-watch was often carried with the chain displayed over the chest as a visible sign of the owner's control over time and existence. Oscar Montelius, who as a chronology-constructor successfully tried to control past time, was also portrayed with an easily visible pocket-watch chain (Figure 3.4).

It would seem that time was used in Sweden during the late nineteenth century as a means of discipline in society in general as well as in archaeology. In society, time was used to discipline the Swede to become a useful citizen in an increasingly organised and centralised society (Broberg 1991: 889). In archaeology the controlling of time through the creation of chronological order was an essential part of the establishment of archaeology as a modern science.

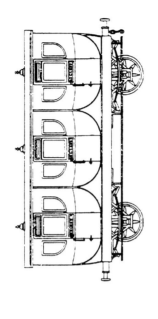

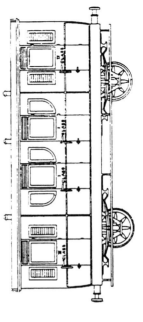

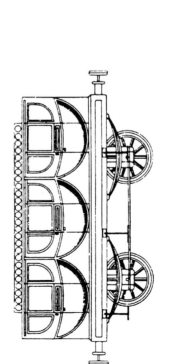

Figure 3.3 The typological series – the archaeological method for creating chronological order – illustrated by the development of the railway carriage

Source: After Montelius (1899): 262–263

Figure 3.4   Oscar Montelius (1843–1921) at the time of his retirement from the Central Board of National Antiquities. As in earlier portraits (cf. Rydh 1937) the pocket-watch chain is well displayed. Painting by Emerik Stenberg in 1913

Source: The Antiquarian-Topographical Archive, Stockholm

DISREGARDING FOLKLORE

In folklore there was little concern with the dating of ancient monuments. Instead it was the monuments themselves and their location in the landscape that attracted attention. In his study of Irish folklore Henry Glassie has made a similar observation:

> It is not the date that matters, it is the place. Time passes, but land endures, demanding attention. For most people, history's purpose is to enrich the world they inhabit by explaining the origin of some feature on the landscape – a twisted river, a spot bare of grass, the name for a meadow – for that is the most obvious way the past forces itself on the present, and the past unalive in the present is not history.
>
> (Glassie 1982: 196)

To folklore tradition dates are alienating, to archaeology they are essential. With the more solid chronological frameworks of the late nineteenth century, the scholarly status and ambition of archaeology grew considerably. The focus on chronological problems and the use of the typological method made archaeological interest centre on artefacts, while interest in ancient monuments diminished (cf. Selinge 1978: 76). Interest in the latter was often restricted to the artefacts they might contain. This increased the distance between archaeologists and the general public. While the monuments and the stories told about them continued to attract common people's interest, archaeologists focused on the dating of artefacts and considered the stories told about monuments to be superstition without scientific value.

The antiquarian loss of interest in folklore is, for example, evident from a regional survey of ancient monuments that started in western Sweden during the 1870s. This survey, known as the 'Gothenburg Survey' (*Göteborgsinventeringen*) continued with some breaks for half a century (cf. Bertilsson and Winberg 1978). The survey differed from its predecessors by a sharp restriction to the recording of prehistoric monuments. The survey has been described as 'extremely successful' since it ignored 'churches, folklore, the recording of local dialects, and much more that previously had encumbered the antiquarian work and reduced its value' (Sarauw and Alin 1923: 16, my translation). This appreciation is an evident illustration of how making archaeology a discipline altered antiquarian work. Antiquarians continued to have contact with local people concerning the presence of ancient monuments, but they were no longer interested in the stories locals could tell about them. From now on antiquarians were collecting archaeological 'data', and these were not to be confused with unlearned speculation. Hereby the antiquarians founded an interpretative supremacy concerning the understanding of ancient monuments (cf. Figure 3.5). By virtue of this supremacy, locals were no longer considered as partners in a dialogue but were reduced to informants

Figure 3.5 Hans Hildebrand (1842–1913), the director-general of the Central Board of National Antiquities, in his official uniform adorned with the Swedish grand cross, inspecting excavation work in 1904. The uniform stresses the supreme antiquarian position

Source: The Antiquarian-Topographical Archive, Stockholm

and potential objects for adult education. This attitude created a split between the antiquarian authorities and the general public.

At approximately the same time, ethnology was established as a modern science and a separate discipline. In ethnology interest focused on the material aspects of the old peasant culture in Sweden and the folklore did not attract much attention. In practice, the scientific organisation of archaeology and ethnology meant that the folkloristic traditions concerning ancient monuments were now outside the field of research of both disciplines.

FOCUSING ON MEANING

During recent years archaeology has focused interest on the interpretation of meaning. In line with postmodern debate in general it has been acknowledged that the meaning of ancient monuments is not restricted to the time when they came into being. On the contrary, they have repeatedly attracted attention and been ascribed meaning throughout history (cf. e.g. Bradley 1993; Burström 1989, 1993, 1996a, 1996b; Burström *et al.* 1996; Chippindale 1983; Holtorf 1996; Olsen 1990: 200–201; Strömberg 1995).

Ancient monuments are no longer looked at as just carriers of information about prehistory; they are also considered to have cultural value (Burström 1993: 7). This consists of the multitude of meanings that we and earlier generations have ascribed to the monuments and the ones they will be ascribed in the future. An essential part of monuments' cultural value is formed by the folklore surrounding them. A truly meaningful archaeology – that is, an archaeology full of meaning – must take into consideration the many contexts in which ancient objects have been ascribed meaning. Thereby, archaeology will cross the borders of what are traditionally considered other disciplines, and the search for meaning will become a joint venture (Burström 1996a: 39).

The interest in different kinds of meaning is a good base for professionals to reconsider their interpretative supremacy and start a dialogue with the general public. Such a dialogue once existed but was broken when archaeology was established as a separate discipline and a modern science. Now, after more than a century of well-disciplined archaeology, I believe it is high time to reopen that dialogue.

REFERENCES

Baudou, E. (1995) 'Politik, vetenskap och folkliga föreställningar. Olika syn på rannsakningarna – exemplet Norrland.' In E. Baudou and J. Moen (eds) *Rannsakningar efter antikviteter – ett symposium om 1600-talets Sverige,* pp. 155–174. Kungl. Vitterhets Historie och Antikvitets Akademien, Konferenser 30. Stockholm: Almqvist & Wiksell International.

46   Mats Burström

Baudou, E. and Moen, J. (eds) (1995) *Rannsakningar efter antikviteter – ett symposium om 1600-talets Sverige*. Kungl. Vitterhets Historie och Antikvitets Akademien, Konferenser 30. Stockholm: Almqvist & Wiksell International.

Bertilsson, U. and Winberg, B. (1978) 'Bohuslän – ett experimentområde.' *Fornvännen* 73: 97–107. Stockholm.

Bradley, R. (1993) *Altering the Earth. The Origins of Monuments in Britain and Continental Europe*. The Rhind Lectures 1991–92, Monograph Series Number 8. Edinburgh: Society of Antiquaries of Scotland

Broberg, G. (1991) 'Hur mycket är klockan?' In G. Broberg (ed.) *Gyllene Äpplen. Svensk idéhistorisk läsebok*, pp. 876–892. Stockholm: Atlantis.

Burström, M. (1989) 'Kronologi och kontext. Om samtidighetens relevans för den arkeologiska tolkningen.' In M. Burström *et al.* (eds) *Mänsklighet genom millennier. En vänbok till Åke Hyenstrand*, pp. 37–41. Stockholm: Riksantikvarieämbetet.

Burström, M. (1993) *Mångtydiga fornlämningar. En studie av innebörder som tillskrivits fasta fornlämningar i Österrekarne härad, Södermanland*. Stockholm Archaeological Reports, Number 27. Stockholm: Stockholm University.

Burström, M. (1996a) 'Other generations' interpretations and use of the past: the case of the picture stones on Gotland.' *Current Swedish Archaeology*, 4: 21–40.

Burström, M. (1996b) 'Skalunda hög. Historier kring en hög.' In E. Holmström (ed.) *Mellan bronssköld och JAS-plan – glimtar av Lidköpingsbygdens historia*, pp. 78–92. Lidköping: Lidköpings kommun.

Burström, M., Winberg, B. and Zachrisson, T. (1996) *Fornlämningar och folkminnen*. Stockholm: Riksantikvarieämbetet.

Chippindale, C. (1983) *Stonehenge Complete*. London: Thames and Hudson.

Glassie, H. (1982) *Passing the Time in Ballymenone. Culture and History of an Ulster Community*. Philadelphia: University of Pennsylvania Press.

Gräslund, B. (1987) *The Birth of Prehistoric Chronology. Dating Methods and Dating Systems in Nineteenth-Century Scandinavian Archaeology*. New Studies in Archaeology. Cambridge: Cambridge University Press.

Holtorf, C.J. (1996) 'Towards a chronology of megaliths: understanding monumental time and cultural memory.' *Journal of European Archaeology* 4: 119–152.

Klindt-Jensen, O. (1975) *A History of Scandinavian Archaeology*. London: Thames and Hudson.

Löfgren, O. (1987) 'Människan och tiden.' In J. Frykman and O. Löfgren *Den kultiverade människan*, pp. 21–44. Skrifter utgivna av Etnologiska sällskapet i Lund 11. Malmö: Liber.

Lundmark, L. (1989) *Tidens gång och tidens värde*. Stockholm: Författarförlaget Fischer & Rye.

Medelius, H. (1989) 'Om bondens år och arbetets tid.' *Människan och Tiden*. Katalog för utställning på Läckö slott, pp. 71–80. Skövde: Västergötlands turistråd

Montelius, O. [1885] (1986) *Om tidsbestämning inom bronsåldern med särskildt afseende på Skandinavien*. Kungl. Vitterhets Historie och Antikvitets Akademien. Handlingar, Del 30, Stockholm. Translated into English as *Dating in the Bronze Age with Special Reference to Scandinavia* (1986), trans. Helen Clarke. The Royal Academy of Letters, History and Antiquities. Stockholm: Almqvist & Wiksell International.

Montelius, O. (1899) 'Typologien eller utvecklingsläran tillämpad på det menskliga arbetet.' *Svenska Fornminnesföreningens Tidskrift*. Tionde bandet. pp. 237–268. Stockholm.

Olsen, B. (1990) 'Roland Barthes: from sign to text.' In C. Tilley (ed.) *Reading Material Culture. Structuralism, Hermeneutics and Post-Structuralism*, pp. 163–205. Oxford: Basil Blackwell.

Rydh, H. (1937) *Oscar Montelius. En vägrödjare genom årtusenden*. Stockholm: Åhlén & Söners Förlag.

Sarauw, G. and Alin, J. (1923) *Götaälvsområdets fornminnen*. Skrifter utgivna till Göteborgs Stads trehundraårsjubileum genom jubileumsutställningens publikationskommitté III. Göteborg: Göteborgs Stad.

Selinge, K.-G. (1978) 'Fornlämningsregistret som forskningsunderlag. Några synpunkter med norrländska exempel.' *Fornvännen* 73: 75–90. Stockholm.

Ståhle, C.I. (ed.) (1960) *Rannsakningar efter antikviteter. Band I, häfte I*. Stockholm: Kungl. Vitterhets Historie och Antikvitets Akademien.

Strömberg, M. (1995) 'Fornminne med många uttolkare. Ales stenar inspirerar fackmän och allmänhet.' *Ale. Historisk tidskrift för Skåne, Halland och Blekinge* 4: 1–15.

Trigger, B.G. (1989) *A History of Archaeological Thought*. Cambridge: Cambridge University Press.

Welinder, S. (1994) *Strindberg som arkeologikritiker*. Stockholm: Almqvist & Wiksell International.

CHAPTER FOUR

BACK TO THE FUTURE

Resonances of the past in myth and material culture

MIRANDA J. GREEN

ABSTRACT

The central tenet of this essay is the hypothesis that a sense of past pervaded the earliest extant mythic literature of Ireland and Wales, in the same way as there is evidence, from archaeology, of interactive 'discourse' between different phases of prehistoric and early historical periods. It is contended that apparent linkages between the symbolism of these mythic texts and the material culture of religious expression in earlier periods – not only in Britain and Ireland but also in western Europe as a whole – consisted of genuine and deliberate attempts, by the constructors of the myths, to enter into a 'folkloric' dialogue with their past. Such resonance of pre-Christian cultic activity within later mythic constructs is predicated in part on admittance of the active influence of oral tradition, whose genesis may lie centuries earlier than the myths into which it fed. A second valid model within which to explain connections between material culture and later myth depends on the presence of archaeological evidence pertaining to early ritual surviving to the time in which the myths were constructed which, it is proposed here, may have provided conscious or unconscious inspiration to medieval storytellers.

This paper addresses the issue of linkages – genuine and apparent – between folklore and the archaeology of later prehistoric and Roman period Europe. A great deal of Welsh and Irish medieval mythic literature, compiled within a Christian context, contains allusions that appear to relate to elements of pre-Christian imagery and cult practice, as reflected in the material culture of Britain and parts of Europe during the later first millennium BC and earlier first millennium AD. The problems inherent in the acknowledgement of linkages between medieval texts and material pertaining to earlier pagan ritual are those concerned with dislocations in chronology and in spatial continuity: the earliest Irish myths may have been written down in the seventh or eighth century AD, but the earliest Welsh mythic literature probably dates no earlier than the tenth or eleventh century. Similarly, it is difficult to comprehend the apparent correspondences between descriptions of supernatural heroes in Welsh and Irish myth and their putative prototypes, which consist of pagan cult-images whose distribution is largely Continental rather than British or Irish.

This essay seeks both to present some of the evidence for 'linkages' and to propose models which may contribute to an understanding of the mechanisms that may have been in place to enable such connections. One of the basic tenets underpinning the arguments presented here is that a sense of past may have been an important element not only in the creation of myth but also in the socio-religious organisation of people living in later prehistoric, Roman and medieval communities. It is not argued that the past necessarily had meaning to later societies, in terms of depth or identity, but that the detritus of former human groups may have been recognised as being – at one and the same time – different (or 'other'), on the one hand, yet linked to the ancestors (and/or the supernatural), on the other. Additionally, the material culture of earlier human activity may have sometimes played a part in legitimising the political behaviour of later communities (Holtorf 1998: 30). Whether or not these interactions between pasts were associated with perceptions of the supernatural or with secular power-politics, elements of the past perhaps acquired a certain *dignitas* or reverence in antiquity; such an attitude would help to explain the apparent interweaving of allusions to pre-Christian cultic material into the medieval mythic tradition. It will be contended later in this essay that one of the mechanisms for the intrusion of earlier material culture into later texts is the observation of the physical remains of that earlier stratum by the storytellers who were responsible for relating mythic tales or the writers who codified them. That such observation could and did occur can sometimes be clearly demonstrated, for instance, by the records of Giraldus Cambrensis (Gerald of Wales), a prolific twelfth-century author who compiled copious notes on his travels. In March 1188, Gerald set out from Hereford Cathedral on a journey through Wales, undertaken as a recruiting tour for the Crusades (Kightly 1988: 28; Knight 1988: 3). On his arrival at Caerleon he made the following comments:

> Caerleon is of unquestioned antiquity. It was constructed with great care by the Romans, the walls being built of brick. You can still see many vestiges of its one-time splendour. There are immense palaces which, with the gilded gables of their roofs, once rivalled the magnificence of ancient Rome . . . There is a lofty tower, and beside it remarkable hot baths, the remains of temples and an amphitheatre . . .
>
> (Gerald of Wales 1978: 114)

Giraldus' journey, which was completed in about 1191 (Roberts 1988: 96–97), contains elements that were clearly 'lifted' wholesale from

Geoffrey of Monmouth's 'historical' romance, the *History of the Kings of Britain*, written some 50 years earlier, but Gerald's description of Caerleon clearly arises from first-hand observation. Gerald's account indicates quite unequivocally that some monuments of Roman date were not only highly visible but – in some cases – virtually intact in the medieval period. That being the case, there is no reason to doubt that other travellers, some of whom came home to Ireland and Wales and constructed mythic tales – such as the *Táin Bó Cuailnge* or the *Pedeir Keinc y Mabinogi* – also observed and noted the standing monuments or other remnants of earlier, pre-Christian, material culture. My contention is that certain of these observations, particularly those pertaining to pagan cult-imagery or evidence for ritual practice, were woven into medieval mythic literature whose authors used such material as inspiration, either to develop the personae of heroes or as a basis for depicting the supernatural world: some possible examples of such borrowing will be examined later in this study. First, however, I wish briefly to explore the concept of retrospective sanctity, the notion that communities in European antiquity acknowledged a sacred or symbolic past with which they interacted in ways that are sometimes archaeologically visible.

WHEN PASTS COLLIDE

Time and again, it appears that communities consciously interacted with the material culture – and thus arguably with the minds behind it – of their forebears (Bradley 1987: 1–17): this is evident in the use of both monuments and artefacts. In a recent paper Richard Hingley clearly demonstrated such diachronic interaction in the prehistoric landscape of Atlantic Scotland, where several Neolithic chambered tombs have not only produced later prehistoric finds but were clearly sometimes themselves adapted for re-use as habitation structures. Hingley interprets such evidence as the result of local communities, between the ninth and first century BC, interacting with their ancestral landscape and perhaps 'deliberately reinventing monumental aspects of the past as part of active strategies related to the projection of contemporary identity' (Hingley 1996: 231–243). The re-use of tombs as dwelling places for the living, in particular, seems likely to have been – at least in part – the result of a desire to establish or maintain contact with the dead, perhaps as a means of asserting identity within the context of an ancestral pedigree; such a practice may have engendered a sense of place and have enhanced feelings of close relationships between past and present, dead and living, at locations which were perceived as thresholds between worlds.

A practice essentially similar to the later prehistoric use of tombs in Scotland has been noted elsewhere in Britain, notably in Wessex: thus, Howard Williams (1997) presented evidence which he argued should be understood as deliberate re-use of 'ancient and ruinous monuments', dating from the prehistoric and Roman periods, as Anglo-Saxon burial places. Dark (1993: 132–146) similarly discusses the use of prehistoric ceremonial monuments during the Roman period. In Ireland, there is evidence that some Neolithic passage graves, such as Newgrange (Co. Meath), were foci for later activity. Barry Raftery has described the great mound of Newgrange as a 'magnet to travellers from the provincial Roman world' (1994: 210–211) and interprets Roman finds from the vicinity of the tomb as the belongings of visitors who looked upon the ancient site as a centre of pilgrimage.

In addition to the re-use or re-visitation of 'ancestral' monuments in antiquity, it is possible to recognise a converse phenomenon, that is the practice involving the inclusion of archaic material in sacred structures of later periods, arguably as deliberately selected offerings the value of which was enhanced by a recognition of otherness associated with what was perceived either as past human activity or as evidence for a supernatural presence. Such perceptions may account for the presence of early Bronze Age barbed-and-tanged arrowheads in Merovingian tombs (Alcock 1963: 171; Evans 1897: 354). It is difficult to explain such occurrences other than as the result of ritual behaviour involving deliberate sepulchral deposition of strange objects (whether or not they were perceived as belonging to earlier cultures, or even of human manufacture), on account of their presumed numinous or talismanic properties. A phenomenon which bears a strong resemblance to the occurrence of Bronze Age flints in early medieval graves is the deposition of prehistoric stone or flint axes in Romano-Celtic temples, particularly in northern France; these implements are often found in groups, sometimes deliberately smashed (Adkins and Adkins 1985: 69–75). Most striking among such antique Roman temple deposits is the hoard of stone tools from a sanctuary at Essarts (Seine-Maritime) which consisted of seventy Palaeolithic and Neolithic stone axes (de Vesly 1909: 84–92; Horne and King 1980: 408; King 1990: 139). The frequency with which Stone Age objects are found in Gaulish temples of Roman date is consistent with their presence as votive objects; the practice of deliberate ritual destruction is a common treatment accorded sacred metalwork during the Iron Age and Roman periods, its purpose apparently being symbolically to remove such pieces from the profane world and transfer them to the realms of the supernatural, in the same way that animals (and occasionally humans) were slaughtered in acts of sacrifice (Bradley 1990; Green 1996: 191–203, 1998a). It appears as if, in common with the deposition of early Bronze Age material in early medieval burial contexts, Stone Age implements were carefully selected as offerings to Romano-Gaulish divinities. It is tempting here to see such behaviour as illustrative of retrospective sanctity, of a belief that because these tools clearly belonged to different human groups, who had earlier inhabited the land on which the shrines were erected, they were perceived as part of the ancestral landscape. Their removal to the temples could thereby have been a deliberate act of veneration, designed to propitiate the ancient local spirits. Here again, however, the possible supernatural dimension should be noted: Roman writers such as Pliny (*Natural History* XXXVII, 9) and Suetonius (*Life of Galba* VIII, 4) allude to the supernatural origin of stone axes.[1]

MEDIEVAL MYTH AND THE ARCHAEOLOGY OF PRE-CHRISTIAN PAGANISM

The mythic texts of Ireland and Wales were compiled – for the most part – by medieval Christian clerics, between the eighth and twelfth centuries AD. However, despite the religious affiliations of their redactors, these texts possess a strongly pagan content, in which supernatural beings and the inhabitants of the Otherworld play a prominent role. Moreover, firm links appear to exist between some elements of these myths and features of earlier British, Irish and European material culture belonging to the early Iron Age and Roman periods (Green 1990: 13–28). Leaving aside – for the moment – problems concerning chronological discrepancies between the time the myths were composed and the archaeology of pre-Christian paganism, it is possible to cite certain persuasive illustrations of such apparent correspondences.

The descriptions of the mythic Otherworld, as presented, for example, in the Irish *Táin* and the *Leabhar Gabhala* and in the Welsh *Pedeir Keinc y Mabinogi* paint a kaleidoscopic picture of a spirit-world or afterlife which bears a close resemblance to earthly life at its best. A central focus of this never-never land, especially in Ireland, is the Otherworld feast over which particular gods presided and where ever-replenished food and drink were supplied (Mac Cana 1983: 34–35, 127; O'Rahilly 1946: 120–122). One of the best-known episodes is the story of Mac Da Tho's pig, in which just such a banquet is described (Cross and Slover [1936] 1988: 199–207). In another story, in the First Branch of the Mabinogi, Annwfn, the Welsh Otherworld, was visited by Pwyll, Lord of Dyfed, who participated in a sumptuous feast therein. 'Of all the courts he had seen on earth, that was the court best furnished with meat and drink and vessels of gold and royal jewels' (Jones and Jones 1976: 6; see also Jackson 1961–7: 83–99).

Feasting also appears to have been an important element in pre-Christian funerary (and other) rituals in Iron Age Britain and Europe. Some rich Hallstatt tombs of the earliest Iron Age contained equipment for communal feasting: the grave of the chieftain buried at Eberdingen-Hochdorf (Baden-Württemberg) in about 530 BC was furnished with sufficient platters and drinking horns for a nine-person banquet, together with implements for the preparation of meat; a great 400 litre capacity Greek cauldron (its residues showing that it once contained a liquor fermented from honey) stood at the foot of the funerary couch on which the dead man lay (Biel 1991). That eating and drinking played a prominent role in later funerary ritual is amply illustrated by some very late Iron Age tombs, for example at Welwyn Garden City (Hertfordshire), a grave of the so-called Aylesford–Swarling tradition dating to the late first century BC, which contained six Italian wine amphorae and thirty-six pots, as well as a silver cup and bronze wine-strainer as testament to the serious business of wine consumption (Stead 1991). The lavish tomb assemblages found at Goeblingen-Nospelt in Luxembourg are witness to the presence of similar and broadly coeval funerary feasting rituals across the English Channel. One of the Goeblingen graves contained wine amphorae, bronze-bound stave buckets, a bronze strainer, pan and cauldron and more than fifty ceramic vessels (Metzler 1991).

Cauldrons are associated with symbolic and regenerative feasting in both myth and pre-Christian material culture. In early Irish texts, cauldrons are presented as being closely associated with the Otherworld *bruidhen* or hostel, their function being the preparation of large quantities of food and drink. The Insular god most closely linked with cauldrons was the Daghdha, a chief of the Tuatha De Danann (the divine race of Ireland whose activities are described in the *Leabhar Gabhala*); his cauldron was gigantic and inexhaustible, capable of containing a stew of entire animals and vast quantities of milk, meal and fat (Green 1998b; Mac Cana 1983: 64–66).

The Welsh mythic references to cauldrons display greater complexity and ambiguity: in the *Pedeir Keinc Y Mabinogi* and in a thirteenth-century poem entitled *Preiddeu Annwfn* (the Spoils of Annwfn), cauldrons are associated not only with plenty, renewal and feasting but also with death. Thus, in the Second Branch, a cauldron of Irish origin is described as having the apparent power to raise soldiers from the dead, but these warriors were speechless zombies who were clearly on loan from the infernal regions (Jones and Jones 1976: 29). This same cauldron displayed its capriciousness: in the hands of its owner's enemies, it resurrected fighting men who turned and attacked him.

The ambivalent nature of Welsh mythic cauldrons is expressed with even greater clarity in *Preiddeu Annwfn*, which chronicles a mythical raid on the Otherworld by the British hero Arthur, who sought to carry off a great cauldron as loot; the distinct persona of the vessel was such that it would only consent to cook the food of a brave man and could be heated only by the breath of virgins (Haycock 1983; Jones and Jones 1976: xxv). In the tenth-century story *Culhwch ac Olwen*, Arthur was once again involved in cauldron rustling, this time in Ireland whence he returned with the great 'Cauldron of Diwrnach' filled with all the treasures of Ireland, but only at the cost of nearly all his forces (Jones and Jones 1976: 116).

One of the most striking features of these mythic cauldrons is their connection with the Otherworld and thus – directly or indirectly – with both death and regeneration. This may be significant in terms of the ritual treatment of cauldrons in later Bronze Age and Iron Age Britain and Europe. Such containers appear to have had a primary function as ceremonial cooking vessels (Gerloff 1986) but the pattern of their deposition after use reflects symbolic practices that are repeated over time and space, although not necessarily without hiatus in each dimension. In the first place, cauldrons were recurrently and deliberately deposited, sometimes full of metalwork, in aquatic locations – rivers, lakes or marshes – in later prehistoric Europe, apparently as a ritual act (Green 1998b).[2] Such occurrences may be associated with sacrificial cultic practice which involved both the consignment of a valuable piece of ceremonial equipment to the spirit powers dwelling in the infernal regions and its permanent removal from the earthly world.[3] Additionally, water, as both a life-force and a destroyer, may have been perceived as possessing similar paradoxical qualities to the cauldrons themselves. The association of death is amply illustrated in ancient Classical literature. In Greek ritual practice, the sacrificial blood of animal victims was collected in a sphageion, a special blood container; this vessel is clearly represented on Greek vase paintings of the sixth and fifth centuries BC (Durand 1989). Interestingly, the Greek geographer Strabo, writing in the late first century BC/early first century AD but probably deriving his material from the earlier Syrian Greek philosopher Poseidonios (Tierney 1959–60: 189–275), records cultic practice among the north European tribe of the Cimbri, in which a cauldron was also used to catch the sacrificial blood of human victims, war prisoners whose throats were cut in an act of divination, to seek to foretell victory for the tribe (Geographia VII: 2, 3). The grisly assemblage from the cave at Byci Skála in Moravia, dating to the sixth century BC, perhaps links cauldrons directly with sacrificial practice: depositions in the cave included the dismembered bodies of about forty people, together with the quartered bodies of two horses and a cauldron containing a human skull (Parzinger *et al.* 1995).

The association of cauldrons with death as displayed by their use in sacrificial ritual may account for their frequent burial in sepulchral contexts during the Iron Age, Roman and sub-Roman periods in Britain and Europe. Iron Age cauldron graves are exemplified by Hochdorf and Goeblingen (already cited on pp. 52–3); those of Roman date include vessels from Zügmantel and Köngen in Germany (Hawkes 1951) and a miniature bronze cauldron from a cremation grave at Tarland in northern Scotland (Piggott 1953). At Westland in Norway, cauldrons were placed in graves over a period between AD 375 and 575 (Hauken 1991). The best known Anglo-Saxon sepulchral cauldron finds are those from Sutton Hoo in East Anglia (Evans 1983).

It appears that both the archaeology of cauldrons and their role in Welsh and Irish myth are indicative of a shared symbolism, despite the chronological disparity in the two forms of evidence. The material culture of medieval cauldrons and synchronous secular literature, such as the Laws of Hywel Dda (Jenkins 1986: 39, 192), suggest that, as in earlier periods, cauldrons possessed high status as feasting vessels, over and above their function as domestic culinary equipment. However, what is missing is the association between medieval use of cauldrons and their symbolism as ambiguous vessels of plenty, death and regeneration that is so apparent both in myth and in the pre-medieval archaeological record. If such commonality between myth and earlier material culture is not to be dismissed as coincidence, then we need to look for mechanisms to explain such linkage (see p. 49).

A powerful motif running through both Irish and Welsh mythic litera-ture is that of shape-shifting: supernatural beings possessed the power to transform themselves, both in age and between human and animal form. Thus in the *Táin*, the diabolical battle-furies, variously named Morrigan and Badbh, appeared on the battlefield as hideous hags or carrion crows picking over the spoils of the slain or as shrieking doom-laden portents, calculated to unman the most stalwart warrior (Green 1995: 41–45; Hennessy 1870–72: 37; Herbert 1996). In the Welsh narratives, shape-shifting is generally presented as punitive rather than voluntary: a number of episodes revolve around the transformation of people into animals because of some misdemeanour. Thus, in *Culhwch ac Olwen*, Twrch Trwyth – an enchanted boar – is the object of one of Culhwch's quests to win the hand of Olwen. When questioned as to the origin of his misfortune, Trwch Trwyth replied that God (presumably the Christian God) blighted him with boar-shape on account of his evil ways. In the Fourth Branch of the Mabinogi, Gwydion and his brother Gilfaethwy were turned into three successive pairs of beasts (deer, wolves and swine) because of their conspiracy to rape King Math's virgin footholder Goewin (Jones and Jones 1976: 61–63), an act which seriously under-mined Math's sovereignty.[4]

There are Irish counterparts to the punitive/vengeance shape-shifting theme: in the Fionn Cycle, for example, Finn's wife Sava suffered from the vengeful action of a certain 'Black Druid' who, in jealous rage at her spurning of his attentions, turned her into a doe; her child Oisin ('Little Deer') retained this animal affiliation to some extent, though he grew up as a man (Mac Cana 1983: 104). The mythic theme of meta-morphosis is, of course, closely associated with the supernatural world. It involves divine beings who were either the shape-shifters or the per-petrators of transmutation as directed towards others.

Elements in the pagan religious iconography of the later Iron Age and Roman period in northern and temperate Europe may have had some influence on the generation of these later skin-turners. There are several instances of what may be termed therianthropic images, depictions that display features of both human and wild animal form. The most striking group consists of horned beings, anthropomorphic figures with antlers' or bulls' horns, and occasionally (like the Pan of Classical mythology) with hooves or animal ears. Antlered images are widely distributed over space and time: the earliest Iron Age examples are two petroglyphs in the Naquane group at Val Camonica, near Brescia in north Italy, which date to the seventh and fourth centuries BC (e.g. Priuli 1988: 78, no. 134); a similar image appears on the Danish Gundestrup Cauldron (Kaul *et al.* 1991), on a late Iron Age silver coin from the British Midlands (Boon 1982), and on several Gallo-Roman monuments, including those from Reims (Espérandieu 1913, no. 3653), Saintes in Aquitaine (Espérandieu 1908, no. 1319) and Sommerécourt, Haute-Marne (Espérandieu 1915, no. 4839). The recently discovered pair of red deer antlers, pierced as if for wear as a headdress, in a Roman context at Hook's Cross, Hertfordshire (Green 1997: 58–59 and Tony Rook personal communication) may have been designed for such an image, but it may – instead – have been worn by a shaman. Bull-horned images have a similarly wide distribution: depictions of Roman date include a bronze head from Lezoux (Green 1992: 235, fig. 8.22) and stone carvings from northern Britain, for example at Maryport and Netherby in Cumbria (Ross 1961: figs 1 and 2). Anthropomorphic figures of pre-Roman date include the fifth-century BC janiform male statue from Holzgerlingen in Germany (Megaw 1970, no. 14) and the late Iron Age bucket escutcheon from Boughton Aluph in Kent (Green 1976: 230); horned beings also appear on some Iron Age coin issues (Allen 1980: 133–134). A seated, cross-legged bronze image from Bouray (Essonne) is probably of second–first century BC date; it depicts a being with a hornless, overlarge head, but with hooves (Joffroy 1979, no. 78). Apart from those with horns, other therianthropes include the later Iron Age stone figure of an anthropomorphic being with a large, erect-crested boar superimposed on his torso (Espérandieu 1938, no. 7702); and a pelt-clad figure from Cirencester in Gloucestershire (Green 1986: 220, fig. 102).

Triplism and a focus on the human head form my final two areas of comparison between myth and material culture. These two forms of image possess a common feature inasmuch as they each reflect ways of expressing the divine rather than presentation of specific god-types. Triads or triple beings are ubiquitous elements in the Welsh and Irish mythic imagery: the Irish battle-furies, mentioned earlier in connection with shape-shifting, were triple entities; likewise, the powerful Insular goddess Macha possessed triple aspects and personae, as did Brigit (Condren 1989: 23–43; Herbert 1996; McCone 1982, 1990; O'Catháin 1995), and there are numerous other examples in the *Táin* and the *Leabhar Gabhala*. In the Welsh texts, Branwen (in the Second Branch of the Mabinogi) is described variously (according to the translation) as one of the three fairest women in the land or one of three matriarchs (Jones and Jones 1976: 26). As we have seen, the punishment meted out to the trickster Gwydion and his brother by Math, following their dishonouring of Goewin, was their metamorphosis into three successive animals, during which time the couple produced three sons, each of whom also began life as a beast:

> The three sons of false Gilfaethwy,
> Three champions true,
> Bleiddwn, Hyddwn, Hychdwn Hir.
> (Jones and Jones 1976: 63)

The singing birds of Rhiannon (ibid.: 38, 115–116), which have a direct Irish counterpart in the three magical healing birds of the goddess Clíodna (Mac Cana 1958: 105–107, 1983: 50–54), repeat the triadic formula.

The religious iconographic repertoire of Gaul and Britain during the Roman period includes a wide range of triple forms: the most common triadic depiction is that of the triple mother goddess, who appears as three women (generally not identical), seated – or occasionally standing – side by side, accompanied by children, animals and examples of the earth's bounty: fruit or bread. British triple mother images include a cluster from Cirencester or its environs (Henig 1993, nos. 116–119) and from Hadrian's Wall (Coulston and Phillips 1988, nos. 173–176). They occur all over Gaul, particularly in Burgundy and the Lower Rhône Valley, for example at Vertault, near Châtillon-sur-Seine (Espérandieu 1911, nos. 3373, 3377–8) and Lyon (Espérandieu 1910, nos. 1741–2), and on the Rhine frontier, especially around Cologne and Bonn (Espérandieu 1938, nos. 6307, 6560, 7760, 7761). Other triads include three-faced/headed images, for instance from Corleck (Co. Cavan) in Ireland (Raftery 1994: 185–186; Rynne 1972: 79–96), Scotland (Megaw and Simpson 1979: 478–479), Reims (Green 1989: 172–174, figs 76, 77; Espérandieu 1913, nos. 3651–9) and Lyon (Audin 1975: 15); and triple-horned depictions, usually bulls (Boucher 1976: 171; Colombet and Lebel 1953: 112) but occasionally boars (Dayet 1954: 334–335) and even humans (Deyts 1976, no. 21).

The perception of the human head as a talismanic symbol pervades Irish and Welsh myth: in the *Táin*, the Ulster hero Conall Cernach possessed a gigantic head which, when severed, was used as a vessel for containing milk; the head endowed the liquid with magical properties, so that the Ulstermen who drank it were immediately re-invigorated after suffering desperate battle-fatigue (Dillon 1933; Lehner 1989; Mac Cana 1983: 97–98). In the Second Branch of the Mabinogi, the head of the supernatural hero Bendigeidfran (Bran the Blessed) possessed independent life after decapitation and was kept, uncorrupted, by his followers for many years until its final burial (Jones and Jones 1976: 38–40).

The archaeological record of pre-Roman and Roman period paganism in temperate Europe contains a great deal of evidence for the veneration of the human head. Skulls are repeatedly found in contexts that appear to reflect their sanctity: those placed in niches (and heads carved in stone) in pre-Roman sanctuaries such as Roquepertuse and Entremont near Marseilles (Benoit 1969, 1981) and the skulls found deliberately deposited in disused grain-storage pits at Iron Age Danebury (Cunliffe 1992: 69–83, 1993: 100–112) are just some of many instances of the ritual use of human heads for which there is evidence in many regions of Europe. Classical writers, such as Livy (X, 26, XXIII, 24) and Diodorus Siculus (V, 29, 4) allude to the practice of ritual head-hunting in Gaul in the first century BC. Iconography, too, displays an emphasis on the head: human faces frequently appear as motifs in a pre-Roman Iron Age art whose repertoire is otherwise notably lacking in realistic representation of the human form. On certain images of Iron Age and Roman date, the head is exaggerated in proportion to the rest of the body: the hooved bronze statuette from Bouray (p. 56) and that of a stone-carved mother goddess from Caerwent in South Wales (Brewer 1986, no. 14, pl. 6) illustrate this tradition. Moreover the practice of depicting heads alone, as representative of entire images, which was particularly prevalent in northern Britain during the Roman period (Ross 1974: 94–171), also points to the persistent perception of the head as a focus for special veneration.

ANCESTRAL VOICES: MEDIEVAL STORYTELLERS AND ANCIENT SURVIVALS

If the apparent linkages between medieval myth and earlier material culture are the result of anything other than pure coincidence, then it is necessary to present models to help explain the mechanisms through which such connections could have come about. It is my suggestion that a relationship or interaction existed between mythic functionaries (story-tellers, poets and redactors) and their past, in much the same way as later communities of antiquity interacted with the human landscape of their ancestors (pp. 50–51). One method by which this might occur is through oral tradition. In discussing the construction of the *Pedeir Keinc y Mabinogi*, Sioned Davies comments

> it would seem that the tales, or parts of them, were transmitted orally for centuries before they were safeguarded in manuscript form and therefore the material, or part of it certainly, can claim to have its roots in the distant past.
>
> (Davies, 1993: 9)

If this is so, then it is by no means impossible that some of the Welsh mythic episodes had their genesis in the pre-Christian period. Davies argues (1993: 10) that the *Pedeir Keinc* demonstrably belongs to the story-telling genre, but that these tales were part of the repertoire of the pro-fessional storyteller, the *cyfarwydd* (rather than simply transmitted from parents to children within the family context), whose livelihood was the entertainment of medieval courts. Sometime (maybe centuries) later, the tales were codified, written down by someone, who could have been a *cyfarwydd* himself, or a scribe writing from a storyteller's dictation, or – most likely of all – a skilled and artistic composer of literature. The identity of the author of the Four Branches is not known for certain, but it may have been a cleric: the names most frequently linked with the stories are Sulien, Bishop of Saint David's and his son Rhigyfarch (ibid.: 13–14). Certainly, as was the case in Ireland, the monasteries were great foci for learning in medieval Wales.

Irish myth may well have been similarly generated by a combination of oral transmission and professional literary composition. Patricia Kelly makes a comment about the Insular heroic tales which is virtually identical to that of Davies on Wales: 'It would seem to be a general rule that early Irish sagas are sited in times long anterior to the date of composition' (Kelly 1992: 72). The redactors of the Insular myths were almost certainly early medieval Christian clerics: the monasteries were the main centres of learning, and were probably far more active in this regard than the royal courts, the other foci for education. The 'primitive' nature of the tales, particularly the *Táin*, and their overt paganism are highly suggestive of a substantively pre-Christian element in their oral composition, even though they were crystallised within a monastic Christian milieu. The feeding of – perhaps quite early – oral transmission into mythic literature is one model which can be presented to explain some of the apparent correspondences between medieval text and pagan material culture. However, there is an alternative (or additional) model which has been largely ignored: the hypothesis that early medieval clerics actually observed the remains of pagan cult material within the landscape or listened to accounts of its presence from other witnesses.

In the mid sixth century AD, 'an irritating monk named Gildas' (Ashe 1968: 44) allegedly wrote a *liber querulus* (a complaining book) entitled *De Excidio Britanniae*, in which he denounced the moral lapses of the contemporary rulers of Britain; the earliest surviving manuscript of the work dates to the eleventh century. There has been considerable controversy surrounding the authorship, date and authenticity of the *De Excidio*, but the consensus is that it is a genuinely early work, probably composed between AD 515 and 530 and that it is likely to be a single, integral text, the product of a British cleric (O'Sullivan 1978: 46–76, 179–180). In Chapter 4, Gildas specifically observes the presence of visible pagan monuments:

> I shall not enumerate the devilish monstrosities of my land, numerous almost as those that plagued Egypt, some of which we can see today, stark as ever, inside or outside deserted city walls: outlines still ugly, faces still grim. I shall not name the mountains and hills and rivers, once so pernicious, now useful for human needs, on which, in those days, a blind people heaped divine honours.
>
> (*De Excidio Britanniae* 4, 2–3: trans. Winterbottom 1978, 17)

We can ignore the passionate anti-pagan rhetoric of the passage; what is interesting is the comment that pagan images were still present in the British landscape centuries later (it can be assumed) than their manufacture. Gildas was by no means the only early medieval cleric to notice remnants of the pre-Christian past; Gregory of Tours, in his *Glory of the Confessors*, for instance, recounts how the sixth-century cleric Hilary, Bishop of Poitiers, condemned pagan sacrificial practices at a lake in the vicinity of Javols in the Cevennes (de Nie 1987: 223; Van Dam 1988: 19).

One of the stumbling blocks encountered in any attempt to make links between pagan cult-imagery and medieval myth is the spatial disparity between the two types of source: the authors of the mythic texts wrote within the context of Ireland and Wales whereas a large proportion of the pagan image-types are seldom found in British or Irish locations but are heavily concentrated on the continental mainland. But it must be remembered that some early Irish monks travelled widely within Europe. Such travels were undertaken for the glory of God and many clerics embarked upon what was known as the *peregrinatio pro Dei amore* (the journey for the love of God), to spread the faith, to establish new monastic centres and to seek to become closer to the divine presence far from their ancestral roots. One of the most vigorous and wide-ranging of these early Insular Christian travellers was Columbanus, who was born in AD 543. Pope Pius XI commented on his work: 'The more experts study the most obscure problems of the Middle Ages, the clearer it becomes that the renaissance of Christian learning in France, Germany and Italy is due to the work and zeal of St Columban' (Lehane 1994: 147). Columbanus set out for Europe from Abbot Sinell's monastery at Lough Erne in north-west Ireland, arriving in Brittany in about 591. By this time the Christianity established in Gaul by the Frankish king Clovis nearly one hundred years before had all but dissolved back into paganism. Columbanus travelled around eastern France, was welcomed at various royal courts, and settled in Alsace, founding a monastery at Annegray, where he stayed until his expulsion by the Burgundian king Theodoric in 612. The exiled monk and his companions were escorted through Burgundy and northern France via Nevers, Orléans and Tours to Nantes and the Atlantic coast, where their guards put them on a ship for Ireland. But, as so often occurred in connection with the lives of early saints, a miracle intervened and the monks were returned to the French shore, travelled to Burgundy and thence to the Rhineland, Switzerland and, eventually, Rome; in this venture, Columbanus was aided by Theodoric's hated cousin the Merovingian king Chlotar II. Columbanus died a year after his arrival in Italy (Lehane 1994: 147–182; Walker 1957).

The life of Columbanus demonstrates very clearly that some early medieval clerics travelled widely within Europe. The places visited by this particular monk are precisely the regions for which there is a wealth of evidence for pagan religious iconography: northern and eastern France and the Rhineland. It is quite possible that clerics like Columbanus observed such images and, in this way, pagan motifs may have been – consciously or unconsciously – integrated within both the orally transmitted mythic tales and the written redactions. Similarly, the products of pre-Christian ritual practice, such as the deposition of cauldrons in marshes and lakes, may have been seen, perhaps in the course of everyday activities like fishing, reed-gathering or peat-cutting. Some cauldrons may have been recovered, perhaps even re-used in the early Christian period, but the circumstances of their discovery could quite easily become incorporated into local folklore. Observation of pagan material culture by clerics and others may thus have generated interaction between past and present.

A clear example of the reaction of the composers of medieval Irish myth to their ancestral past relates to the great Neolithic passage graves, such as Newgrange and Lough Crew in Co. Meath (Herity and Eogan 1989: 58–60). These massive mounds were interpreted by the originators of the myths as *sídhe*, the dwelling places of the Tuatha Dé Danann after their relegation to an Otherworld underground following the invasion of the Gaels (Hull 1930: 73–89; Lehmacher 1921: 360–64; Mac Cana 1983: 54–71; Raftery 1994: 180). Such monuments were clearly held in high esteem by local Irish communities in the early Christian period, and the kings of the Bregha dynasty seem to have established a royal residence close to the tumulus at Knowth, one of the three huge mounds of the Neolithic Brugh na Bóinne passage-grave cemetery (Mac Cana 1983: 61).

CONCLUSION: CORRIDORS OF TIME

This chapter has examined the hypothesis that communities of the later prehistoric and early historic periods entered consciously and deliberately into symbolic and other relationships with their own past. The evidence cited to support such an argument consists, on the one hand, of demonstrable interaction between the material culture of different periods and, on the other, of apparent linkages between myth and the archaeological record of earlier peoples. The presence of dialogue between pasts can be amply illustrated by the clear impingement by later communities on their ancestral landscape; it is the second form of interaction that is the more difficult to explain. However, two factors – the second largely predicated on the first – lend credence to the possibility that pre-Christian cults and ritual may resonate within the mythic tradition of Wales and Ireland: first, an acceptance that the written myths may owe their genesis to an oral tradition belonging, in origin, to much earlier periods; second, that clerics travelling within and outside Britain may have observed the material remains of pagan belief systems and that such witness caused elements of pre-Christian traditions to become incorporated within the early medieval mythic texts. Whatever the mechanisms for interaction between different phases of the past, and for whatever reasons, a meaningful and symbolic dialogue between pasts seems, on occasion, to have occurred. Such discourse between pasts served both to break down barriers between traditions of different periods and also, perhaps, to legitimise the conceptual framework of the present in terms of the past.

NOTES

1   It is worth mentioning another form of archaism associated with Roman provincial shrines: in his report on the coins from the Harlow sanctuary, Haselgrove (1989) has argued that the occurrence of Iron Age issues on British temple sites may not always be indicative of pre-Roman activity but may rather illustrate deliberate cult practice in which archaic coins were selected as votive gifts to the divine presence in Roman sanctuaries. In this context, it should be noted that huge numbers of Iron Age coins have been discovered on the site of the Wanborough (Surrey) Roman temple (Cheesman 1994: 31–92), although the religious status of the site before the first stone phase of the temple is by no means clear.
2   Examples of ritual deposition of iron cauldrons include those at Llyn Fawr in South Wales, Carlingwark in Scotland, Duchcov in Bohemia and Portglenone in Ireland. References to all these and many more can be found in Green (1998b).
3   It is perhaps significant, in this context, that the origin of the cauldron described in the Second Branch of the Mabinogi was an Irish lake, the Llyn y Peir (Jones and Jones 1976: 30).
4   The curious phenomenon of the footholder seems to have been associated with kingship and the generation of power. In the Laws of Hywel Dda, which are of tenth-century origin, although not codified until the thirteenth century, there is mention of the *troediawc*, the medieval king's male footholder, who symbolised aspects of his sovereignty, including the power to grant clemency and freedom (Carey 1991; Markale 1975: 130–131).

REFERENCES

Adkins, L. and Adkins, R. (1985) 'Neolithic axes from Roman sites in Britain.' *Oxford Journal of Archaeology* 4(1): 69–75.

Alcock, L. (1963) *Dinas Powys. An Iron Age, Dark Age and Early Medieval Settlement in Glamorgan.* Cardiff: University of Wales Press.

Allen, D.F. (1980) *The Coins of the Ancient Celts.* Edinburgh: Edinburgh University Press.

Ashe, G. (1968) *The Quest for Arthur's Britain.* London: Pall Mall Press.

Audin, A. (ed.) (1975) *Musée de la Civilisation Gallo-Romaine.* Lyon: Musée de la Civilisation Gallo-Romaine.

Benoit, F. (1969) *L'Art primitif Méditerranéen dans la Vallée du Rhône.* Aix-en-Provence: Publications des Annales de la Faculté des Lettres.

Benoit, F. (1981) *Entremont.* Paris: Ophrys.

Biel, J. (1991) 'The princely tombs of Hohenasperg (Baden-Wurttemberg)'. In S. Moscati, O.H. Frey, V. Kruta, B. Raftery and Szabó (eds) *The Celts*, pp. 108–112. London: Thames and Hudson.

Boon, G.C. (1982) 'A coin with the head of Cernunnos.' *Seaby Coin and Medal Bulletin* 769: 276–282.

Boucher, S. (1976) *Recherches sur les bronzes figurés de Gaule pré-romaine et romaine.* Paris and Rome: Ecole Française de Rome.

Bradley, R. (1987) 'Time regained: the creation of continuity.' *Journal of the British Archaeological Association* 140: 1–17.

Bradley, R. (1990) *The Passage of Arms.* Cambridge: Cambridge University Press.

Brewer, R.J. (1986) *Corpus Signorum Imperii Romani.* Great Britain, Vol. I, Fasc. 5, *Wales.* London: Oxford University Press/British Academy.

Carey, J. (1991) 'A British myth of origins?' In J. Carey, *History of Religions*, pp. 24–38. Chicago: University of Chicago.

Cheesman, C. (1994) 'The coins.' In M.G. O'Connell and J. Bird, 'The Roman Temple at Wanborough'. *Surrey Archaeological Collections* 82: 1–168.

Colombet, A. and Lebel, P. (1953) 'Mythologie gallo-romaine.' *Revue Archéologique de l'Est et du Centre-Est* 4(2): 112.

Condren, M. (1989) *The Serpent and the Goddess: Women, Religion and Power in Celtic Ireland.* San Francisco: Harper and Row.

Coulston, J.C. and Phillips, E.J. (1988) *Corpus Signorum Imperii Romani.* Great Britain, Vol. I, Fasc. 6, *Hadrian's Wall West of the North Tyne, and Carlisle.* London: Oxford University Press/British Academy.

Cross, Tom Peete and Slover, Clark Harris (eds and trans.) [1936] (1988) 'Mac Datho's Pig.' In T.P. Cross and C.H. Slover (eds) *Ancient Irish Tales*, pp. 199–207. Totowa, NJ: Barnes and Noble Books.

Cunliffe, B. (1992) 'Pits, pre-conceptions and propitiation in the British Iron Age.' *Oxford Journal of Archaeology* 11(1): 69–83.

Cunliffe, B. (1993) *Danebury.* London: English Heritage/Batsford.

Dark, K. (1993) 'Roman-period activity at prehistoric ritual monuments in Britain and in the Armorican peninsula.' In E. Scott (ed.) *Theoretical Roman Archaeology: First Conference Proceedings*, pp. 132–146. Worldwide Archaeology Series, vol. 4. Aldershot: Avebury.

Davies, S. (1993) *The Four Branches of the Mabinogi: Pedeir Keinc y Mabinogi.* Llandysul: Gomer Press.

Dayet, M. (1954) 'Le sanglier à trois cornes du Cabinet des Medailles.' *Revue Archéologique de l'Est et du Centre-Est* 5: 334–335.

De Nie, G. (1987) *Views from a Many-Windowed Tower: Studies of Imagination in the Works of Gregory of Tours.* Amsterdam: Rodopi.

De Vesly, L. (1909) *Les Fana ou petits Temples Gallo-Romains de la Région Normande.* Rouen: Lecerf Fils.

Deyts, S. (1976) *Dijon, Musée Archeologique: sculptures gallo-romains mythologiques et religieuses.* Paris: Editions de la Réunion des Musées Nationaux.

Dillon, M. (1933) *Táin Bó Fráich.* Dublin: Dublin University Press.

Durand, J.-L. (1989) 'Ritual as instrumentality.' In M. Detienne and J.-P. Vernant (eds) *The Cuisine of Sacrifice among the Greeks,* pp. 119–128. Chicago: Chicago University Press.

Espérandieu, E. (1908–38) *Recueil Général des Bas-Reliefs de la Gaule Romaine et Pré-Romaine.* Vol. II (1908), Vol. III (1910), Vol. IV (1911), Vol. V (1913), Vol. VI (1915), Vol. VIII (1922), Vol. XI (1938). Paris: Leroux.

Evans, A.C. (1983) 'The bronze cauldrons.' In *The Sutton Hoo Ship-Burial by R. Bruce-Mitford,* edited by A.C. Evans (ed.), London: British Museum Publications.

Evans, J. (1897) *The Ancient Stone Implements Weapons and Ornaments of Great Britain.* London: Longmans.

Gerloff, S. (1986) 'Bronze Age class A cauldrons: typology, origins and chronology.' *Journal of the Royal Society of Antiquaries of Ireland* 117: 84–115.

Green, M.J. (1976) *A Corpus of Religious Material from the Civilian Areas of Roman Britain.* British Archaeological Reports (BS) no. 24, Oxford: BAR.

Green, M.J. (1986) *The Gods of the Celts.* Gloucester: Alan Sutton.

Green, M.J. (1989) *Symbol and Image in Celtic Religious Art.* London: Routledge.

Green, M.J. (1990) 'Pagan Celtic religion: archaeology and myth.' *Transactions of the Honourable Society of the Cymmrodorion,* pp. 13–28.

Green, M.J. (1992) *Animals in Celtic Life and Myth.* London: Routledge.

Green, M.J. (1995) *Celtic Goddesses: Warriors, Virgins and Mothers.* London: British Museum Press.

Green, M.J. (1996) 'Concepts of sacrifice in later prehistoric Europe.' In K. Jones-Bley and M.E. Huld (eds) *The Indo-Europeanization of Northern Europe,* pp. 191–203. Journal of Indo-European Studies Monograph no. 17, Washington D.C.

Green, M.J. (1997) *Exploring the World of the Druids.* London: Thames and Hudson.

Green, M.J. (1998a) 'Humans as ritual victims in the later prehistory of western Europe.' *Oxford Journal of Archaeology* 17(2): 169–189.

Green, M.J. (1998b) Vessels of death: sacred cauldrons in archaeology and myth.' *Antiquaries Journal* 78: 63–84.

Haselgrove, C. (1989) 'Iron Age coin deposition at Harlow Temple, Essex.' *Oxford Journal of Archaeology* 8(1): 73–88.

Hauken, T.M. Dahlin (1991) 'Gift-exchange in early Iron Age Norse society.' In R. Samson (ed.) *Social Approaches to Viking Studies,* pp. 105–112. Glasgow: Cruithne Press.

Hawkes, C.F.C. (1951) 'Bronze-workers, cauldrons and bucket-animals in Iron Age and Roman Britain.' In W.F. Grimes (ed.) *Aspects of Archaeology in Britain and Beyond: Essays presented to O.G.S. Crawford,* pp. 172–199. London: H.W. Edwards.

Haycock, M. (1983) '*Preiddeu Annwfn.* The figure of Taliesin.' *Studia Celtica* 18: 52–78.

Henig, M. (1993) *Roman sculpture from the Cotswold region. Corpus Signorum Imperii Romani.* Great Britain, Vol. I, Fasc. 7. London: Oxford University Press/British Academy.

Hennessy, W.W. (1870–72) 'The ancient Irish goddess of war.' *Revue Celtique* 1: 32–55.

Herbert, M. (1996) 'Transmutations of an Irish goddess.' In S. Billington and M. Green (eds) *The Concept of the Goddess,* pp. 141–151. London: Routledge.

Herity, M. and Eogan, G. (1989) *Ireland in Prehistory.* London: Routledge.

Hingley, R. (1996) 'Ancestors and identity in the later prehistory of Atlantic Scotland: the reuse and reinvention of Neolithic monuments and material culture.' *World Archaeology* 28(2): 231–243.

Holtorf, C. (1998) 'The life-histories of megaliths in Mecklenburg-Vorpommern (Germany).' *World Archaeology* 30: 23–38.

Horne, P.D. and King, A.C. (1980) 'Gazetteer of Romano-Celtic temples in continental Europe.' In W. Rodwell (ed.) *Temples, Churches and Religion:*

Recent Research in Roman Britain, Part III, pp. 369–555. British Archaeological Reports (BS) no. 77. Oxford: BAR.

Hull, V. (1930) 'The four jewels of the Tuatha Dé Danann.' *Zeitschrift für Celtische Philologie* 18: 73–89.

Jackson, K.H. (1961–67) 'Some popular motifs in early Welsh tradition.' *Etudes Celtiques* 11: 83–99.

Jenkins, D. (trans.) (1986) *The Laws of Hywel Dda.* Llandysul: Gomer Press.

Joffroy, R. (1979) *Musée des Antiquités Nationales, St-Germain-en-Laye.* Paris: Editions de la Réunion des Musées Nationaux.

Jones, G. and Jones, T. (trans.) (1976) *The Mabinogion.* London: John Dent.

Kaul, F., Marazov, I., Best, J. and de Vries, M. (1991) *Thracian Tales on the Gundestrup Cauldron.* Amsterdam: Najade Press.

Kelly, P. (1992) 'The Táin as literature.' In J.P. Mallory (ed.) *Aspects of the Táin,* pp. 69–95. Belfast: The Universities Press.

Kightly, C. (1988) *A Mirror of Medieval Wales. Gerald of Wales and his Journey in 1188.* Cardiff: Cadw.

King, A.C. (1990) *Roman Gaul and Germany.* London: British Museum Publications.

Knight, J.K. (1988) *Caerleon Roman Fortress.* Cardiff: Cadw.

Lehane, B. (1994) *Early Celtic Christianity.* Cardiff: Constable.

Lehmacher, G. (1921) 'Tuatha Dé Danann.' *Zeitschrift für Celtische Philologie* 13: 360–364.

Lehner, R.P.M. (1989) 'Death and vengeance in the Ulster Cycle.' *Zeitschrift für Celtische Philologie* 43: 1–10.

Mac Cana, P. (1958) *Branwen, Daughter of Llyr: A Study of the Irish Affinities and of the Composition of the Second Branch of the Mabinogi.* Cardiff: University of Wales Press.

Mac Cana, P. (1983) *Celtic Mythology.* London: Newnes.

Markale, J. (1975) *Women of the Celts.* London: Cremonesi.

McCone, K. (1982) 'Brigid in the seventh century – a saint with three lives.' *Perítia* 1: 107–45.

McCone, K. (1990) *Pagan Past and Christian Present.* Maynooth: An Sagart.

Megaw, J.V.S. (1970) *Art of the European Iron Age.* New York: Harper and Row.

Megaw, J.V.S. and D.D.A. Simpson (1979) *Introduction to British Prehistory.* Leicester: Leicester University Press.

Metzler, J. (1991) Late Celtic horsemen's graves at Goeblingen-Nospelt. In S. Moscati, O.H. Frey, V. Kruta, B. Raftery and Szabó (eds) *The Celts,* pp. 520–521. London: Thames and Hudson.

O'Catháin, S. (1995) *The Festival of Brigit, Celtic Goddess and Holy Woman.* Dublin: DBA Publications.

O' Neil, H. and Grinsell, L. (1961) *Gloucestershire barrows. Transactions of the Bristol and Gloucestershire Archaeological Society* 79.

O'Rahilly, T.F. (1946) *Early Irish History and Mythology.* Dublin: Dublin Institute for Advanced Studies.

O'Sullivan, T. (1978) *The De Excidio of Gildas. Its Authenticity and Date.* Leiden: E.J. Brill.

Parzinger, H., Nakvasil, J. and Barth, F.E. (1995) Bycí Skála Höhle: Ein hallstattzeitliche Höhlenopferplatz in Mähren. *Römisch-Germanische Forschungen* 54, Mainz.

Piggott, S. (1953) 'Three metalwork hoards of the Roman period from southern Scotland.' *Proceedings of the Society of Antiquaries of Scotland* 87: 1–51.

Priuli, A. (1988) *Incisioni Rupestri della Val Camonica.* Collana: Torino: Quaderni di Cultura Alpina.

Raftery, B. (1994) *Pagan Celtic Ireland. The Enigma of the Irish Iron Age.* London: Thames and Hudson.

Roberts, B.F. (1988) 'Gerald the writer.' In C. Kightly (ed.) *A Mirror of Medieval Wales. Gerald of Wales and his Journey of 1188,* pp. 96–97. Cardiff: Cadw.

Ross, A. (1961) 'The horned god of the Brigantes.' *Archaeologia Aeliana* 39(4): 59–85.

Ross, A. (1974) *Pagan Celtic Britain.* London: Cardinal/Sphere.

Rynne, E. (1972) 'Celtic stone idols in Ireland.' In C. Thomas (ed.) *The Iron Age in the Irish Sea Province,* pp. 79–98. Council for British Archaeology Research Report no. 9. Oxford: CBA.

Sauer, E. (1996) *The End of Paganism in the North-Western Provinces of the Roman Empire: The Example of the Mithras Cult.* British Archaeological Reports (IS) no. 634. Oxford: BAR.

Stead, I.M. (1991) 'The Belgae in Britain: the Aylsford culture.' In S. Moscati, O.H. Frey, V. Kruta, B. Raftery and Szabó (eds) *The Celts,* pp. 591–595. London: Thames and Hudson.

Thorpe, L. (trans.) (1978) *Gerald of Wales. The Journey through Wales and the Description of Wales.* Harmondsworth: Penguin.

Tierney, J.J. (1959–60) 'The Celtic ethnography of Posidonius.' *Proceedings of the Royal Irish Academy* 60: 189–275.

Van Dam, R. (trans.) (1985) *Gregory of Tours: Glory of the Confessors.* Liverpool: Liverpool University Press.

Walker, G.S.M. (ed.) (1957) *Sancti Columbani Opera.* Dublin: Dublin Institute for Advanced Studies.

Williams, H. (1997) 'Continuity through discontinuity? The power of the ancient place in Romano-British and early Anglo-Saxon burial practices.' Lecture delivered at the Theoretical Roman Archaeology Conference, University of Nottingham, 11–13 April 1997.

Winterbottom, M. (trans.) (1978) *The Ruin of Britain and Other Works.* London: Phillimore.

CHAPTER FIVE

OF THUNDERBIRDS, WATER SPIRITS AND CHIEFS' DAUGHTERS

Contextualising archaeology and Ho-Chunk (Winnebago) oral traditions

JOHN STAECK

ABSTRACT

Analysis and revaluation of Paul Radin's turn of the century corpus of Ho-Chunk oral traditions open substantive new avenues for interpreting the late prehistoric and protohistoric archaeological records of the North American Upper Midwest (Figure 5.1). Contextualisation of these traditions within the archaeological record yields insights into previously inaccessible actor-specific experiences and world views. In turn, the concomitant contextualisation of archaeological data within the oral traditions allows the development of new interpretive models for sociopolitical organisation and development during the late prehistoric and early historic eras.

INTRODUCTION

The Ho-Chunk are a Siouan-speaking people with close linguistic ties to the Chiwere-speakers, the Ioway, Oto and Missouri. Europeans first made direct contact with the Ho-Chunk in 1634 along or adjacent to the western shore of Lake Michigan between modern-day Chicago, Illinois and Green Bay, Wisconsin (La Potherie 1911; Lurie 1978). These people were reported to be fierce warriors who controlled access to the territory west of Lake Michigan, territory the French government and fur-trade industries strongly desired to exploit. The Ho-Chunk, however, were not inclined to deal with the Native American allies of the French

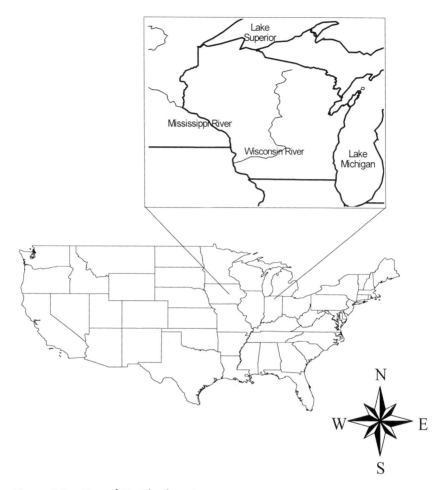

Figure 5.1   Map of Ho-Chunk region

and stymied attempts at westward expansion of trade routes into the middle of the seventeenth century (La Potherie 1911; Staeck 1994).

Archaeologists and ethnohistorians have inferred a link between the Ho-Chunk and the Upper Mississippian traditions in the Western Great Lakes, especially to Oneota (Mott 1938; Overstreet 1976, 1978, 1993). More recently, equally compelling arguments have suggested a link between at least portions of the Chiwere–Ho-Chunk speaking populations and the earlier Late Woodland Effigy Mound tradition (e.g. Hall 1993; Salzer 1996; Staeck 1994, 1996). These latter arguments follow distantly upon the published Ho-Chunk claim that they were the authors of the Late Woodland period's Effigy Mound tradition (Radin 1911), a claim that continues today.

Unfortunately, attempts to attribute Ho-Chunk or proto-Ho-Chunk authorship to either Oneota or Effigy Mound manifestations have been muddled by the ethnohistoric record of the Ho-Chunk and the relative lack of material available on the Chiwere-speaking populations (Lurie 1978; Staeck 1994). Thus, archaeologists have been left with a choice between inferring a Ho-Chunk affiliation with Oneota or Effigy Mound without direct evidence – apparently in direct contradiction of the ethno-historic documents – and postulating a more traditional 'Woodland' lifestyle for these people. In either case, however, it has been essentially impossible to identify a typical Ho-Chunk archaeological signature that has any great time depth in the region.

This paper uses unpublished oral traditions to evaluate the problem outlined above, and then suggests that there is good reason to explore further the potential connections between the Ho-Chunk and either or both the peoples responsible for Upper Mississippian and Effigy Mound material culture.

ORAL TRADITIONS AS A CORPUS OF DATA

One of the most significant resources which bears directly on this issue but which has heretofore been little utilised is the large corpus of Ho-Chunk oral traditions collected by Paul Radin during the first three decades of the twentieth century. Although a large number of these tradi-tions have been published (e.g. Radin 1911, 1915a, 1915b, 1923a, 1926a, 1926b, 1948), the original transcriptions of these tales and the various multiple versions of many of them have never been systematically analysed for what they might reveal about past social and political organisations.

Radin himself was primarily concerned with preserving a record of Ho-Chunk life as he knew it and with pursuing his interests in what he termed native literary traditions. Given the severe disruptions endured by the Ho-Chunk (and most indigenous peoples) as a result of Euroamerican colonialism, however, it is difficult to assess the depth of time during which the lifeways observed by Radin had persisted. Lurie (1978) discusses several areas where Radin may have erred in interpreting his observations. Indeed, many Ho-Chunk to this day claim that Radin's interpretations 'hit the target but miss the mark'.

Certain oral traditions, those known as *waikan* (literally 'that which is true'), are typically conservative elements of Ho-Chunk culture (Radin 1915a, 1926a, 1926b, 1945, 1948, 1955, 1956) and are often mobilised to help define and preserve ethnic identity and beliefs (Radin 1945; Staeck 1994, 1996). *Waikan* are forms of sacred narrative, though in a way that Radin (1945) found hard to quantify. Essentially, although *waikan* are not alive or directly imbued with spiritual identities, their recounting forms links between the present and the past, including the areas of the past that Westerners might label both history and religion. This connection compels raconteurs to adhere to certain rules and limitations, including the necessity to recount the traditions as accurately as possible. It is important to note that the responsibilities associated with performing *waikan* are taken most seriously by those Ho-Chunk adhering to traditional world views (cf. Radin 1923, 1945).

If one accepts that such traditions contain reflections of the social structure or structures that the authors and subsequent raconteurs perceived, then the traditions have the potential to provide modern researchers with glimpses of such structures. In effect, the data Radin collected provide a rich and largely untapped avenue for modelling and contextualising past Ho-Chunk culture. The current research emphasises structural, symbolic and structural-functional approaches to generating a model for pre-modern Ho-Chunk social structure (cf. Douglas 1966, 1970; Dundes 1968, 1984; Firth 1973; Lévi-Strauss 1953; Turner 1967).

The term oral tradition has been adopted in this paper to refer to multiple forms of formulaic oral communication, but particularly important for the current volume are those traditions that pass information between generations. Because belief in either the events recounted in the traditions or the culturally relevant messages passed on by the traditions is held in common by members of an identity group, belief and knowledge of such narratives contribute to the formation of a common identity. Hence, it has been argued that oral traditions serve to reinforce salient identity, in both the physical recounting of tales and the actions depicted in the tales (Blom 1969; Braroe 1975; Gluckman 1962; Goffman 1956, 1959, 1963a, 1963b; Orso 1974; Peacock 1968).

CONNECTING SOCIAL STRUCTURE, ORAL TRADITIONS AND ARCHAEOLOGY

The term social structure is used in this paper in accord with Lévi-Strauss' (1953) discussion of the concept. For our purposes, then, social structure serves to model and condition relations between members of different groups that interact on a regular or frequent basis, although these structures are not necessarily heavily emphasised by members of either group when interacting solely with members of their own cultural groups. This type of structure is implicit in the differing views of style in archaeology. Wobst (1977), for example, has argued that style serves as a messaging behaviour that is largely ignored by close relations and people who interact with the messaging group regularly, but is identified and interpreted by people who are at a greater social distance from the messaging group. One of the numerous implications of Wobst's model is that style is organised along social structural lines and that the analysis of style and its applications can be used to help reconstruct social structure. In turn, this has implications for the identification of salient identities through archaeological analysis.

Similarly, Sackett's (1990) categorisation of style into active and passive roles touches upon this same topic. Accordingly, passive style exists as a product of cultural preferences but becomes active when someone recognises the style as foreign or different. According to Sackett's model, this realisation tends to occur at the juncture of group boundaries, such as between different ethnic groups or different cultural groups. Active style, on the other hand, functions as discussed by Wobst, that is, active style is a deliberate message sent to define ethnic or cultural identity.

This distinction becomes more important when Upham's (1990) arguments relating style to political organisation are taken into account. Upham argues that from the perspective of political control and style, isochrestic variation really can be subdivided into isochrestic and heterochrestic (unequal in use) aspects, each defining different elements of political structure. According to this approach, once a population reaches some sort of critical mass, in terms of the number of people per fixed amount of territory, communities are forced to become larger and more complex. As a function of this, style is used by some people in the form of emblems to define political authority and, in turn, these symbols are restricted from being used by people not directly associated with the political structure.

This argument closely approximates Schortman's (1989) discussion of political symbolism and development in Mesoamerica and is implicitly present in many other conceptualisations of stylistic variation (Hodder 1982, 1990; Plog 1976, 1980, 1983, 1990; Sackett 1990; Wiessner 1990; Wobst 1977). Such views of style agree that distinctions between salient identities may be reflected in stylistic variation. Upham (1990) also points out the importance of style and symbol to social structure as well as defining the means (e.g. style and symbol) through which social structure is signalled across cultural unit boundaries.

On a more specific level, the distinction between intended social structure and realised social structure has direct implications for identifying material traces of the Ho-Chunk as well as for understanding their ethnogenesis. Lurie (1978), for example, has suggested that the historically recorded Ho-Chunk clan and moiety system may represent a transitional adaptation in social structure. That is, the Ho-Chunk had envisioned or were moving towards a different social structure but were essentially trapped in the one recorded historically as a result of the profound changes brought about by contact with Europeans. An additional aspect to this argument is that the Ho-Chunk have traditions regarding rapid depopulation through both warfare and disease. Such dramatic change in population levels may have had a profound effect upon social structure so that, by the time anthropologists came to be involved with the Ho-Chunk, these people were undergoing a transition to a social system more adapted to their new natural and social environments (Lurie 1978; Radin 1923). In either event, however, some elements of social structure should be expected to reflect previous behaviours and ideology while others reflect more recent adaptation. It is argued here that the Ho-Chunk perform-ance elements, particularly oral traditions, contain implicit references to multiple variations of social structure and, consequently, document shifts in Ho-Chunk social structure. In fact, Lévi-Strauss has commented that 'The field of myth, ritual and religion seems nevertheless to be one of the more fruitful for the study of social structure' (1953: 548).

These threads converge in preparing archaeologically testable models for Ho-Chunk ethnogenesis and identity marking (Staeck 1994). By con-textualising the sub-text of oral traditions, that is the repetitively portrayed connections between characters, identity and social obligations, within socio-anthropological theory, archaeologists can infer the presence of social behaviours that were not recorded ethnographically. In this fashion archae-ologists can predict material cultural corollaries to the perceived social actions and then gather data pertaining to such behaviours. Ultimately the presence of the perceived behaviours may or may not be substantiated archaeologically, but in any event we will at least have had the opportunity to explore this realm of past social organisation.

RESULTS

Matricentred behaviour

Among the most significant results of the current research is the identi-fication of consistent references among the Ho-Chunk to matricentred, hierarchical behaviours (Staeck 1994). Such behaviours are rarely associ-ated with traditional Woodland lifestyles and are more frequently seen among agricultural populations, such as the Iroquois, Cherokee and various Muskogean-speaking peoples.

Throughout all of the tales collected by Radin, matrilocality or uxori-locality and representations of privileges afforded to women dominate the actions of the tales. For example, in the important tales 'The Red Horn' and 'Blue Horn's Nephews', there are clear descriptions of males becoming village leaders through marriage. In the former tale, the char-acter Turtle marries the daughter of a village chief and the next day announces that he has been made chief. He then settles down to live in his wife's village as its political leader. In 'Blue Horn's Nephews', an unnamed warrior marries the two daughters of a village chief and is consequently made the new chief. No change in residence occurs since the warrior is from the same village as his new wives. Both tales clearly illustrate the pattern discussed above. In neither case does the old chief disappear or die in the course of the story; rather it appears as though he is simply replaced. Also of significance, in neither tale is there mention of resentment or other political ramifications as a result of the transfer of power. It appears as though the transfer is a normal part of society. In both cases, the male either relocates or remains in the village of his wife or wives. Similar events are described or implied in numerous other Ho-Chunk tales, such as 'The Chief's Daughter and the Orphan', 'The Thunderbird', 'The Man who Visited the Thunderbirds', and 'The Woman who Loved her Half-Brother'. Indeed, in all tales examined in this research in which a marriage takes place involving the daughter of a chief, the groom is subsequently appointed village chief.

In 'Blue Horn's Nephews' and 'The Red Horn' we also see another important feature of this matricentred behaviour. In these tales the process of marriage and ascension to political power is as described above but involves polygyny. In the Blue Horn tale, an unnamed warrior of great renown marries the two daughters (sororal polygyny) of the village leader and is shortly thereafter elevated to the village chieftainship. At the opening of the tale, the warrior is depicted as a poor and violent husband. He has numerous wives and treats them all badly. Yet, because he is such an accomplished warrior, and no one in the village can kill him, he courts or pursues any woman he chooses. During the course of the story, the warrior tries to marry the chief's eldest daughter by telling her that if she does not consent, the warrior will kill the chief. Rather than have her father killed and be taken by force, the eldest daughter flees the village in the hope of dying in the wilderness. She is eventually saved by the chief of the Water Spirits, Blue Horn, and thus becomes his adopted sister. The action repeats itself with the chief's remaining daughter and she too is adopted by the Water Spirit.

Blue Horn eventually returns the women to their village and persuades the warrior to return all of his current wives to their original families. The warrior agrees to this because Blue Horn is the most powerful of all Water Spirits and even the invulnerable warrior cannot kill him. Following the return of his first wives, the warrior marries both of the chief's daughters. Under the guidance of Blue Horn, the marriages are successful and the warrior is made chief shortly after the two women consummate the marriage.

In the Red Horn tale there is a parallel polygynous situation, though in this case Red Horn's wives are unrelated. Indeed, his second wife is a red-haired giantess from a population that Red Horn's people are at war with. In both the Red Horn and Blue Horn tales, though, the women give birth to children who, in fact, are the mythical twins. These twins set the world straight and free it from evil spirits. Importantly, however, the actions of the twins in the two tales are parallel but differ in one significant fashion. In 'The Red Horn' the twins, in one of their first adventures, rescue and regenerate their father and his companions after they are captured and killed by giants. Blue Horn's nephews, however, return from their grand mission of freeing the world of evil and find that their uncle (*deega*, mother's brother) has been captured and killed by Thunderbirds.[1] They set out to avenge his death and manage to slay many Thunderbirds before finding the remains of their uncle and regenerating them. The point to be gleaned here is that these tales are quite different from one another and that they reflect different narrative sequences, each reflecting different social structures. As argued elsewhere (e.g. Staeck 1994), it would appear that the Red Horn tale represents a more recent temporal era than does the Blue Horn tale.

Hierarchical behaviour

Just as with matricentred behaviour, there is also a strong pattern of hierarchical behaviour represented in the tales. Significantly, though, this behaviour seems to be focused upon women. As mentioned previously, the Red Horn myth illustrates the passage of political power to Turtle through his marriage to the chief's daughter. The circumstances and the manner through which the marriage is arranged provide important insights into Ho-Chunk values and social stratification.

On the night the marriage is arranged, Turtle and three other warriors are about to lead a war party on a dangerous but very prestigious war path. The village chief has agreed to the war party only because of the reputations of the four men leading it. As was common among the Ho-Chunk, the four leaders are ranked according to their prestige and perceived abilities. The most prestigious of the leaders is Red Horn, who either is himself a Water Spirit or has been blessed by these creatures. Second in importance is Wolf, a warrior or spirit from the Wolf clan, third is Storms-As-He-Walks, a warrior or spirit from the Thunderer clan, and fourth is Turtle, who has no apparent affiliation with any clan. Indeed, Turtle is traditionally a random mythical character but is always a hero. Nonetheless, he is often portrayed as a trickster-like figure who leads people into, and out of, trouble.

During the final night of preparations, the war party has assembled and is singing. The myth explains that during this night of singing it was customary for women to present moccasins to men they favoured. If moccasins were given by an unmarried woman to an unmarried man, it was agreed that they would marry upon the man's return from the war path. It is during this night that the daughter of the chief comes to the war party's fire with moccasins. She is the first person who is allowed to offer moccasins to members of the war party. Selecting the most prestigious of the warriors, she first offers the moccasins to Red Horn, who declines to accept them. Embarrassed, the chief's daughter, whose title is translated by Radin (1948) as 'princess', offers the moccasins to Wolf and Storms-As-He-Walks and on both occasions is again rejected. Finally, she moves to offer the moccasins to Turtle, who takes them before they are formally given. The princess, now betrothed to Turtle, leaves the camp very much embarrassed.

During the same night, an elderly grandmother sends her granddaughter to the war party with moccasins. The tale describes the granddaughter as being fearful of rejection because those 'superior to herself' (Radin n.d.) had been rejected by the warriors. This single statement suggests other women, in addition to the chief's daughter, had offered moccasins to members of the war party and had been rejected. The reference to superiors, coupled with the apparently disenfranchised status of the girl (she has been raised by her grandmother and is therefore probably an orphan), also suggests that some form of social rules existed which allowed women to offer moccasins in a particular order. Given that the chief's daughter is first to be allowed to offer moccasins, and that the orphaned girl identifies herself as relatively low in the order which determines such offerings, a strong inference for the presence of a social hierarchy is made.

The privileges of this hierarchy, however, are not always cast in a flattering light by the tale. Red Horn, for example, accepts the moccasins from the orphan girl while rejecting those from the chief's daughter. Similarly, it is Turtle, the least of the war party's leaders, who accepts the moccasins from the chief's daughter, grabbing them from her hand before they can be properly offered to him. The woman is embarrassed in view of the entire village as it becomes clear that she offered moccasins to the leaders of the party in order of their prowess as warriors and has been rejected by all but Turtle. Turtle's acceptance, however, saves the woman little face as he violates existing rules of etiquette and precedence by grabbing the moccasins from her hands before they are offered. Thus, the chief's daughter is humiliated despite her privileged status.

On the other extreme, the most prestigious of all the warriors, Red Horn, accepts an offer of marriage from a woman who is among the lowest ranking females in the village. The implications are that the Ho-Chunk society described in the tale valued achieved status and worth (the orphan proves to be an excellent wife and mother) as much as ascribed status. Nonetheless, social hierarchy is depicted as an important, functioning part of society.

The presence of respect for both achieved and ascribed status suggests that the Ho-Chunk may have shared concepts of complementariness between the genders. Most Native American societies divide labour and ownership according to principles of intra- and extragroup activities, with females engaging primarily in intragroup activities and males in extragroup activities. If we accept that ascribed status is tied to matrilineages then females would inherit some level of status. Males, on the other hand, may inherit a certain level of status, as described by references to many heroes being the sons of chiefs, but it is their actions which mark their actual status in society.

For example, in 'The Chief's Daughter and the Orphan' the hero becomes an acceptable marriage partner and leader through his actions, not his distant and, according to Radin (1926a), unknown relationship to a former chief. These actions prove the hero to be a great hunter (he always finds and kills game) and spiritually powerful (he brings the chief's daughter back from the grave). Similar patterns are exemplified in 'The Red Horn', where Turtle proves to be an incapable leader and unwilling warrior despite his marriage to the chief's daughter, while Red Horn is seen as a role model for his village. Likewise, similar patterns exist in the Thunderbird tales where males achieve status among new societies, regardless of their past, while females are ascribed a social rank at the outset.

A caveat to this system appears to be that it is less rigid for males than for females. Males of unknown or average status can marry a chief's daughter and themselves become chiefs, as evidenced by the legends 'The Chief's Daughter and the Orphan', 'Blue Horn's Nephews' and both of the Thunderbird tales discussed here. In each case, males of unknown or unremarkable status prove themselves to be powerful warriors, hunters or spiritually blessed and marry into a chieftainship. Their social mobility is upward and there are no constraints, other than personal shortcomings, which limit this mobility.

On the other hand, females of high status, especially the daughters of chiefs, appear to be more rigidly constrained, being pressured to marry wisely, despite an apparent free choice of marriage partner. In the tales 'The Woman who Married her Half-Brother', 'The Woman who Married a Snake', and 'The Chief's Daughter and the Orphan' we are told that a chief's daughter can marry whomever she likes. In the case of 'The Woman who married her Half-Brother' this privilege extends even to marrying a half-brother without fear of censure from the community. Additional support for such behaviour is found in the activities at the war party's fire in 'The Red Horn' and in a passage in 'Blue Horn's Nephews'. In the former, the chief's daughter offers moccasins to the highest ranking male and, as she is rejected, descends the social hierarchy until she finds a prospective mate who accepts. Likewise, the latter tale contains a passage explaining how the chief's daughters initially rejected the attentions of the warrior as they were free to marry anyone they chose.

Finally, evidence for this behaviour is also found in other forms of performance among the Ho-Chunk. Frank Speck (notes on file at the American Philosophical Society) has collected a class of Ho-Chunk flute songs restricted in use to chiefs' daughters. According to Speck, chiefs' daughters are free to court any individual they choose. The songs which accompany such courting are used exclusively by these women and cannot be performed by others. It is interesting to note that in most American Indian cultures, flute songs are generally performed by males during courting activities and only rarely by females. The significance is that males are usually perceived to be the initiators of mating activities. In the Ho-Chunk case, this seems to be reversed.

Yet, despite this apparent freedom, the women in the tales are always concerned that their choice of marriage partner might be beneath their station and thus cause them embarrassment. In the tale 'The Chief's Daughter and the Orphan', the woman's consternation over loving an orphan, traditionally a symbol of low social rank among the Ho-Chunk (Lurie personal communication 1990), causes her death. Taken in combination, the tales suggest that there is an unstated restriction which requires women of high status to marry high-status males.

This stricture is only mitigated in cases where the male has proved himself an exceptional figure and has achieved a high status as a warrior, hunter or spiritually powerful man. (Spiritually powerful does not necessarily indicate that the individual is a shaman, rather that he is considered to be blessed by spirits and has the ability to withstand supernatural attack.) It is the hero's achievements which mitigate the social barriers between the chief's daughter and the orphan in that tale. Similar achievements by the heroes of both Thunderbird legends discussed here enable high-status women to marry the men. Likewise, in 'Blue Horn's Nephews' it is his achieved status as an invincible warrior which eventually allows the warrior to marry the chief's daughters.

A STRUCTURAL CAVEAT?

Given the nature of structuralism and symbolic analyses involving concepts of complementary opposition, it is possible that the interpretations discussed above might be viewed as inverted from the actual cultural situation. Such an argument centres on the idea that in worlds of folklore, or in dealing with the spirit world, there is often a tendency to invert actual social practices as a way to distinguish between the world of humans and the realm in which the characters in the traditions perform.

While this is certainly the case in some situations, two lines of evidence indicate that the worlds recounted in the traditions discussed above are not inverted. First, the tales under consideration belong to the class of oral tradition the Ho-Chunk call *waikan*, or that which is true. This class of tradition includes literal histories and does not typically allow for stylistic freedom of the magnitude required to invert entire social systems (Radin 1915a, 1926a, 1926b, 1945, 1948, 1955, 1956). In part this is due to the nature of possessing the right to relate such tales and the connection between these tales and the perceived past, including ancestors, of the Ho-Chunk (Staeck 1994). Structural inversions can and do take place within Ho-Chunk oral traditions, though. They are clearly distinguished as *woorak*, however, a term which can be translated as 'that which is said'. As defined by Radin, the collector of these tales, there is a clear distinction between *waikan* and *woorak* so there is little chance that the traditions discussed here could be misclassified.

On a second level there is the consistency with which the interrelations between characters in the tales are recounted. It seems likely that, were the social system of the Ho-Chunk reversed in the traditions analysed here, there would be some level of inconsistency between different raconteurs. In fact, however, there is complete consistency across more than the thirty tales examined for this study, including multiple versions of the same tale provided by different informants, and between the three primary informants who provided the information to Radin. Significantly, Radin had each of his informants separately record their information in a phonetic text which he then translated. This took place over a period of more than five years and it is unlikely that the informants were influenced by some sort of interviewing process which biased their transcriptions so that the tales matched. Coupled with the consistency between the tales and the historical accounts composing the data set it seems unlikely, though not impossible, that the traditions discussed here represent an inverted world view.

CONCLUSIONS

Taken as a package, the Ho-Chunk tales suggest the presence of social behaviours more indicative of a socio-politically complex society than of a generalised Woodland society. There is good reason to expect that political power was tied to both achieved and ascribed status and that, at least among high-status females, matrilocality or uxorilocality was expected behaviour. Throughout the tales characters regularly manipulate implicit social rules in order to achieve increased social status and prestige. Similarly, there is evidence which suggests an implicit social hierarchy, especially for women, and this may be tied to their position as potential determiners of leadership. Such a system is seen repeatedly in the pressures placed on high-status females (chiefs' daughters) to marry well in order both to avoid embarrassing their brothers and to secure a suitable mate who will eventually become a political leader.

The system that emerges from the analysis of the traditions is one in which there is strong impetus towards actor-based manipulation of an implicit social system. Such manipulations regularly emphasise increased status through marriage and prowess in hunting, spiritual power and warfare. In most respects this system more closely approximates Hayden's (1995) transegalitarian model for constructing power and prestige (especially in the form of aggrandisement) than it does traditional anthropological models for an egalitarian, hunting and gathering population (e.g. Radin 1923).

For the archaeologists, then, there are several ramifications from this situation. First, we need to move away from static constructions of past social structures in the Upper Midwest and adopt interpretive models that are both more dynamic and actor-specific. Second, we must seek to postulate and, where feasible, test associations between Ho-Chunk antecedents and socio-politically complex archaeological cultures. Typically such associations would be postulated to include only the Upper Mississippian tradition Oneota sites and, more tangentially, the Middle Mississippian site of Aztalan (e.g. Hall 1962; Lurie 1972; Overstreet 1993;

Staeck 1991). As noted previously, however, there is also reason to suspect that the socio-political organisation of peoples associated with Effigy Mound materials approached or was parallel to that possessed by people affiliated with Oneota material culture. In either event, though, it is clear that archaeologists concerned with Ho-chunk ethnogenesis may wish to focus their energies on either or both Oneota and Effigy Mound manifestations. Finally, we need to accept the probability that our classificatory systems, ranging from ordering of traditions through morphological typologies, currently function to homogenise a complex network of unique human behaviours.

Such ramifications raise serious questions about how archaeologists view the Effigy Mound and other Late Woodland traditions. Too often such traditions seem to be relegated to an entry on a timeline, recognised only in order to fill the temporal gap between the highly visible Hopewell and Mississippian cultures (Staeck 1996). This, coupled with nearly a century of ignoring the traditions of peoples such as the Ho-Chunk, has resulted in the substantial gaps between history, archaeology and oral tradition outlined at the outset of this paper. It is only with the careful reconsideration of indigenous oral traditions that we can begin to generate archaeologically testable models that can help us to visualise the intricacies of past social systems.

NOTE

1   Thunderbirds are empyrean beings associated with lightning, thunder and often rain. Among the Ho-Chunk they are often referred to as Thunderers, though for consistency with Radin the term Thunderbird has been retained.

REFERENCES

Blom, J.-P. (1969) 'Ethnic and cultural differentiation.' In F. Barth (ed.) *Ethnic Groups and Boundaries*, pp. 74–85. Boston: Little, Brown.

Braroe, N.W. (1968) 'Continuity and change in the development of a pre-literate state.' *Anthropologica* 10: 3–27.

Braroe, N.W. (1975) *Indian and White: Self-Image and Interaction in a Canadian Plains Community*. Palo Alto: Stanford University Press.

Douglas, M. (1966) *Purity and Danger: An Analysis of the Concepts of Pollution and Taboo*. London: Routledge and Kegan Paul.

Douglas, M. (1970) *Natural Symbols: Explorations in Cosmology*. New York: Pantheon.

Dundes, A. (1968) 'Oral Literature.' In J. Clifton (ed.) *Introduction to Cultural Anthropology*, pp. 117–129. Boston: Houghton Mifflin.

Dundes, A. (ed.) (1984) *Sacred Narrative: Readings in the Theory of Myth*. Berkeley: University of California Press.

Firth, R. (1973) *Symbols: Public and Private*. London: Unwin Hyman.

Gluckman, M. (ed.) (1962) *Essays on the Ritual of Social Relations*. Manchester: Manchester University Press.

Goffman, E. (1956) 'On the nature of deference and demeanor.' *American Anthropologist* 58: 473–502.

Goffman, E. (1959) *Encounters: Two Studies in the Sociology of Interaction.* Indianapolis: Bobbs-Merrill.

Goffman, E. (1963a) *Behaviour in Public Places: Notes on the Social Organisation of Gatherings.* New York: Free Press.

Goffman, E. (1963b) *Stigma: Notes on the Management of Spoiled Identity.* Englewood Cliffs, NJ: Prentice-Hall.

Hall, R.L. (1962) *The Archaeology of Carcajou Point.* Madison: The University of Wisconsin Press.

Hall, R.L. (1993) 'Red Banks, Oneota, and the Ho-Chunk: views from a distant rock.' *The Wisconsin Archaeologist* 74: 10–79.

Hayden, B. (1995) 'Pathways to power: principles for creating socioeconomic inequalities.' In T.D. Price and G. Feinman (eds) *Foundations of Social Inequality*, pp. 15–86. New York: Plenum.

Hodder, I. (1982) *Symbols in Action.* New York: Academic Press.

Hodder, I. (1990) 'Style as historical quality.' In M.W. Conkey and C.A. Hastorf (eds) *The Uses of Style in Archaeology*, pp. 44–51. Cambridge: Cambridge University Press.

La Potherie, C.C. Le Roy Bacqueville de (1911) *History of the Savage Peoples Who Are Allies of New France,* edited by E.H. Blair. Cleveland: The Arthur H. Clark Company.

Lévi-Strauss, C. (1953) 'Social structure.' In A. Kroeber (ed.) *Anthropology Today: An Encyclopedic Inventory.* pp. 524–53. Chicago: University of Chicago Press.

Lurie, N.O. (1972) 'An Aztalan-Ho-Chunk Hypothesis.' Ms. on file, Anthropology Program, Luther College, Decorah, Iowa.

Lurie, N.O. (1978) 'Ho-Chunk.' In B. Trigger (ed.) *Handbook of North American Indians: Northeast,* pp. 690–707. Washington: Smithsonian Institution Press.

Mott, M. (1938) 'The relation of historic Indian tribes to archaeological manifestations in Iowa.' *Iowa Journal of History and Politics* 36(3): 227–314.

Orso, E.G. (1974) 'Folklore and identity.' In T. Fitzgerald (ed.) *Social and Cultural Identity: Problems of Persistence and Change,* pp. 24–38. Athens: University of Georgia Press.

Overstreet, D.F. (1976) 'The Grand River, Lake Koshkonong, Green Bay and Lake Ho-Chunk phases: eight hundred years of Oneota prehistory in Eastern Wisconsin.' Ph.D Dissertation, Department of Anthropology, University of Wisconsin–Madison.

Overstreet, D.F. (1978) 'Oneota settlement patterns in Eastern Wisconsin.' In B.D. Smith (ed.) *Mississippian Settlement Patterns*, pp. 21–49. New York: Academic Press.

Overstreet, D.F. (1993) 'McCauley, Astor, and Hanson – candidates for the provisional Dandy phase.' *Wisconsin Archaeologist* 74: 120–196.

Peacock, J. (1968) *Rites of Modernization.* Chicago: University of Chicago Press.

Plog, S. (1976) 'Measurement of prehistoric interaction between communities.' In K. Flannery (ed.) *The Early Mesoamerican Village*, pp. 255–72. New York: Academic Press.

Plog, S. (1980) *Stylistic Variation in Prehistoric Ceramics: Design Analysis in the American Southwest.* Cambridge: Cambridge University Press.

Plog, S. (1983) 'Analysis of style in artifacts.' In B. Siegel (ed.) *Annual Review of Anthropology* 12, pp. 125–142. Palo Alto: Annual Reviews.

Plog, S. (1990) 'Sociopolitical implications of stylistic variation in the American southwest.' In M.W. Conkey and C.A. Hastorf (eds) *The Uses of Style in Archaeology*, pp. 61–72. Cambridge: Cambridge University Press.

Radin, P. (n.d.) Field notes housed at the American Philosophical Society Library, Philadelphia.

Radin, P. (1911) 'Some aspects of Ho-Chunk archaeology.' *American Anthropologist* (N.S.) 13: 517–538.

Radin, P. (1915a) *Literary Aspects of North American Mythology*. Anthropology Series of the Canada Geological Survey, No. 6, Museum Bulletin 16.

Radin, P. (1915b) *The Social Organisation of the Ho-Chunk Indians, an Interpretation*. Anthropology Series of the Canada Geological Survey No. 6, Museum Bulletin 16.

Radin, P. (1923) 'The Ho-Chunk tribe.' In *37th Annual Report of the United States Bureau of American Ethnology*, pp. 35–550.

Radin, P. (1926a) 'Literary aspects of Ho-Chunk mythology.' *Journal of American Folk-Lore* 39: 18–52.

Radin, P. (1926b) 'Ho-Chunk myth cycles.' *Primitive Culture* 1: 8–86.

Radin, P. (1945) *The Road of Life and Death*. Bolligen Series 5. New York: Pantheon Books.

Radin, P. (1948) *Winnebago Hero Cycles: A Study in Aboriginal Literature*. Indiana University Publications in Anthropology and Linguistics 1. Bloomington, IN: Indiana University.

Radin, P. (1954) *The Evolution of an American Indian Prose Epic: A Study in Comparative Literature*, Part 1. Special Publication of the Bollingen Foundation No. 3. Reprinted Princeton, NJ: Princeton University Press.

Radin, P. (1955) 'The literature of primitive peoples.' *Diogenes* 12: 1–28.

Radin, P. (1956) *The Trickster: A Study in American Indian Mythology*. London: Routledge.

Sackett, J.R. (1990) 'Style and ethnicity in archaeology: the case for isochrestism.' In M.W. Conkey and C.A. Hastorf *The Uses of Style in Archaeology*, pp. 32–43. Cambridge: Cambridge University Press.

Salzer, R.J. (1987) 'Preliminary report on the Gottschall site (47Ia80).' *The Wisconsin Archaeologist* 68: 419–72.

Salzer, R.J. (1996) 'C-14 assays on ceramic components at the Gottschall site.' Paper presented at the Midwest Archaeological Society Conference, 9–12 October 1996, Beloit, Wisconsin.

Schortman, E.M. (1989) 'Interregional interaction in prehistory: the need for a new perspective.' *American Antiquity* 54: 52–65.

Staeck, J.P. (1991) 'New directions in interpretation: Chiwere myth traditions and the late prehistoric of the western Great Lakes.' Paper presented in the symposium entitled Plains Woodland Interactions at the 36th Annual Midwest Archaeological Conference, 18–20 October, La Crosse, Wisconsin.

Staeck, J.P. (1994) 'Archaeology, identity, and oral traditions: a reconsideration of late prehistoric and early historic Ho-Chunk social structure and identity as seen through oral traditions.' Unpublished Ph.D. Thesis, Rutgers University, New Brunswick.

Staeck, J.P.(1996) 'Ranking, marriage, and power: reflections of Ho-Chunk oral traditions on Effigy Mound transegalitarian strategies for developing power and prestige.' Paper presented at the Midwest Archaeological Society Conference, 9–12 October 1996, Beloit, Wisconsin.

Turner, V. (1967) *The Forest of Symbols: Aspects of Nbembu Ritual*. Ithaca: Cornell University Press.

Upham, S. (1990) 'Analog or digital: toward a generic framework for explaining the development of emergent political systems.' In S. Upham (ed.) *The Evolution of Political Systems: Sociopolitics in Small-scale Sedentary Societies*, pp. 87–115. Cambridge: Cambridge University Press.

Wiessner, P. (1990) 'Is there a unity to style?' In M.W. Conkey and C.A. Hastorf (eds) *The Uses of Style in Archaeology,* pp. 105–112. Cambridge: Cambridge University Press.

Wobst, H.M. (1977) 'Stylistic behaviour and information exchange.' In C. Cleland (ed.) *For the Director: Research Essays in Honor of James B. Griffin*, pp. 317–342. Ann Arbor: Museum of Anthropology, University of Michigan.

CHAPTER SIX

FEMINISM, PAGANISM, PLURALISM

LYNN MESKELL

ABSTRACT

Within a post-processual archaeology all voices are supposedly welcomed and a plurality of positions is considered necessary, especially when they encompass an engendered or feminist perspective. This postmodern, multivocal milieu is inclusive rather than exclusionary, since it seeks to provide a forum for previously silent groups and those who have social and political vested interests in the construction of archaeological knowledge. From this theoretical standpoint the voices of feminists, ecofeminists, archaeofeminists, Goddess worshippers and pagans must all be considered as legitimate discourses and given validity alongside scholarly accounts of the past. While the intention is admirable, in theory, academia remains reticent in seriously considering, let alone publishing, alternative histories and New Age narratives. Pagans and Goddess worshippers maintain their own publications, journals and conferences. The end result is that little overlap or dissemination of ideas actually takes place and separate spheres are rigorously upheld. In this paper I argue that in reality archaeologists, post-processual and otherwise, are generally resistant to many alternative discourses and that their theoretical premises bear little relation to academic praxis. Furthermore, I argue that the central projects of feminism and paganism are often at odds with archaeology (each field is also internally fragmented). Essentially, these specific constructions of knowledge need to exist as separate entities, though cross-referencing is still inevitable. At present these narratives of difference cannot be reconciled within the current disciplinary framework of archaeology.

The very fact that this volume exists is testament to a changing academic climate, one which acknowledges other voices and other constructions of knowledge. That they can exist side by side is the result of a post-processual archaeology where all voices are supposedly welcomed and a plurality of positions is considered necessary. This postmodern, multivocal milieu is inclusive rather than exclusionary, since it seeks to provide a forum for previously silent groups and those who have social and political vested interests in the construction of archaeological knowledge. From this theoretical standpoint the voices of feminists, ecofeminists, archaeo-feminists, Goddess worshippers and pagans must all be considered as legit-imate discourses and given validity alongside scholarly accounts of the past. My point is that whilst the intention is admirable, the outcome in reality usually falls short. At present there is little scholarly overlap and the dis-ciplinary boundaries are firmly in place. Feminists continue to write their books on theoretical and experiential issues, including archaeology only to provide the long time depth for women's oppression. Goddess wor-shippers, pagans and alternative archaeologists run their own journals and publishing houses, having little input from their institutionalised counter-parts. And archaeologists continue to write their own narratives within their own disciplinary milieu, claiming intellectual superiority, either implicitly or explicitly. So where is the pluralism, multivocality and dia-logue that we have been told characterises the 1990s? It would seem that this is simply wishful thinking on a grand scale.

Often when academics make forays onto the sacred ground of pagans and Goddess worshippers they are met with great hostility, as if an archaeological search for meaning is tantamount to the purposeful destruction of contemporary spiritualist movements. In my own case, one article on the Goddess and New Age archaeology (Meskell 1995) became embroiled in a highly personalised and polarised battle, where I symbol-ised the 'stuffy academic' and Goddess worshippers were the bearers of real knowledge, experience and real feminism (see Sjöö 1996). We are fooling ourselves if we imagine that we all play by the same rules, or that we can sustain lively intellectual debates on topics which lie at the heart of people's life experience. However, archaeologists are also responsible for the great divide. Generally they are not willing to take part in con-temporary debates, to write for other groups in a non-academic forum, or to produce books which disseminate archaeological knowledge to the general public. There are of course exceptions, people like Chris Chippindale and Barbara Bender for example. In the academic environ-ment, such writing is not always valorised and anyone who becomes a populariser is usually pigeonholed as such. Even the terms we use are highly loaded: *popular* is synonymous with superficial, non-rigorous, gloss-ing. The fringe becomes the periphery, a no man's land where chaos and mythology reign supreme – one is reminded of the old saying when one goes off the map, 'there be dragons'. Unlike many, I do not see these internecine differences as revolving around reductionist concepts such as domination and resistance, or oppressor versus oppressed. From my own experience with pagans and Goddess worshippers in Australia and the UK, I know many of these people to be highly educated, articulate, mobilised individuals who have their own means of publishing and disseminating material, organising conferences and mastering cyberspace. Surf the net and see. It is simply wrong to see academia as the oppressive ivory tower, and everyone else as agitating anarchists. Many simply do not care for our academic musings and are satisfied to create independent narratives, such as Goddess groups.

FEMINIST FORAYS

Taking this one step further I want to tie in the Goddess worship with feminism, since the two are often conflated (Meskell 1996). There is a noticeable trend in feminist texts, primarily those with an interdisciplinary focus, which seeks to incorporate developments in archaeology and anthropology. Since feminism has had a longer and more noticeable effect on anthropology, most feminist writers feature recent and well-documented work, like that of Rubin, Ortner, Rosaldo, Zihlman or Moore. Recent work in social and biological anthropology is restated, illustrating the insights gleaned from a feminist perspective. However, the story is very different when it comes to summarising archaeological contributions. As an example, I would like to draw on a recent textbook, published by Judith Lorber (Lorber 1994) called *Paradoxes of Gender*. After several excellent chapters outlining the offerings of anthropology, Lorber launches into an analysis of the Neolithic using the narratives of Marija Gimbutas (e.g. Gimbutas 1982, 1989, 1991). Suddenly we are launched from French feminist philosophy and Foucault, to a reconstructed Neolithic Çatalhöyük where a utopian existence was enjoyed by all – but mainly women. We all know the story: things were peaceful, creative, vegetarian and Goddess-centred . . . that is until men ruined it by bringing increased technology, metallurgy, warfare, etc. Gimbutas' sexist revisioning of history is used, as it generally is, to explain the suppression of women and the source of their imposed inequality. This represents another search for origins, an aetiological trope which has been vigorously critiqued by feminists themselves for being an androcentric paradigm (e.g. Brown 1993; Conkey and Tringham 1995).

It is surprising at the end of the twentieth century, when feminism is reaching new intellectual heights and archaeology is gradually becoming socially aware, that such interdisciplinary ignorance is still possible. Gimbutas is invoked by various writers, the Neolithic is a particularly popular destination, and Çatalhöyük is the feminist site *par excellence*. This is not a unique instance. Perhaps the connection is that feminists too are not really interested in current archaeological reformulations, since the political picture archaeologists like Gimbutas offer is more sympathetic to the cause. This genre, often termed mythopoetics, has an inherent structure which not only makes the past a more habitable place, a utopian existence which we must actively seek to replicate, but offers a reassuring archetype which potentially provides the model for the next millennium. The past is not only a foreign country we desire to colonise, it is our way back to the future.

So in this instance all three movements interact with each other – feminism, Goddess worship and archaeology. Gimbutas certainly took advantage of the women's movement and feminism to promote and sell her work, moving from New England to California and radically altering her scholarship in the process. She then became an integral part of the feminist movement, without being explicitly a feminist. This is a clear example of how disciplines can become intertwined and are complicit in the production of popular narratives. Moreover, it suggests that plurality and multivocality are not easily achieved without some loss of integrity, since we all know that not all pasts are equal. For archaeologists it is disconcerting that other disciplines revive outdated scholarship rather than address recent research. Feminist and pagan writings on Çatalhöyük are a clear example of this. However, we seem to be caught in a contradictory bind. On the one hand mainstream archaeology has little contact with alternative archaeologies, pagans and Goddess worshippers, and fails to incorporate their particular narratives. On the other, archaeologists have failed to acknowledge their intellectual heritage, and in fact many of our ideas and concepts can be traced back to mythology and writers interested in pagan histories. Therefore, archaeology is not free from outside influence; it has just failed to recognise its historical setting. Again Çatalhöyük is a case in point. The construction of the site in the modern mind is not simply the product of archaeology. I would argue that it is an amalgam of paganism, archaeology, fiction and Goddess-based interpretations (Figure 6.1). Two archaeologists who wrote about the site were embroiled in a mixture of all those narratives and I would argue that they are exemplars of the construction process. I want to look more closely at the specific narratives of Marija Gimbutas and James Mellaart (Mellaart 1962, 1964, 1965, 1966, 1967, 1975; Mellaart et al. 1989).

VISIONS OF ÇATALHÖYÜK

I would like to look at Mellaart first, because his vision of Çatalhöyük set the scene for Gimbutas and other writers of Goddess archaeology. In fact, little rewriting was necessary because Mellaart was already using the language of magic and paganism. Typical of many excavators in the 1960s, Mellaart (1965: 77) was also at pains to stress that the site was the biggest, best and the ancient antecedent of Western civilisation itself: 'Çatal Hüyük shines like a supernova among the rather dim galaxy of contemporary peasant cultures.' Moreover, the lasting effect of the site itself was felt not in the Near East but in Europe, according to Mellaart (1965: 77), since it introduced to the latter agriculture, stock breeding and the 'cult of the Mother Goddess, the basis of our civilisation'. From the outset, there was only one Goddess at the site. According to Mellaart (1964: 119), she was the 'Great Goddess, mistress of life and death, protectress of women, patroness of the arts ... at this period there can be no doubt that the

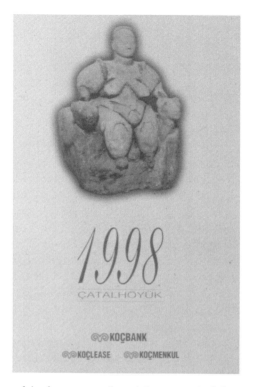

Figure 6.1   Image of the famous Çatalhöyük figurine, which featured on a calendar for Koç Bank in Turkey

supreme deity was the Great Goddess'. It seems clear that the initial record-ing of Çatalhöyük was largely influenced by decidedly Greek notions of ritual and magic, especially that of the Triple Goddess – maiden, mother and crone. These ideas were common to many at that time, but probably originated with Jane Ellen Harrison, Classical archaeologist and member of the famous Cambridge Ritualists (Harrison 1903). One wonders where the inspiration for such strong convictions emanated from. Possibly Frazer's *The Golden Bough* (Frazer [1922] 1993: 331) in which he states, on sur-veying all evidence, that 'a great Mother Goddess, the personification of all the reproductive energies of nature, was worshipped under different names but with a substantial similarity of myth and ritual by many peoples of Western Asia'. Ronald Hutton believes it goes back further, to Gerhard in 1849, and this was later taken up by Classicists (Hutton 1997: 92–93). This notion of ritual and magic, coupled with the sensational nature of the material, seems to have inspired Mellaart's narrative of Çatalhöyük. This is not commonly recognised within academia, yet was certainly taken up by pagans, Goddess worshippers and feminists.

It is interesting to examine the common assumptions held about Çatal-höyük as a result of Mellaart's excavations through the subsequent narratives produced. Many begin with the belief that the site is the foremost Goddess site in a truly global sense, and this is largely due to the efforts of Gimbutas. They assume the Goddess was worshipped there. This doesn't mean just any female deity, rather the universal, monolithic entity of the Great Goddess. She was the Neolithic 'virgin' according to Gimbutas, and her effigies had shared characteristics with figurines from the Aegean and Europe.

Following on from the work of Gimbutas, Eisler (1991: 3–4, 8) claims that Çatalhöyük was essentially free from armed conflict and socially equitable; however, the highest power was bestowed upon female deities. Eisler tells us that archaeologists, like Mellaart, have proved sites like Çatalhöyük were peaceful, matrilineal communities where women held high social positions, such as priestesses. Basically, there is a unified vision of Çatalhöyük, inspired by the original excavator's vivid reconstructions and sanctioned by Gimbutas' universal gynocentric narrative. This vision is still so pervasive that current excavations of the site have to 'dig through' Mellaart's prior work, both literally and metaphorically. The site is so steeped in his reconstructions, interpretations and terminology that it will take some time before a new Çatalhöyük can emerge.

In questioning why the fervour about the site is so strong, one might look to Weber's concepts about the roots of structured inequality. If inequality, whether it be class- or sex-based, is socially constructed, then it should be possible to find examples where the *status quo* was different. So the desire to elevate Çatalhöyük can be seen as the search for a utopian model, which doubly serves as an explanatory story and a template for change. We might also turn to Hobsbawm's idea about the invention of tradition (Hobsbawm 1983). This invention is seen as a common trope which is deployed as a means of conferring legitimacy upon certain prac- tices (of a ritual or symbolic nature) throughout society, which implies continuity with the past. Contemporary desires are appeased by the creation and maintenance of myths about the past: this is particularly strong at the time of writing due to millenarian sentiments.

In sum, I would argue that these archaeologists – at one time very con- servative scholars – created the narratives which New Age archaeology has subsequently adopted. However, they were indelibly influenced by mytho- logical studies when they created their interpretations. We are never free from the impact of the fringe and some of our most evocative archaeolog- ical interpretations cannot be extricated from that complex maze of associ- ations. So who influenced whom, and who is responsible for our intellectual heritage? Whether it is Margaret Murray and Egypt, Jane Ellen Harrison or Arthur Evans for Greece, Jacquetta Hawkes or Marija Gimbutas and Europe, or James Mellaart's Çatalhöyük – archaeology, wicca, paganism and Goddess veneration share a long and interwoven trajectory. Taking the Huttonian hard line, academics themselves may have unwittingly been the founders of a new religion. Can we legitimately indict the fringe when they have simply been following archaeologists, albeit somewhat outdated ones. I would suggest that disciplinary and alternative archaeology share a long, sometimes fruitful, yet often unhappy relationship. Often they fail to acknowledge each other or to recognise their reliance and responsibility. In that sense real pluralism has a long way to go before it transcends tokenism and trendiness. Yet the starting point for all these groups has always been the evocative nature of the material remains from the past and the people of antiquity. Our greatest responsibility is to them.

REFERENCES

Brown, S. (1993) 'Feminist research in archaeology. What does it mean? Why is it taking so long?' In N.S. Rabinowitz and A. Richlin (eds) *Feminist Theory and the Classics*, pp. 283–371. New York: Routledge.

Conkey, M.W. and Tringham, R.E. (1995) 'Archaeology and the Goddess: exploring the contours of feminist archaeology.' In D.C. Stanton and A.J. Stewart (eds) *Feminisms in the Academy*, pp. 199–247. Ann Arbor: University of Michigan.

Eisler, R. (1991) 'The goddess of nature and spirituality: an ecomanifesto.' In J. Campbell and C. Musés (eds) *In All Her Names: Explorations of the Feminine in Divinity*, pp. 3–23. San Francisco: HarperCollins.

Frazer, J. [1922] (1993) *The Golden Bough*. Ware: Wordsworth Editions.

Gimbutas, M. (1982) *The Goddesses and Gods of Old Europe*. Los Angeles: University of California Press.

Gimbutas, M. (1989) *The Language of the Goddess*. San Francisco: HarperCollins.

Gimbutas, M. (1991) *The Civilisation of the Goddess*. San Francisco: HarperCollins.

Harrison, J.E. (1903) *Prolegomena to the Study of Greek Religion*. Cambridge: Cambridge University Press.

Hobsbawm, E. (1983) 'Introduction: inventing tradition.' In E. Hobsbawm and T. Ranger (eds) *The Invention of Tradition*, pp. 1–14. Cambridge: Cambridge University Press.

Hutton, R. (1997) 'The Neolithic great goddess: a study in modern tradition.' *Antiquity* 71: 91–99.

Lorber, J. (1994) *Paradoxes of Gender*. New Haven: Yale University Press.

Mellaart, J. (1962) 'Excavations at Çatal Hüyük. First preliminary report, 1961.' *Anatolian Studies* 12: 41–65.

Mellaart, J. (1964) 'Excavations at Çatal Hüyük, 1963.' *Anatolian Studies* 14: 39–119.

Mellaart, J. (1965) *Earliest Civilisations of the Near East*. London: Thames and Hudson.

Mellaart, J. (1966) 'Excavations at Çatal Hüyük, 1965. Fourth preliminary report.' *Anatolian Studies* 16: 165–191.

Mellaart, J. (1967) *Çatal Hüyük: A Neolithic Town in Anatolia*. London: Thames and Hudson.

Mellaart, J. (1975) *The Neolithic of the Near East*. London: Thames and Hudson.

Mellaart, J., Hirsch, U. and Balpinar, B. (eds) (1989) *The Goddess from Anatolia*. Rome: Eskenazi.

Meskell, L.M. (1995) 'Goddesses, Gimbutas and New Age archaeology.' *Antiquity* 69: 74–86.

Meskell, L.M. (1996) 'Review of *The Concept of the Goddess*, edited by S. Billington and M. Green.' *Norwegian Archaeological Review* 29: 117–120.

Sjöö, M. (1996) 'Snidy and dishonourable. Letter to the Readers' Forum.' *The Ley Hunter* 124: 29–30.

CHAPTER SEVEN

APOCALYPSE PAST/FUTURE

Archaeology and folklore, writ large

KATHRYN E. L. DENNING

ABSTRACT

In many recent best-selling 'fringe' books related to archaeology, such as The Mayan Prophecies *(Gilbert and Cotterell 1995) and* Keeper of Genesis *(Bauval and Hancock 1996), there is a common theme – the idea that in the remains of 'extinct' civilisations, there are not only clues to the fate which will befall our own society, but sources of ancient wisdom which, if interpreted correctly, may help us to avoid cataclysm. These works and others like them are provocative because they resonate with traditional Judaeo-Christian apocalyptic literature, both in form and in effect, using other-worldly revelations about the past and future to guide understanding and action in the present. Apocalyptic narratives can act as powerful historical forces – stories to live and die by – particularly at significant junctures in time, such as the upcoming millennium. Thus, it is of interest that apocalyptic/revelatory threads also run through more 'orthodox' writings in archaeology. The idea that peoples of the past can tell us something crucially important about our own future has always been in the background of much archaeological research, but in this time of environmental degradation, instability and rapid social change, such themes have begun to appear in more specific forms, and in sharper relief, provoking questions about the use of the past in the present, and about archaeologists as tellers of stories.*

If we recall that our history's end has not yet been written, and that we ourselves are its coauthors, then perhaps we will come to see that no ending is inevitable, and that the saving bliss of catastrophe is a luxury we can ill afford.

(O'Leary 1994: 228)

During several years of researching prehistory's importance to people in Britain, and the many forms which its interpretation takes, multiple lines of connection between archaeology and folklore quickly became evident to me. There are, for example, frequent links between archaeological sites and local traditions or legends in Britain, as well as the strong tendency for avocational researchers there to be interested in both, rather than either subject in isolation. This is intriguing territory indeed. But if one adopts a broader definition of folklore, moving outwards from 'the traditional beliefs and stories of a people' (*Concise Oxford Dictionary*) to include all stories, including religious narratives, which play an important role in societies today, there emerge many more lines of connection with archaeology. One example is that of Western apocalyptic writings, both secular and religious, for these versions of history can easily be seen in parallel to modern archaeologically based narratives. Followed far enough, these lines intertwine in surprising ways, and put fairly ordinary observations about the popularity of archaeology, or the importance of history, into larger contexts – contexts which archaeologists may find worthwhile to consider as they read and write upon their subject, for the archaeologist's role in modern society can be more substantial than is sometimes assumed.

Archaeology is important socio-politically, and not only in explosive situations like India's Ayodhya (Ascherson 1998), but also in the way that archaeologically based narratives are woven, just as folklore is, into the very fabric of our lives. This has increasingly been the subject of study for scholars, especially those concerned with national and ethnic identities and their representation and construction through archaeological material (e.g. Kohl and Fawcett 1995; Piccini 1997; Ronayne 1997). But there is another dimension in which archaeology is socially consequential, which is becoming ever more obvious now, in a time when idle conversation often turns to the fast-approaching year AD 2000. Archaeology is also important because of the role it plays in generating narratives about the way our world will end. These narratives in turn are important socially (not just to academics and ideologues) because human beings understand and describe their world through stories, and more than that, because stories help us to situate ourselves, as individuals and as groups, in time. More significantly still, stories – whether born of history, religion, science or myth – tell us how to live. And sometimes, they tell us how to die.

THE MILLENNIUM COMETH[1]

A former professor from Taiwan named Hon-Ming Chen is now the leader of God's Salvation Church, and has been, at least until recently, patiently waiting in a Texan suburb with 150 devoted followers for God to return to Earth. Specifically, they were waiting at 3513 Ridgedale

Drive in Garland, with a 'spacecraft' made of radial tires, plywood and lamp posts, where they spent each day reading Chen's books and praying in preparation for God to come in a spaceship, to save all humanity from nuclear war. But, despite Professor Chen's assurances that on Wednesday 25 March 1998, 'the Almighty will make a preliminary appearance on Channel 18 of every TV set in the world' – interestingly enough, the Home Shopping Network in Texas – God has so far been a no-show (Perkins and Jackson 1998: 24).

This is, by now, a familiar sort of story, for there is an increasing amount of coverage in the media about activities relating to the end of this millennium. Interest is not climbing only in isolated religious groups, however; this is a secular phenomenon too, and has been growing steadily for decades (Russell 1978: 23; Zamora 1982). The word 'apocalypse', allusions to the Book of Revelation and even photographs of the Four Horsemen, are showing up with amusing regularity in tabloid newspaper headlines, while elements of the storyline from Revelation are often used in movies, in fiction and vividly in comic books. One particularly lurid tale of extraterrestrial invasion even opens with a line from Revelation: 'And I saw another sign in heaven, great and marvelous, seven angels having the seven last plagues' (Wheeler 1996). This is not surprising, for it can be argued that the obsession with extraterrestrials now gripping much of the West is a result of this end-of-the-millennium, end-of-the-world-as-we-know-it mindset. Certainly, the themes of extraterrestrial visitation and the end of the current world order were blended in some of the most popular Hollywood films of the late 1990s, from *Independence Day* to *Men in Black*, *Contact*, *Sphere* and *Starship Troopers*. Themes of mass destruction by inexorable natural forces are played out in *Deep Impact*, *Armageddon* and, in different ways in *Titanic*, *Volcano*, *Twister* and the remake of *Godzilla*. Cities or even countries being laid waste are apparently almost prerequisite to engaging the American movie-going public's attention; and as Ralph Melcher commented, 'at the end of the Millennium the highest achievement of popular culture is the construction of the perfect disaster' (1998: 2).

Of course, academics are not exempt from end-of-the-world fervour, and so there has also been a proliferation of scholarly interest in social behaviour as the millennium approaches. There seems to be a new sociological, historical or literary book out every week analysing apocalyptic or millenarian movements, or offering general comment on what has come to be known as 'pre-millennial tension'. There are also many very popular books being published which are specifically preoccupied with dramatic ends to ancient civilisations, and with looking to sources of ancient wisdom which may help us to avoid a dramatic end of our own. As an archaeologist with an interest in the ways in which 'alternative prehistory' over the last century can illuminate the influences operating on academic archaeologists, and also an interest in the complex relationships between accepted and marginalised discussions of the past, I have found this to be well worth examining in considerable detail. As that is a book in itself, however, I will here only sketch, at the most general and omissive level, some areas of connection between such popular books, apocalypses and their social role, and archaeological writing.

APOCALYPSE

It is probably wise to begin with what 'apocalypse' means. For most of us, in general usage, the word 'apocalypse' means disaster, or the end of the world. Bible readers may even have some more specific images in mind, like the Four Horsemen bringing unspeakable cataclysm, the blowing of trumpets, fire in the sky and the sea turning to blood, or plagues of exceptionally nasty locusts, and stars falling into the sea, poisoning the water. But actually, the word 'apocalypse' properly means 'revelation'.

The essence of apocalypse is captured by Revelation 6:1–8, where the four Beings, in sequence, lead St John by the hand to show him the Horsemen, crying 'Come and see!' Similarly, all the events we associate with 'the apocalypse' – again, the Horsemen, various scenes of destruction and heavenly intervention – are integral to the story, but it is St John's experience, his revelation, that is apocalyptic. The Four Horsemen are not the bringers of the apocalypse: they are characters in the story which is *itself* the substance of the apocalypse.

Thus, biblical scholars speak of 'apocalypses', including the apocalypse of Daniel, of St John as written in Revelation, the apocalypses of Zachariah, Isaiah, Joel, Enoch, Baruch, Ezra, Abraham, and the apocalypses of Greco-Roman, Gnostic and Persian origin (Hellholm 1983). Apocalypse or 'apocalyptic' is in fact a literary genre, including narratives dealing with divine revelation through dream, vision or supernatural intermediary. These narratives usually pertain to eschatology, or 'the study of the End Times', but not invariably. Sometimes they emphasise the bad things that are going to happen to everyone on the face of the earth, and sometimes they emphasise the subsequent happiness for the righteous in the glorious kingdom of God.

Apocalyptic is complex, and there is a great deal written about it, not only about interpretation of the texts themselves, but also about their purposes. Most pertinent here is the observation made by Christopher Rowland, in his book *The Open Heaven* (1982), that Judaeo-Christian apocalyptic writings did not deal only with what was to come – they covered past, present and future, explaining history and contemporary events in terms of prophecies for what lay ahead. This is critical to their interpretation. In short, they sought not only to relate divine wisdom about the future, but to provide an understanding of all history.

Bernard McGinn, in his book *Visions of the End*, wrote that

> The structure and meaning of time, the meeting place of this age and eternity, are consistent concerns . . . The desire to understand history – its unity, its structure, its goal, the future hope which it promises – is not a passing interest or momentary whim, but a perennial human concern. A sense of belonging in time, as well as the need to understand the special significance of the present, is the anthropological root of apocalyptic systems of thought.
>
> (McGinn 1979: 30)

One could say that it is also the root of the disciplines of history and archaeology. These different studies and writings are all about our place in time, our place in history, and our relationship to the beginning and the end.

But more than this, in our modern era, archaeology provides some of the raw material of revelation. Voices from the past replace divine messages. And accordingly, popular archaeology books have at least partly replaced traditional religious wisdom in guiding our thought about who we are, where we've been, where we're going, and how we should live.

POPULAR ARCHAEOLOGY, REVELATION AND ESCHATON

The popular archaeology books that will be discussed here have the elements that can be considered the chief hallmarks of apocalyptic. They tell elaborate stories based on epiphanies (revealed, in this case, by the archaeological record), make eschatological statements, and also make comments on the state of society today and recommendations for our future action. There are many books with similar themes, so only two of the most recent bestsellers will be discussed here. These are also, happily, two of the better ones, which are at least somewhat grounded in the interpretation of material archaeological reality.

The Mayan Prophecies, published by Adrian Gilbert and Maurice Cotterell in 1995, is an international bestseller which revolves around the notions of the end of the world and of revealed wisdom from another sphere. Their claim is, essentially, that in some Mayan carvings, particularly the Lid of Palenque, there are secret messages that can be decoded and understood. Further, the authors argue that the Mayan obsession with calendars concerned cycles of sunspots. They then relate sunspots to dramatic drops in human fertility, and thus explain what they claim is the hitherto enigmatic Mayan collapse. It is all entwined with the Popol Vuh, the sacred Mayan book which can itself be considered an apocalypse of sorts, concerned as it is with prophecy, the past and the future. Based on the Mayan calendar, Cotterell and Gilbert make specific predictions for the year 2012, of the greatest catastrophe that mankind has ever known. We are to expect a reversal of the magnetic field, pole changes, giant floods, submerged landmasses, a drop in temperature . . . the works. We are entreated to sit up and take note while we still can.

The second popular archaeology book may become even more widely read. My copy of the best-selling *Fingerprints of the Gods* bears the notable cover blurb, 'a Quest for the Beginning and the End'. But the author, Graham Hancock, was just warming up with his proposal that Antarctica is the place to look for the high civilisation that spawned all others. Its recent sequel, *Keeper of Genesis*, by Hancock and Robert Bauval (of *The Orion Mystery* fame), says that the monuments of the Giza acropolis, together with the ancient texts and rituals which are linked to them, were specifically designed to transmit a message to us, across time. They say that this specially encoded message pertains to the predecessors of the ancient Egyptian civilisation, and to their quest for immortality and the transcendence of their physical being. Once again, the authors plead with us to take heed, for if we can decode and understand this message, it could mean a wonderful renaissance for humanity and the solution to many of our problems.

This theme is played out, too, in another very popular book of a somewhat different kind. Unlike *The Mayan Prophecies* and *Keeper of Genesis*, however, this one is written as fiction, but fiction of that particular New Age sort which is implied to be deeply truthful at its core. *The Celestine Prophecy* has spent years on bestseller lists, and millions of copies are in print (*The Economist*, 7 December 1996, p. 6). The cover reads:

> In the Rain Forests of Peru, an ancient manuscript has been discovered. Within its pages are 9 key insights into life itself – insights each human being is predicted to grasp sequentially, one insight then another, as we move towards a completely spiritual life on earth.

(Here we have both the elements of revealed wisdom from a distant archaeological source, and in this case, a happy ending – a jolly eschatology.) Although this book is presented as fiction, the author James Redfield, a sociologist, also puts out a special newsletter chronicling his experiences with the spiritual renaissance now occurring on our planet. There is also a sequel – *The Tenth Insight*, presumably based on a new Mayan manuscript inexplicably found in Peru – and a series of spin-offs, including *Celestine Prophecy* Pocket Guides, Experiential Guides and audio tapes. Indeed, there is a full-blown *Celestine Prophecy* industry and, apparently, the books are being used by spiritual study groups the world over. The specifically archaeological slant seems more a rhetorical device used for legitimation than anything else, but it is difficult to suppose that all the book's earnest readers reject the central premise, that the Maya were the source of these prophecies and they disappeared because, by raising their energy vibrations through meditation, they actually crossed over into a higher plane, transcending all materiality and even death.

Typically, most archaeologists respond to such books with derision, or respond not at all. The books are seen as either bad archaeology or nothing to do with archaeology. However, this is underestimating the complexity of these narratives and of their position within society, not to mention taking a rather narrow view of archaeology. There are more productive ways to look at the situation.

These books are hugely popular around the world. People's lives are changed by them, and their views of the past and future transformed. Why should that be so? Archaeologists often suspect that books like *The Mayan Prophecies*, *Keeper of Genesis* and *The Celestine Prophecy* are so well received as historical or cultural reading by the general public simply because of an appetite for the supernatural and the sensational in place of the human and the ordinary. This may be part of it, but it is just as likely that their popularity is due to the way they are written. This is not to say that they are presented in an accessible style, because sometimes such books are overly long, every bit as dense as an archaeological site report, and twice as boring. Rather, they may well be popular because they use the age-old formula of the apocalypse, which tells us about the beginning and the end, where we are in relation to them, and what we can do about it. This formula continues to have great resonance for people today, as it always has (Russell 1978). The implications of this, in the context of the creation and relation of history, are worth considering.

APOCALYPSES WITHIN SOCIAL HISTORY

All old stories – whether folklore, religion or history – must be seen in the social and political contexts of their origination and perpetuation, and the early Judaeo-Christian apocalypses are no exception (Hanson 1979). They were written in times of great oppression. For example, the Book of Daniel was written when Antiochus Epiphanes was attempting to annihilate Judaism, and St John wrote Revelation from prison, convinced, correctly, that tribulations lay ahead for the churches of Asia Minor (Russell 1978: 16).

And so, biblical scholars consider that these writings were in part about revenge and a reversal of power (Hanson 1979). Indeed, in the Book of Enoch, it says that 'the evil doers [will] be consumed, and the power of the guilty be annihilated' and that 'This Son of man . . . shall hurl kings from their thrones and their dominions . . . Darkness shall be their habitation, and worms shall be their bed' (Laurence, 1995: 178, 51). In Revelation 19 and 20, John describes the triumph of God and the angels over the False Prophet and the Great Beast – who are best understood as representing political figures – as well as the subduing of the eternal characters of Satan and the Dragon. But more than revenge, the apocalypses, especially the Revelation, were letters of consolation to the oppressed, for there is a happy end for the righteous, after all the carnage is finished. These writings did not intend to incite rebellion or active resistance against the oppressors of the day, because the final war between good and evil would take place in heaven, not on earth, and God would deliver the protagonists from their enemies (Rowland 1982).

But the historical context of the perpetuation of apocalypses is not necessarily the same as that of their origination. In reference to some American apocalyptic movements, Hanson points out that today, 'no longer are war and desolation prerequisites for the apocalyptic response. A vague feeling of dissatisfaction with modern life seems sufficient basis for laments over "the late great planet earth"' (1979: 427).[2] However, what remains – regardless of the reality of the oppression – in apocalyptic narratives is what Rowland called 'an insistence on the working out of God's will through the processes of history' (1982: 159). History is seen as a trajectory which people cannot change. But in practice, that does not mean that people do not choose how to act, for they do. They can make the choice to be passive and let history take its course, or they may become very proactive, because although the trajectory cannot be changed, the end can be hastened.

An example of the latter behaviour may be found in the 1997 millenarian mass suicide of the Heaven's Gate group in California – thirty-seven people killed themselves in the belief that a spaceship following in the wake of Comet Hale–Bopp would take their spirits to a higher plane. It was generally considered to be a bizarre anomaly, but this is not the only way to see it. If one actually peruses the group's web site or official literature, and reads beyond the sensationalist news coverage, it becomes apparent that this was not merely an isolated group of lunatic UFO enthusiasts, but that the eschatology of the Heaven's Gate group was based on traditional tenets held dear by many Western Christians; in short, their doctrine was the syncretic end result of combining 'apocalyptic Christian bits and pieces with folk myths of our own contemporary culture' (Gould 1997: 53). Baudrillard made sense of acts like this when he wrote:

> Whole communities have gone to the point of putting their lives on the line to hasten the advent of the Kingdom. And since this has been promised to them at the end of time, all one has to do is put an end to time, immediately (and personally).
>
> (Baudrillard 1997: 4)

And so they did, just as many others have before them, and others will again.

Just as the contexts of perpetuation of apocalyptic are highly varied, O'Leary relates that the roles played by apocalyptic beliefs in recent centuries, and the political consequences of those beliefs, are diverse – apocalyptic cannot be seen as only radical, only conservative, only encouraging passivity, or only a call to arms (1994: 12). But what remains constant is the high human cost. Gould makes it clear that the price has been exacted many times, in many places. He writes that 'the fusion of Christian millennialism with traditional beliefs of conquered (and despairing) people has often led to particularly incendiary, and tragic, results', citing as examples the nineteenth-century defeat of the Xhosa of South Africa and the Ghost Dance movement of Native Americans in the late 1800s, which led to the massacre at Wounded Knee (Gould 1997: 52).

It is critically important that, despite the striking drama of these human tragedies, these were not anomalies or deviations from 'normal history', although this is how they are usually represented. Millennial history specialist Richard Landes asserts that, traditionally, historians of apocalypticism, messianism and chiliasm have had difficulty transforming their observations into 'productive historical analysis' – that although they 'have identified a number of times and places where eschatological beliefs played a central role in a culture's imagination (e.g., first century Palestine, fifth century Mediterranean, thirteenth century Europe, seventeenth century England, eighteenth century America, nineteenth century China)', such phenomena have been considered as contained events (Landes 1996: 165). Landes argues that there has been a significant and systematic underestimation of apocalyptic beliefs as 'normal' historical forces, and that careful study of their influence in history is warranted, given that 'in favorable circumstances, apocalyptic beliefs can launch mass movements capable of overthrowing (and forming) imperial dynasties and creating new religions' (ibid.). Landes submits that apocalyptic rhetoric – as analysed in exhaustive detail by O'Leary (1994) – is given its persuasive force by 'apocalyptic time', which he defines as 'that perception of time in which the End of the World (variously imagined) is so close that its anticipation changes the behavior of the believer' (Landes 1996: 165). Clearly, this is an important phenomenon of history; however, although 'such perceptions of time operate on several levels of cognition, of individual, group, and mass psychology', and have often been studied by social scientists such as anthropologists and sociologists, Landes contends that historians have not often dealt with apocalyptic time.

> The historian, however, has been largely removed from the subject because his documents almost always reflect the perspectives or the editorial blade of post-apocalyptic, normal time, with its retrospective knowledge that the end did not come.
>
> (Landes 1996: 165)

And so Landes argues that historians must think again, for an awareness of this perception of time and its effects on the believer's behaviour is essential to understanding the historical influence of eschatology on society. Most importantly, Landes suggests that this understanding is in turn essential to a real comprehension of our modern age, steeped as it is in the resurgence of religious fundamentalism worldwide (ibid.: 166).

Apocalyptic movements, then, emerge and spread in both unpredictable and predictable places, have the force of inexorability behind them, act in themselves as strong and underestimated historical forces, and seem to be particularly relevant on the world stage at the moment. They provide narratives that can and do guide people's actions in a very real way, for stories specifically about the end of the world, or of a world, are exceptionally powerful in their effect on people. Archaeologists contribute to those narratives – these stories to live and die by – both directly and by implication, as the popular works discussed in the previous section remind us, and as professional academic archaeologists have long been aware.

ARCHAEOLOGY AND APOCALYPSE: ADAPTING THE FORMULA AND CHANGING THE ENDING

It is, by now, a commonplace observation that narratives created by archaeologists to explain the past are coloured by what we see happening around us in the present. What is less considered, but surely equally important, is the fact that in turn, these stories about the past shape people's view of our future. Some have written about this, and some have acted upon it.

In his *History of Archaeological Thought*, Bruce Trigger acknowledges the power that archaeology has to contribute to the narratives by which people today understand their current situation and choose how to live. For example, he wrote that 'cataclysmic' evolutionary archaeology encourages a world view which

> attributes the shortcomings of a world economy to largely immutable evolutionary forces rather than to specific and alterable political and economic conditions that have evolved under American hegemony. This explanation has attracted a willing audience among the insecure middle classes of Western nations, who are anxious to believe that they are not responsible for the fate they fear is overtaking them.
>
> (Trigger 1989: 323)

Trigger retains the hope, however, that archaeology can also have the 'ability to act as a positive force in human history' (1995: 279). This is a hope that other archaeologists share. The best example, worth discussing at some length, comes from Paul Bahn and John Flenley's 1992 book, *Easter Island, Earth Island*. The line on the cover, 'A message from our past for the future of our planet', is a noteworthy parallel to the theme central to *The Mayan Prophecies* and *Keeper of Genesis*.

Bahn and Flenley, rather than fixating on the traditional questions of how Easter Island's inhabitants got there and how they made those amazing statues, concern themselves with the evidence surrounding the culture's violent decline, after centuries of peace and stability. They ask: 'What cataclysm could have had such a devastating impact on the island's culture?' (1992: 9), and introduce their case without mincing words:

the answer to this question carries a message that is of fundamental importance to every person alive today and even more so to our descendants. Given the decline of the island's culture, we should consider the parallels between the behaviour of the Easter Islanders in relation to their limited resources and our cavalier disregard for our own fragile natural environment: the earth itself. This is more, therefore, than an account of the rise and fall of an extraordinary prehistoric culture . . . it is, indeed, a cautionary tale relevant for the future of all humankind.

(Bahn and Flenley 1992: 9)

The ecological catastrophe that befell Easter Island centred on the disappearance of the once-abundant palm trees. Without trees, there could be no canoes to go deep-sea fishing, erosion became a problem and fresh water supplies dried up. As the stresses increased, there was war, a drastic population decline and a rapid degeneration of the society. Finally, the great statues were toppled over and mutilated, providing a powerful metaphor for the end of a 'golden age'. European visitors later on reported that to the Easter Islanders, 'even driftwood was looked on as a treasure of inestimable value, and a dying father frequently promised to send his children a tree from the kingdom of shades' (Bahn and Flenley 1992: 172).

It is a gripping tale, but what is especially relevant to this discussion is the way that Bahn and Flenley chose to tell it. There were three main factors that contributed to the complete deforestation of the island: drought, tree cutting and rats eating the trees' seeds. Where others have argued for climate being the most important variable, Bahn and Flenley choose to emphasise the factor which was under human control. Their message was this:

Easter Island is small, and its ecosystem relatively simple. Whatever one did to alter that ecosystem, the results were reasonably predictable. One could stand on the summit and see almost every point on the island. The person who felled the last tree could see that it was the last tree. But he (or she) still felled it.

(Bahn and Flenley 1992: 214)

A more poignant historical parable is hard to imagine. Yet, surprisingly, some might read such a powerful true story about humanity's relationship with the natural world and remain unmoved. Stephen Jay Gould, in making the point that it is not only the socially downtrodden or oppressed who hold millenarian beliefs, relates this intersection of apocalyptic thought and ecology:

James Watt, Ronald Reagan's unlamented secretary of the interior, a deeply conservative thinker and prominent member of the Pentecostal Assembly of God, stated that we need not worry unduly about environmental deterioration (and should therefore not invest too much governmental time, money, or legislation in such questions) because the world will surely end before any deep damage can be done.

(Gould 1997: 50)

It is at this point that the real importance of the intersection of apocalypse and archaeology becomes clear. It is here that the spheres of political philosophy, eschatology and archaeology come together, and – at the risk of sounding prophetic – it is here that the line must be drawn. And indeed, although Bahn and Flenley use many elements of traditional apocalypses in their writing, including the ideas of revelation of wisdom from another dimension and the situating of the reader within a timeline, there is a crucial departure from the formula which makes all the difference: Bahn and Flenley reject inevitability, they reject the notion that we are on a historical trajectory which cannot be changed, and in so doing, they put the responsibility for our future back, squarely, on our human shoulders. They write that the Easter Islanders

> carried out for us the experiment of permitting unrestricted population growth and profligate use of resources, destruction of the environment, and boundless confidence in their religion to take care of the future. The result was an ecological disaster leading to a population crash. A crash on a similar scale (60 per cent reduction) for the planet Earth would lead to the deaths of about 1.8 billion people . . . Do we have to repeat the experiment on this grand scale? . . . Would it not be more sensible to learn from the lesson of Easter Island history, and apply it to the Earth Island on which we live?
>
> (Bahn and Flenley 1992: 213)

Bahn and Flenley have written this book in the knowledge – almost instinctive to historians, archaeologists and prophets alike – that stories about the past and the future are the axes around which revolve the worlds of listeners in the present. This is the point made by Landes and others, above, that apocalypses are historical forces in themselves. But Bahn and Flenley depart from the traditional formula because they place the making of future history in human hands. In a work which is both honest and courageous, they deliberately use the revelatory might of archaeology, with their ecological agenda made transparent and their eschatology explicit.

Trigger (1995) implies that archaeological narratives about the course of history can neatly excise a population's political conscience. Bahn and Flenley hope that archaeological narratives can help restore ecological responsibility and save us from ourselves. Perhaps it is also true that the manner in which archaeologists represent past societies can affect the future in ways which are less direct but no less important.

In journals of political science and international relations, one can often see reviews of books like *Anticipating the Future: Twenty Millennia of Human Progress* (Buzan and Segal 1998). In this case, the book starts at the beginning, with prehistory, charts what the authors consider to be the (progressive) trajectory of human development, and makes predictions for the future on that basis. This is significant, not just because books like this exist, but because of who reads them and why. High-profile popular futurists Toffler and Toffler (1998) reviewed *Anticipating the Future* for

Foreign Affairs, for a readership that is not just intellectually curious about what the coming years will bring, but is actively involved in designing corporate and political strategies for survival in those years. The extent to which prophecies like those of Buzan and Segal can actually shape the future through this influence is inevitably difficult to ascertain, but the potential cannot be neglected. Books forcefully combining humanity's history and future have undeniable power; those who doubt need only see Marx and Engels ([1848] 1988) and a textbook of twentieth-century European history for an effective reminder.

Toffler and Toffler, committed to a view of history as discontinuous, punctuated by massive revolutions or waves, disagree with Buzan and Segal's continuist stance, but moreover, claim that such a stance 'blinds them to some of the most important changes that lie ahead' (1998: 136). More specifically, Toffler and Toffler argue that although both ways of interpreting history have merit, their own model of 'wave conflict' – strife between societies on opposite sides of historical discontinuities, 'rural vs. urban, agrarian vs. Industrial' – might enable one to 'do a better job of anticipating hot spots before they blast their way into the headlines' (ibid.). Toffler and Toffler suggest that a better academic understanding of the processes of world history, from its very beginning, could help the international community prevent the human tragedies of Bosnia, or better interpret the actions of the Taliban in Kabul. Perhaps, then, millennium or no millennium, now is the time for archaeologists to take stock of their role in the production of social knowledge for the future.

CONCLUSION

Our world is growing smaller and the communities in which we live are growing larger. Traditional stories are told not only from one to another in villages, but replicate themselves in news reports on the Internet. They change, die and are reborn in different forms, and never cease to exert an influence on the minds of those they touch. Indeed, they are living forces in themselves.

So if we take the word 'folklore' writ large, at its broadest and most forward-looking; if we conceive of 'archaeology' at its most extensive, meaning the study and the creation of the past in the present; if we understand popular books with unusual theories about the ancient Egyptians and the Maya not as somehow deviant, but as indicators of what matters to people, and how they read history; if we see 'apocalypses' as revelatory stories situating ourselves in relation to the beginning and the end; if we recognise the role of the archaeologist in creating narratives which can be understood as apocalypses; and if we are concerned that these narratives be forces for good . . . then perhaps the intersection of archaeology and folklore, history and story, is a stranger, more important and more remarkable place than is usually suspected.

There is a suggestion embedded in popular alternative archaeology books like *Keeper of Genesis* and *The Mayan Prophecies*, and echoed by critics like Trigger, that part of archaeology's task is to help us recover ancient knowledge which we desperately need today to avert disaster. This may or may not be so, but one thing is clear. Archaeology has never been only about that which has gone before. It is also about that which is yet to come.

NOTES

1   I am finishing this final draft at precisely 514 days and 13 hours before the new millennium. (At least, this is true according to the school that arbitrarily designates 1 January 2000 as the first day of the new era. See Gould (1997) for alternative notions.) I have included references to current events, and presently popular books and films, although this will undoubtedly make this contribution seem dated quickly. But this essay is dated, and a product of its time; I see no reason to camouflage this fact. It is my hope, however, that the larger point will stand the test of time and remain thought-provoking for later readers.

2   Similarly, O'Leary remarks that

> The early Christians who responded favorably to the book of Revelation were, by most historical accounts, subject to intense persecution that included execution and public torture. If the largely middle-class group of fundamentalist Christians in the United States who today form the core of [apocalyptic prophet] Hal Lindsey's [very extensive] readership believes itself to be similarly persecuted, this is surely a rhetorically induced perception; for there is an obvious difference between being torn apart by lions in front of cheering crowds and being forced to endure media onslaughts of sex, violence, and secular humanism. As one critic puts it, 'the crucial element is not so much whether one is actually oppressed as whether one feels oppressed'; and this is always a subject for persuasion.
>
> (O'Leary 1994: 11)

ACKNOWLEDGEMENTS

First and foremost, my thanks go to Cornelius Holtorf and Amy Gazin-Schwartz for organising the Folklore session at TAG 96, and for their considerable patience and helpful suggestions. I also appreciate the audience's responses during that session, and input from those who listened to other papers exploring similar themes in Lampeter, Sheffield, Winnipeg, Manchester and London. My thanks also go to John Collis, Mike Parker Pearson, John Barrett and Mark Edmonds, all of Sheffield Archaeology, for their conversations with me, and to Darrell Hannah of Biblical Studies at Sheffield, David Mutimer of I.R. at Keele and Mark Knackstedt of the University of Western Ontario, who shared very helpful insights at critical stages in this paper's development. None of them should be held responsible for the ideas herein, however, especially since I haven't always taken their advice . . . at least, not yet. The research for this paper was carried out with the support of a Commonwealth Doctoral Fellowship and a Social Sciences and Humanities Research Council of Canada Doctoral Fellowship; I am most grateful to both organisations.

REFERENCES

Ascherson, N. (1998) 'India's real doomsday machine.' *The Observer*, 17 May: 28.
Bahn, P. and Flenley, J. (1992) *Easter Island, Earth Island*. London: Thames and Hudson.
Baudrillard, J. [1992] (1997) 'Pataphysics of the Year 2000.' Trans. Charles Dudas. URL: http://www.ctheory.com
Bauval, R. and Hancock, G. (1996) *Keeper of Genesis: A Quest for the Hidden Legacy of Mankind*. London: Heinemann.
Buzan, B. and Segal, G. (1998) *Anticipating the Future: Twenty Millennia of Human Progress*. London: Simon and Schuster.
Gilbert, A. and Cotterell, M. (1995) *The Mayan Prophecies*. Shaftesbury: Element.
Gould, S.J. (1997) *Questioning the Millennium: A Rationalist's Guide to a Precisely Arbitrary Countdown*. New York: Harmony Books.
Hancock, G. *Fingerprints of the Gods*.
Hanson, P.D. (1979) *The Dawn of Apocalyptic: The Historical and Sociological Roots of Jewish Apocalyptic Eschatology*. Rev. edn. Philadelphia: Fortress Press.
Hellholm, D. (ed.) (1983) *Apocalypticism in the Mediterranean World and the Near East*. Tübingen: Mohr.
Kohl, P.L. and Fawcett, C. (eds) (1995) *Nationalism, Politics, and the Practice of Archaeology*. Cambridge: Cambridge University Press.
Landes, R. (1996) 'On owls, roosters, and apocalyptic time: a historical method for reading a refractory documentation.' *Union Seminary Quarterly Review* 49: 165–185.
Laurence, R. (trans.) (1995) *The Book of Enoch the Prophet*. San Diego: Wizard's Bookshelf.
Marx, K. and Engels, F. [1848] (1988). *Manifesto of the Communist Party*, trans. F. Engels. New York: International Publishers.
McGinn, B. (1979) *Visions of the End: Apocalyptic Traditions in the Middle Ages*. New York: Columbia University Press.
Melcher, R. (1998) 'Godzilla.' *Ctheory: Theory, Technology, and Culture* 21(1–2), Event-Scene 58. URL: http://www.ctheory.com/
O'Leary, S.D. (1994) *Arguing the Apocalypse: A Theory of Millennial Rhetoric*. Oxford: Oxford University Press.
Perkins, R. and Jackson, F. (1998) 'Spirit in the sky.' *Fortean Times* 109: 24–26.
Piccini, A. (1997) ' "Good to think": the consumption of Celtic heritage in Wales.' Paper given at the Theoretical Archaeology Group conference, University of Bournemouth, December.
Redfield, J. (1992) *The Celestine Prophecy*. New York: Bantam.
Ronayne, M. (1997) 'Wounded attachments: practising archaeology from "the outside".' Paper given at the Theoretical Archaeology Group conference, University of Bournemouth, December.

Rowland, C. (1982) *The Open Heaven: A Study of Apocalyptic in Judaism and Early Christianity.* London: SPCK.

Russell, D.S. (1978) *Apocalyptic: Ancient and Modern.* Philadelphia: Fortress Press.

Toffler, A. and Toffler, H. (1998) 'The discontinuous future: a bold but over-optimistic forecast.' *Foreign Affairs* 77(2): 134–139.

Trigger, B. (1989) *A History of Archaeological Thought.* Cambridge: Cambridge University Press.

Trigger, B. (1995) 'Romanticism, nationalism, and archaeology.' In P. Kohl and C. Fawcett (eds) *Nationalism, Politics, and the Practice of Archaeology*, pp. 263–279. Cambridge: Cambridge University Press.

Wheeler, D. (1996) *Leonard Nimoy's Primortals*, vol. 2(6). Boca Raton: BIG Entertainment.

Zamora, L.P. (ed.) (1982) *The Apocalyptic Vision in America.* Bowling Green: Bowling Green University Press.

CHAPTER EIGHT

SONGS REMEMBERED IN EXILE?

Integrating unsung archives of Highland life

JAMES SYMONDS

ABSTRACT

In this paper I will explore the ways in which folklore material has been collected in the Western Isles over the past one hundred and fifty years, with particular reference to the island of South Uist. It is my intention to situate the actions and motivations of collectors within a broader anthropological framework, and to examine why this rich corpus of folklore material has generally failed to inspire studies in historical ethnography. Drawing upon songs collected by the late John Lorne Campbell and others in the Outer Hebrides and Nova Scotia, I will demonstrate how these collections can be used to illustrate the routines of daily life, and to provide insights into individual perception and experience. The paper calls for an integration of folkloric material with excavated evidence, and presents examples from South Uist and Cape Breton.

> There is no sorrow worse than this sorrow
> the dumb grief of the exile
> among villages that have strange names
> among the new rocks.
> The shadows are not his home's shadows
> nor the tales his tales
> and even the sky is not the same
> nor the stars at night
> ('There is No Sorrow', from *The Exiles*
> by Iain Crichton Smith)

The Highlands and Western Isles, or Outer Hebrides, of Scotland evoke poignant images of a geographically remote place where 'folklore and history visibly meet' (Dorson 1973: 75). Here folklorists and historians search for the essence of a 'traditional culture', a way of life that has

somehow evaded the ravages of modernisation (Figure 8.1). The perception of the Gaelic-speaking Highlands as a timeless place of 'otherness'
emerged in the late fourteenth century and has galvanised over the course
of the past two hundred and fifty years (Devine 1994: 1). A large amount
of ink has been spilled in an effort to disentangle elements of 'traditional'
Gaelic culture from outside influences, a search for authenticity that has
been termed the 'quest for culture' (Macdonald 1997). In this paper I
do not intend to contribute to this ongoing debate. I will instead explore
the ways in which folklore material has been collected in the Western
Isles over the past one hundred and fifty years, with particular reference
to the island of South Uist. It is my intention to situate the actions and
motivations of collectors within a broader anthropological framework,
and to examine why this rich corpus of folklore material has generally
failed to inspire studies in historical ethnography.

It is, in my opinion, a matter of great sadness that the fervent scholarly interest shown by the folklorists who visited the Outer Hebrides in
the 1860s was not sustained. This may in part derive from the fact that
English-speaking scholars have been unwilling or unable to work with
Gaelic oral tradition (Cheape 1993: 112). However, it is also undoubtedly
the case that material has been overlooked because the nature of the
evidence is not easily defined and it has the unnerving potential to overlap
entrenched disciplinary boundaries: 'it is neither archaeology nor history:
it is too recent to be considered an archaeological source and in most
instances it is not old enough to be obviously historical' (ibid.).

Historical writing about the Highlands has been dominated by the
subject of the Highland Clearances and the profound social and economic
transformations that took place following the introduction of agrarian
capitalism (see Devine 1988, 1994; Hunter 1976). The mental rupture
caused by dispossession and mass emigration has had an enduring effect
upon the formation of identity in modern-day Gaelic-speaking communities in the Outer Hebrides and beyond (Macdonald 1997; Parman
1990). Gaelic folklore has, for example, been collected and appropriated
by the descendants of eighteenth- and nineteenth-century emigrants to
Nova Scotia and other 'New World' destinations. One of the greatest
challenges facing historical inquiry into the Gaelic diaspora is the need
to reunite the strands of tradition that exist in isolation on either side of
the Atlantic, severed by emigration (see Symonds 1999a). With this in
mind, the title of this paper is taken from the late John Lorne Campbell's
book of Gaelic songs, collected from the descendants of Highland
emigrants to Cape Breton in the 1930s (Campbell 1990). I will begin
this paper with a story from the Outer Hebrides.

Figure 8.1 'Grinding corn in Skye.' This photograph of a Skye couple, taken between 1870 and 1908, is typical of the Victorian interest in capturing images of supposed anthropological curiosities

Source: Reproduced courtesy of the George Washington Wilson Collection, University of Aberdeen

THE FAIRY-EGG, AND WHAT BECAME OF IT

> On the stormy coasts of the Hebrides, amongst sea-weed and shells, fisher-men and kelp-burners often find certain hard light floating objects, somewhat like flat chestnuts, of various colours – grey, black, and brown, which they call sea-nuts, strand-nuts, and fairy-eggs. Where they are most common, they are used as snuff-boxes, but they are also worn and preserved as amulets, with a firm or sceptical belief in their mysterious virtues.
>
> (Campbell 1860: i)

This description of 'fairy-eggs' introduces J.F. Campbell's *Popular Tales of the West Highlands*, a collection of tales 'orally-collected' among the Gaelic-speaking Highlanders, and first published in 1860 (Campbell 1860). The supernatural qualities attributed to these curious objects were first commented upon by Martin Martin, who visited the Western Isles more than a hundred and fifty years earlier, and referred to them as 'Molluka beans' (Martin [1703] 1981: 38). At that time white Molluka beans were regarded as powerful talismans. Martin records that they were hung around the necks of children, and were said to turn black if a child was threatened by evil. The beans were also thought to be a potent cure for witchcraft, and were used to purify the milk of cows blighted by a curse (ibid.: 39). Campbell employs the example of the fairy-eggs to demonstrate how the meaning of apparently simple objects can be reworked as cultural milieux change:

> Practical Highlandmen of the present day call the nuts trash, and brand those who wear them . . . as ignorant and superstitious; but learned botanists, too wise to overlook trifles, set themselves to study even fairy-eggs; and believing them to be West Indian seeds, stranded in Europe, they planted them, and some (from the Azores) grew. Philosophers, having discovered what they were, use them to demonstrate the existence of the Gulf Stream, and it is even said that they formed a part of one link in that chain of reasoning which led Columbus to the New World.
>
> (Campbell 1860: ix)

Campbell likened the nuts found on the shores of the Hebrides to stories. The meaning of stories can also change and they can be collected and cultivated and traced back to their roots. His collection of tales was intended to be a contribution to a new science of 'Storyology' (Campbell 1860: xi). It is significant that the first two volumes of *Popular Tales* appeared in 1860, one year after the publication of Darwin's *The Origin of Species*, for although Campbell found little intrinsic value in the frag-ments gathered together by his beach-combing, describing the tales as 'drift rubbish' and 'light mental debris' (ibid.: xii, xvii), it is clear that he perceived the importance of the collection to lie in its ability to throw light upon cultural evolution.

The diffusion of popular tales, Campbell believed, could be used to chart the course of Indo-European 'migratory hordes' that emanated from the plains of Asia and swept across Europe in prehistory, leaving traces of their religion and history in stories wherever they settled. The Hebrides, by virtue of their marginal geographical position on the Atlantic seaboard, provided a fertile delta onto which successive waves of this human stream out-poured and mingled (Campbell 1860: xvi). Campbell was inspired to collect his Gaelic tales by G.W. Dascent, whose *Popular Tales from the Norse* appeared in 1859 (D. Wyn Evans 1964, cited in Dorson 1968: 394). The intellectual stimulus provided by Dascent linked Campbell to a chain of scholarship that incorporated the Norwegians Peter Christian Asbjørnsen and Jørgen Moe, and the German brothers Grimm. Campbell explicitly accepted the Aryan thesis of racial origins promoted by the brothers Grimm and earlier German Romantics, and believed that it was imperative to search out and preserve on record the residues of this ancient diaspora before time intervened to further denude the already highly fragmented assemblage (Dorson 1968: 393).

Problematic as this thesis may be to late twentieth-century scholarship, Campbell's contribution to the study of Gaelic folklore cannot be over-stated. His systematic approach and meticulous attention to detail broke new ground and fired the imagination of generations of folklorists. Among his many innovations was the desire to faithfully transcribe the words of stories as spoken. To this end, and realising the enormity of the task in hand, he recruited and sent out a team of Gaelic-speaking collectors to locate and interview storytellers. Alongside this desire for authenticity ('stories orally collected can only be valuable if given unaltered' (Campbell 1860: xi)) readers are privileged to receive full details on the provenance of stories. Tables of contents appear in the published accounts listing the title of the story, the name and occupation of the storyteller, the date and place where it was collected, and the name of the collector. Campbell published four volumes of *Popular Tales* between 1860 and 1862. The first three volumes contain a total of eighty-six stories, and the fourth com-prises a series of essays on diverse topics ranging from the epic of *Ossian*, the spurious Gaelic poetry published by James McPherson in 1760, to mythology, Highland dress and Celtic art.

The other pre-eminent nineteenth-century Gaelic folklorist worthy of mention in this introduction is Alexander Carmichael. Carmichael was born on the Isle of Lismore, off the coast of Argyll, in 1832. His profes-sion as a Customs and Excise officer led him to travel widely among the Hebrides, and during the second half of the nineteenth century he contributed material to Campbell's *Popular Tales* and to the Skye-born lawyer Alexander Nicholson's, *A Collection of Gaelic Proverbs and Familiar Phrases* (1881) (MacInnes 1994: 8).

Carmichael's greatest achievement lay in the publication of *Carmina Gadelica, Hymns and Incantations, with Illustrative Notes on Words, Rites, and Customs, Dying and Obsolete, Orally Collected in the Highlands and Islands of Scotland*, a six-volume collection of oral folklore, gathered in the Isles of Barra and South Uist during his residence there between 1865 and 1882 (MacInnes 1994: 8). Volumes one and two of the collection appeared in 1900; four subsequent volumes were published posthumously, between 1940 and 1971. Although Carmichael shared Campbell's deeply sentimental and in many ways atavistic view of Gaelic culture, his collection of folklore differs in several important ways. The hymns and incantations reproduced in *Carmina Gadelica* contain a mixture of pagan and Christian lore, and provide an intimate commentary on nineteenth-century Hebridean crofting life. Whereas Campbell 'bagged the tales related in public circles', Carmichael 'coaxed out the hymns, prayers, charms, and blessings sung and intoned secretly and privately' (Dorson, 1968: 402). Here may be found songs and blessings to accompany the everyday tasks of herding, fishing, tending the fire, milking, weaving and grinding corn, as well as hymns and incantations reserved for seasonal celebrations.

Carmichael's deep affection for the people of the Hebrides produced tangible improvements to the conditions of everyday life. He was able, for example, to use his position as a civil servant to persuade the Inland Revenue to abolish the tax on horse-drawn carts and on dogs used for herding in crofting townships (MacInnes 1994: 10). Carmichael's scholarly reputation has nevertheless been marred by the accusation that his published texts lack authenticity, and that the eloquent and highly polished verses have been reworked for popular consumption. This should not, however, be taken to suggest that Carmichael was culpable of a measured deceit, but rather that the works were compiled following the editorial conventions of his day; where several versions of a poem had been collected a composite version taking in all of the best elements was reproduced (see MacInnes 1994: 13).

Before going on to explore in more detail the ways in which the folkloric material gathered by Carmichael and others might be used to shed light upon aspects of everyday life and experience, I will first examine the broader context of nineteenth- and early twentieth-century Gaelic folklore studies in relation to the disciplines of anthropology and ethnography.

THE RISE AND FALL OF ANTHROPOLOGICAL FOLKLORE?

I have thus far intentionally avoided offering any definition for the term folklore. The *Shorter Oxford English Dictionary* defines folklore as: 'The traditional beliefs, customs, songs, tales, etc., preserved in oral tradition among (a group of) people; the branch of knowledge that deals with these; popular fantasy or belief.'

This simple definition does not indicate the diverse aims that have motivated collectors of folklore since the nineteenth century. Nor does it touch upon the sometimes bitter wrangling that has taken place over the status of the subject with the related disciplines of anthropology, ethnology and history. One of folklore's most eloquent advocates, Henry Glassie, has argued that the subject should play a central role in the understanding of human culture. For Glassie, folklore offers:

> a unified program for the study of human beings. Its base is the manifest reality of the individual, the society, and the world. Its thrust is that what we call folklore (or art or communication) is the central fact of what we call culture, and culture is the central fact of what we call history, and that people, as history's force, create the phenomenon we study whatever name we give our discipline.
>
> (Glassie 1982: xiv)

Despite Glassie's plea for a unified approach to culture, one that situates folklore as 'historical ethnography' or 'the ecology of consciousness', and defies the narrow boundaries of disciplinary convention, the study of folklore is still dogged by the reputation of being an esoteric and academically marginal pastime. Other equally troubling perceptions persist, that folklore is a 'dead' body of material preserved by the poorer classes in industrialised countries (Thompson 1966: 226).

The relative paucity of twentieth-century anthropological fieldwork in the Scottish Highlands and Western Isles may be explained by the late nineteenth-century separation of interests that took place between British social anthropologists and 'ethnologically-minded' folklorists (Dorson 1968: 302). This separation of interests has been thoughtfully explored by Malcolm Chapman in his analysis of the construction of Gaelic identity from textual sources (Chapman 1978). Chapman contends that the folkloric paradigm, with its emphasis on survival and tradition, and its reliance upon an evolutionist historicism, became discredited in the early twentieth century, when British social anthropologists turned their attentions towards structural functionalism (ibid.: 182). The influence of work by Radcliffe Brown and Malinowski in New Guinea and East and West Africa led anthropologists to attempt to reconstruct the systemic workings of small-scale indigenous societies prior to British and European colonisation, and to refute the idea that customs were survivals from an earlier period in societal development, arguing instead that customs should be explained in terms of their present function (Layton 1997: 27–28). The emphasis placed on investigating colonial societies had the detrimental effect of diverting the attention of social anthropologists away from British subjects. Whereas folklorists continued to search for the 'primitive' within, social anthropologists began to search for their 'primitives' abroad. In this sense the Scottish Highlands suffered from being both too close to home and not exotic enough to excite the interest of aspiring fieldworkers (Chapman 1978: 182).

This should not be taken to suggest that the Gaelic culture of the Highlands has been neglected; rather that it has been the almost exclusive domain of folklorists and Celtic scholars. Collectors from the School of Scottish Studies in Edinburgh have searched the Highlands and islands for oral tradition since 1951 (Cregeen 1974; Dorson 1973) and have amassed a formidable sound archive of music, songs, tales, customs, beliefs and other 'traditional material'. Yet despite an early commitment to integrate folklore into broader anthropological frameworks, the resulting collection of folklore has been criticised as being indiscriminately collected in the service of the 'historical authentication of a national identity' (Chapman 1978: 184). The same criticism could, of course, be levied at the serried ranks of artefacts held by the majority of state museums. Material collected in such a way faces the danger of conforming to the outdated paradigm of evolutionary historicism and of being reduced to a scrapbook-like collection of fast-fading fragments from a supposedly simple-minded pre-industrial age, an incomplete inventory of the 'pre-rational memories of former days and ways' (ibid.: 121).

This nonetheless remarkable collection of Scottish oral tradition is complemented by the Scottish Ethnological Archive of the National Museum of Antiquities of Scotland, which focuses upon material culture and the living conditions of rural and urban Scots (Fenton 1993). The pioneering efforts of Alexander Fenton have furnished scholars with detailed empirical studies of agricultural practices in the Scottish mainland and the Northern Isles of Orkney and Shetland (see Fenton 1976, 1978a, 1986). But overall, it is fair to say that rather less attention has been given to the islands of the Outer Hebrides (but see Fenton 1978b).

The limited amount of anthropological work that has been undertaken in the Outer Hebrides in the second half of the twentieth century has for the most part been prompted by an interest in the constitution of 'community'. Anthropologists have taken pains to address the highly romanticised history of the Highlands and to examine the ways in which contemporary island communities have been shaped as a consequence of their interaction with outside influences, particularly those from the industrialised Scottish Lowlands (Macdonald 1997: 10). Ethnographers have similarly explored aspects of the material expression of 'traditional' as opposed to 'modern' ideologies in the articulation of local identity (Condry 1980; Ennew 1980; Macdonald 1997; Parman 1972).

LANDSCAPES, THINGS, ORAL TRADITION AND HISTORICAL ARCHAEOLOGY

for long the concerns of rural historians and folklorists have been separated, as if the study of virtually all aspects of folklore . . . was considered something less than respectable . . . despite the fact that very original research has often been done by scholars with the expertise and breadth to incorporate folklore study into a wider disciplinary framework.

(Snell 1989: 218)

> It is the archaeologist's sadness to have to study people through material remains, chipped flint, burnt clay, but it be the ethnographer's madness to try to comprehend the complexity of culture through one kind of expression.
>
> (Glassie 1982: 405)

The growth of post-processual archaeology has spawned a plethora of theoretically informed and emancipatory interpretations of how past communities may have perceived and ordered their surroundings. Within the field of landscape archaeology, pioneered by British prehistorians, scholars have investigated how space and resources are contested and appropriated by social groups, and how power, social relations and social identity are expressed through the medium of encultured landscapes (Bender 1993; Fleming 1990). The phenomenological approach advanced by Christopher Tilley (Tilley 1994) has emphasised the temporal and spatial constitution of society, a development that is in close accord with the theoretical underpinnings of modern cultural geography (see Gregory and Urry 1985) and social theory (Giddens 1979, 1984). Tilley argues that landscape should be viewed not as a 'neutral backdrop' to human action but as an interactive non-verbal text, 'a setting in which locales occur in dialectical relation to which meanings are created, reproduced, transformed' (Tilley 1994: 25).

The approach adopted by Tilley and other post-processualists is thus avowedly humanistic. Individual experience is foregrounded and emphasis is given to historical context, to the particular rather than the general, and to interpretation of meaning, rather than scientific explanation (Whiteley 1998: 13). But is it really possible to reconstruct the thoughts, motivations and actions of long dead people from the material residues they left behind them? The prehistorian Julian Thomas has argued that: 'We cannot put ourselves back into the heads of past people, but we must put people back into the spaces of the past' (Thomas 1993: 74). Clearly, it is impossible to gain insight into the lives of past actors through 'some magical intrusion into their consciousness' (Geertz 1986: 373) and one way of enhancing our understanding is to situate active individuals within an interactive landscape or 'taskscape' (Ingold 1993: 154). Fortunately, the rich and diverse strands of evidence that are available to historical archaeologists, including both written and oral texts, far exceed the sources that are available to prehistorians, and arguably allow far more credible understandings of cognition to be made.

How then can we hope to draw close to people who lived in the past and gain an understanding of their lives? Any attempt to recover meaning must involve the use of imagination, but to avoid straying into some form of spurious empathy this act must be based in hermeneutics, the art of interpreting and understanding. The historical archaeologists Rebecca Yamin and Karen Bescherer-Metheny have described how it is possible to gain some sense of the feelings of those who lived in the past by means of a hermeneutic circle:

Using a manner of reasoning (hermeneutics) that moves back and forth between past and present, between different categories of data, archaeological evidence, oral history, written sources, ethnographic data, anthropological theory, human experience – until the part and the whole begin to make sense.

(Yamin and Bescherer Metheny 1996: xiv)

The interpretation of material culture lies at the centre of this circle of reasoning. In the same way that landscapes should no longer be seen as 'neutral' templates, so artefacts must also be seen to be more than inert materials, the products of technology:

The relationship of behaviour to the material world is far from passive; artifacts are tangible incarnations of social relationships embodying the attitudes and behaviours of the past.

(Beaudry *et al.* 1991: 150)

When seen in this light material culture becomes an active and reflexive medium of social reproduction and individual objects become 'freighted with both social and symbolic significance'.

(Deetz 1994: xix).

What part, if any, can folklore play in the interpretation of this web of significance and meaning? I have indicated that there is an enduring tendency among some British scholars to view folklore as a 'dead body' of material, as incidental survivals from a more simple-minded age. Some of the most strident criticisms that I have encountered against the use of folklore have come from prehistorians. The most frequently voiced criticism is that oral tradition, especially oral history, is made-up and not to be relied upon. Given that most prehistorians work in time scales of whole or part millennia, and freely borrow ethnographic analogies from the modern world as an aid to their interpretations of past human behaviour, often with little regard for context, I find this somewhat ironic. The removal of this misguided perception of oral tradition is surely one of the most challenging problems facing any attempt to provide a more nuanced interpretation of life in the recent past.

The role of oral tradition in social discourse has attracted the interest of a growing number of ethnographers and folklorists, and has recently been reviewed in relation to historical archaeology by Margaret Purser (Purser 1992). Purser stresses that oral narratives are 'purposeful texts that are constantly being created, revised, contested, and validated in complex living situations'. These unwritten texts are of wide-ranging use to the historical archaeologist, displaying the multitudinous ways in which social knowledge and power are manipulated, and also, importantly, shedding light upon the lives and experiences of disenfranchised members of society (ibid.: 26).

If we have the courage to disregard the idea of oral tradition as the fossilised remnants of pre-rational thought we are confronted with a 'milieu of living memory'; far from being detached from the present-day we find that memories of the past (including contradictory ones) endure because they are 'bound to the present for [their] survival' (Hutton 1993: 17). The interwoven threads of oral narrative provide a powerful and reflexive collective mnemonic. Whereas the individual memory allows the passing moment to be captured and re-enacted, at least in representational form, the collective memory fostered by oral tradition allows the death of the individual, and of individual experience, to be overcome.

In this discussion I do not wish to give the impression that the interpretation of oral narratives is in any way simplistic. There are clearly a number of epistemological problems that need to be resolved when one moves from the more conventional archaeological practice of interpreting material culture and stratified layers of soil, to interpreting the alternative, but no less structured medium, of oral transmission. Foremost among these difficulties is the particularistic nature of oral narratives (Purser 1992: 27). How does one mesh the individual voice with broader cultural experience? Our own late twentieth-century Western values have a tendency to privilege individual human agency over institutionalised social forces, and it has been argued that the focus on the individual, which prefigures post-processual interpretative archaeology, unwittingly constructs a past that is 'simply one more version of Protestant individualism' (Grele [1975] 1985: 206, cited in Purser 1992: 27). I would contend that far from reifying the individual agent oral narratives allow us to see through the intricate mechanisms of social reproduction, and expose contradictions and disjunctions within the symbolic and material world. Decoding the various 'rhetorical images' employed in oral narratives offers an insight into the repertoire and power of different forms of representation, a subject worthy of study in its own right (Hutton 1993: 75). Bearing in mind Glassie's belief that 'culture is not a problem with a solution' and that 'studying people involves refining understanding, not achieving actual proof' (Glassie 1982: 13), the study of oral tradition provides the historical archaeologist with alternative 'ways of seeing'.

TIR A' MHURAIN – LAND OF BENT GRASS

> O my country, I think of thee, fragrant, fresh Uist of the handsome youths, where nobles might be seen, where Clan Ranald had his heritage.
> Land of bent grass, land of barley, land where everything is plentiful, where young men sing songs and drink ale.
> ('In Praise of Uist' – an emigrant song cited in displays in Kildonan Museum, South Uist)

The opening verses of *Moladh Uibhist* – In Praise of Uist – speak of the lament of a nineteenth-century emigrant, enticed far from home to Manitoba, 'a cold country, without coal or peat'. The Isle of South Uist lies at the southern end of the Outer Hebrides, or Western Isles, a chain

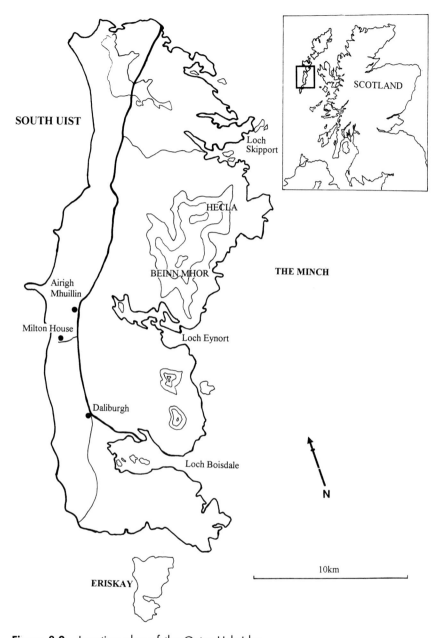

Figure 8.2 Location plan of the Outer Hebrides

of islands situated off the north–west coast of Scotland (Figure 8.2). This 'Long Island' stretches 200 km north–south from the Butt of Lewis to Barra Head. The principal islands are Lewis, Harris, Benbecula, North and South Uist, and Barra.

South Uist is a low-lying island. The landscape, which is virtually tree-less, is one of striking contrasts. Brilliant white sand dunes and a fertile machair plain of shell-sand soils line the west coast. The central portion of the island comprises peat-covered moors and grazing grounds. On the east coast a range of low grey hills rise up to 2,000 feet, and the twin peaks of Beinn Mhor and Hecla. The hills are punctuated by numerous rocky inlets and the major sea lochs of Loch Boisdale, Loch Eynort and Loch Skiport.

The modern-day visitor to South Uist encounters a dispersed settle-ment pattern. The solitary houses are widely spaced among the croft-land, 'moored like square-ended boats on a pale-green marina of pasture and old arable' (Craig 1997: 69). In 1850, prior to the main phase of Clearance, the population of the island numbered almost 7,500; today it stands at a little over 2,200, with 30,000 sheep. The families that remain make a living by small-holding and fishing, and are locked in a constant struggle against fluctuating agricultural markets and the vicissitudes of European Union farming directives. 'A croft', I was told recently by one local resident, is 'a plot of land surrounded by regulations.'

It does not require a great deal of imagination to appreciate the radical changes that have transformed island life over the course of the past 150 years. The most striking facet is the physical depopulation of the land. This process went hand-in-hand with massive out-migration, as pre-nineteenth-century subsistence farming was restyled by landlords to better serve ex-ternal markets and the needs of British imperial expansion (see Macinnes 1988: 70). The Highland Clearances are the subject of intense academic debate, and space does not allow me to enter into a discussion of the complex historiography in this short essay (for discussion see Symonds 1999b). It is perhaps sufficient to say that current historical writing is polarised into two distinct camps. On the one hand there are the writers of what has been termed 'people's history' (Macdonald 1997: 70). This genre has a tendency to depict the victims of Clearance as an honest but simple folk, duped into exile from their ancestral lands by rapacious land-lords (Craig 1997; Hunter 1976; Prebble 1963). Alternatively there are economic historians who have based their accounts upon estate or other official records. These scholars view the Highland Clearances of the nine-teenth century as an inescapable consequence of wider British economic developments, and have been accused by some of being 'landlord apolo-gists' (see Devine 1988, 1994; Gray 1957; Richards 1982, 1985).

ORAL HISTORY AND THE PROBLEM OF OBJECTIVITY

The memory of so genealogical and tradition-minded a people could not have lost the image of so momentous a turn in their history.

(Craig 1997: 9)

Contrary to the opinion of Craig, stories of emigration and physical hardship are hard to find in South Uist. If questioned, people will speak of a time of cruelty, 'when we were little better than slaves', but few individuals can recite tales relating to events prior to the last two decades of the nineteenth century. In South Uist there are no idyllic lost 'golden days', and people prefer to forget the times of hardship, the bad old days 'before the standard of living improved', meaning the 1950s, when the introduction of electricity, running water and improved housing had a widespread impact upon the island.

This is also true of Tiree, where oral tradition is reticent about the physical suffering and hardship that followed the potato famine of the 1840s (Cregeen 1974: 27). The stories that circulate about oppressive acts in the nineteenth century relate to the evil actions of estate factors; more often than not these are aimed at orchestrating hatred against the Earl of Argyll and the clan Campbell, who displaced the MacLeans as lairds of Tiree in the late seventeenth century: 'It seems sometimes that the sufferings of the people of the island in the last century have been remembered and passed on, not for their own sake, but as an illustration of the wickedness of the clan Campbell' (Cregeen 1974: 28).

Work in Sutherland by the anthropologist Paul Basu has found that 'folk-memory' of the Clearances has been replaced by published versions of popular history; 'the accounts of historians such as John Prebble have become the new oral history' (Bangor-Jones 1993: 40, cited in Basu 1997). Sharon Macdonald has noted a similar pattern in Skye, where many of the stories told about the crofters' struggle for land in the 1880s (the 'Land Wars') are reworked from popular published sources (Macdonald 1997: 111). Macdonald attributes the lack of local oral history to the disruption of traditional mechanisms for oral transmission; there are far fewer *ceilidhs* in which to ruminate, mingle and tell stories. Rather than confronting the tragic aspects of recent history individuals choose to distance themselves from events in the past. The strategy of deliberately 'forgetting' the actions of ancestral families serves to reduce friction within the contemporary face-to-face community (ibid.: 114). This brings me back to the important point that representations of the past have a powerful part to play in the constant re-creation of the present. In this sense oral histories are far from objective, but inasmuch as they have been crafted and employed in social discourse, they are never false: 'The importance of oral testimony may lie not in its adherence to fact, but rather in its departure from it, as imagination, symbolism, and desire emerge' (Portelli 1998: 68).

SONGS FOR EVERYDAY LIFE?

The women of nineteenth-century South Uist composed and sang songs to accompany the rhythmical actions of milking, spinning and waulking (or fulling) cloth. These songs stand in stark contrast to the heroic compositions of the male bards, which were more concerned with imparting praise or veiled criticism and related to warfare, the deeds of clan chiefs, and other notable historical events. It was estimated that as many as 200 waulking songs, or *Orain luadhaidh*, survived in South Uist and Barra in the 1930s, but now they are seldom heard (Fay Shaw 1986: 72–73). The process of waulking cloth has been described by Margaret Fay Shaw (see Figure 8.3).

> The ends of a length of a newly woven cloth are sewn together to make it a circle, and the cloth is then placed on a long trestle table and soaked with hot urine. An even number of women sit at the table, say twelve with six a side, and the cloth is passed around sunwise, to the left, with a kneading motion. They reach to the right and clutch the cloth, draw in, pass to the left, with a kneading motion. They reach to the right and clutch the cloth, draw in, push out, free the hands to grasp again to the right. One, two, three, four, slowly the rhythm emerges.
>
> (Fay Shaw 1986: 72–73)

The composition of a typical group of women engaged in waulking in the 1860s is described by Alexander Carmichael:

> Generally the waulking women are young maidens, a few married women of good voice being distributed among them. They sing as they work, one

Figure 8.3 'Wool Waulking', by Keith Henderson, c.1927–8.
Source: Reproduced courtesy of the Talbot Rice Gallery, University of Edinburgh

singing the song, the others the chorus. Their songs are varied, lively, and adapted to the class of work. Most of them are love-songs, with an occasional impromptu song on some passing event – perhaps on the casual stranger who has looked in, perhaps a wit combat between two of the girls about the real or supposed merits or demerits of their respective lovers.

(Carmichael 1994: 600)

The shrunken cloth is treated with reverence, and is 'consecrated' by the women in a ceremony mimicking religious ritual. This action reveals the power of ritual to transform the *status quo*. Beyond the intimate setting of the female gathering the act of consecration could only be performed by a male priest.

> When the women have waulked the cloth, they roll up the web and place it on end in the centre of the frame. They then turn it slowly and deliberately sunwise along the frame saying, with each turn of the web:
>
> This is not second clothing
> This cloth is not thigged
> This is not the property of cleric or priest.
>
> (ibid.)

Sun-wise motion

The sun-wise motion of movement (*deiseal*) recorded in waulking cloth is evident in several other Gaelic activities, and is a superstitution that is taken to impart good luck:

> the ritual performed on New Year's Eve by the lads of the township was of great antiquity and possibly pre-Christian. Known as Hogmanay to the Scots and *A'Challuinn* to the Gaels, it began soon after darkness fell. The sound of boys' voices calling '*A'Challaig seo! A' Challaig seo! Chall O! Chall O!*' was heard in the distance, and when they reached the house they walked around it sun-wise, chanting Hogmanay ballads or *duain* . . . The torch-bearer passed his brand of smouldering sheepskin three times round the head of the wife (a very bad omen if it should go out during the ceremony), and then she produced the three round bannocks which the leader of the boys carefully put in his bag and then gave another one to her in return.
>
> (Fay Shaw 1986: 14)

Margaret Fay Shaw is unable to suggest a reason for this custom, commenting: 'There were probably good reasons originally for these things, but as it was tactless for me to ask I did not hear them' (ibid.: 13). Sun-wise movement, from left to right, was also practised by fishermen turning their boats, and by wedding parties and funerals entering and leaving houses and churchyards. Carmichael provides further evidence for this customary ritual extending into routine agricultural tasks. The sprinkling of water over seed corn in a sun-wise direction was undertaken prior to sowing, in the hope that it would hasten growth; harvesting and the hand-grinding of meal also followed a sun-wise direction.

Carmichael comments that the ritual is a 'combination of paganism and Christianity' (Carmichael 1994: 596).

Traces of these customary rituals survive in South Uist to this day. Excavation in 1997 of a circular stack-base – a simple arrangement of stones used for raising harvested crops off a damp yard surface – revealed that the stones had been placed on the ground in a sun-wise motion. In the absence of dating evidence the stack-base, which stood beside a nineteenth-century blackhouse, was assumed to be of a similar antiquity. However, when the stones were lifted fragments of a plastic Brylcream tub (a container for hair oil) dating from the late 1960s were found sealed beneath them. Subsequent discussions with the tenant of the croft established that he had constructed the stack-base. When questioned as to whether there was a reason for working from left to right, he shrugged his shoulders and replied, 'that is how it is always done'.

Some clues as to the origins of the association of sun-wise motion with fertility and good luck are provided by Robert Dodgshon in his study of the symbolic landscapes of early farming townships in eastern and north-eastern Scotland (Dodgshon 1988). Dodgshon argues that the lay-out of townships was based on a dual classificatory system of sun and shadow, akin to the Scandinavian *sloskifte*. The sun played a pivotal role in Norse cosmologies. Rituals focused upon its ability to differentiate the world into regions of light and dark, and celebrated its diurnal and seasonal movements (see Turvill-Petre 1969, cited in Dodgshon 1988). Symbolic order was imposed upon an uncertain world through a

> ritual of fertility based on a ritual of movement. To harness its powers, one had to establish an accordance with this clear ordination of time and space, starting in the east at dawn and working sun-wise around to the west by sunset.
>
> (Dodgshon 1988: 74)

The sun could also be symbolised by elaborate fire rituals, recalling Fay Shaw's description of the Hogmanay torch-bearer.

Whether or not rituals incorporating a sun-wise motion, which are a widespread occurrence and seem to pervade almost every aspect of daily life in nineteenth-century South Uist, are derived from Norse cosmologies must remain a matter for conjecture. Recent excavations at Kilpheder and Bornish in South Uist have, nevertheless, demonstrated that the Norse presence in the southern Hebrides between AD 800 and 1266 was far more substantial than had been previously supposed (Selkirk 1997: 298). Furthermore, there is evidence to suggest that the Norse incomers underwent a gradual blending of cultural traditions with the resident Christian population (M. Parker Pearson, personal communication; contra Crawford 1981).

TECHNOLOGIES FOR REMEMBERING

Several writers have observed that the act of memory relies on a process of embodiment: 'part of what is remembered are ways of sitting and standing, looking and lounging, hearing and hoping, ruminating and re-collecting'. These sensual actions serve as 'incorporating and inscribing practices' and 'sediment memories in bodily postures' (Urry 1995: 27; Connerton 1989, cited in Urry). This process has been well documented by anthropologists working in African societies. Jan Vansina, for example, has demonstrated how rituals are acted out, and how meaning is im-parted by bodily action, rather than the spoken word (Vansina 1955). The songs performed by Hebridean women to accompany the task of waulking require the synchronisation of thought, action and vocalisation. They are brought alive through the movement of the limbs. Although individual participants change, and the songs become modified and reworked with use, the configuration of the labour remains the same, and provides a structure of commemoration that has the ability to tran-scend generations.

Memory is also grounded in the materiality of daily existence. A favourite chair; a room within a house; a hair brush; an image of a loved one: all of these things may be represented in memory, and articulate the act of remembering. The application of phenomenology to archae-ology, referred to earlier in this chapter, has heightened awareness of the importance of landscape and locality in shaping memory:

> Places help to recall stories that are associated with them, and places exist (as named locales) by virtue of their employment in a narrative. Places, like persons, have biographies inasmuch as they are formed, used and transformed in relation to practice. It can be argued that stories acquire part of their mythic value and historical relevance if they are rooted in the concrete details of locales in the landscape, acquiring material reference points that can be visited, seen and touched.
>
> (Tilley 1994: 33)

The close attention paid to landscape, and to all forms of animal and plant life, by the Gaelic-speaking inhabitants of the Hebrides is well docu-mented (see Gillies 1985). Examples of animals woven into myth and endowed with magical or supernatural qualities are commonplace. During the six years that Margaret Fay Shaw collected folksongs and folklore in South Uist between 1930 and 1935, she recorded many examples. The first bee of summer was said to bring good luck, a cock crowing before midnight was a portent of death. The oyster-catcher, a black and white shore bird with an orange beak, was known as *Gille Brighde*, or the servant of *Brighde*, foster-mother of Christ. It was said that an oyster-catcher had hidden the baby Jesus from enemies beneath a covering of seaweed; ever since that time the bird has worn a cross on its back (Fay Shaw 1986: 13ff).

More sinister supernatural forces lurked within the landscape to trap unsuspecting individuals, as this passage describing the small island of Eriskay reveals:

> By day, the *Ones-that-are-not-remaining* may come and go as they like: by day what is to be may show itself to such as have *The Sight* . . . But the mouth of night is the choice hour of the *Sluagh*, the Host of the dead, whose feet never touch on earth as they go drifting on the wind till the Day of Burning; of the *Fuath*, the Spirit of terror, that 'frightens folk out of the husk of their hearts', of the Washer, who sits at the ford with herself in the twilight; of the slime green-coated ones, the Water-horse . . .
>
> (Murray 1936: 11)

It is easy for us to dismiss such descriptions of supernatural beings as worthless superstition. Yet to do so would mean denying the beliefs that structured people's lives and governed their thoughts, actions and movements. The spectres have their own time, the hours of darkness, but inhabit readily recognisable landscape features – the ford, the loch, the hill-pastures beyond the township – transforming them by night into places of danger. Coping with these superstitions involved the individual and collective embodiment of certain dispositions; the creation of 'durable' and 'transposable' structures generative of improvisatory practices; *habitus* (Bourdieu 1977). These social practices are reflected in domestic architecture – 'It is *not right* to put a window to the West, for on that side the *Sluagh* pass by night, and might throw darts within' – as well as more ephemeral behaviour: water must not be thrown out through the doorway of a house after nightfall, 'because of the dead who come to warm themselves there in the smoke' (Murray 1936: 49).

Within the house activity focused upon a central peat-fire placed directly on the earth floor. The fire provided a fulcrum for daily life and was constantly kept alight by the women of the household. The reverence with which fire was treated is reflected in the Gaelic word for fire – *Aingeal* (angel), implying that it was protected by benevolent spirits (Kissling 1943: 85). At night the fire was smothered or 'smoored' in a customary ceremony that combined Christian imagery with ostensibly pagan fire-ritual. This daily routine, an example of religious syncretism grounded in *habitus*, survived in memory, if not in widespread practice, as late as the 1890s, and was described by Carmichael:

> The embers were evenly spread on the hearth . . . and formed into a circle. The circle is then divided into three equal sections, a small boss being left in the middle. A peat is laid between each section, each peat touching the boss, which forms a common centre. The first peat is laid down in the name of the God of life, the second in the name of the God of peace, the third in the name of the God of Grace. The circle is then covered over with ashes sufficient to subdue but not to extinguish the fire, in the name of the Three of Light. The heap slightly raised in the centre is called '*Tula nan Tir*', the Hearth of the Three. When this smooring operation is complete the woman

closes her eyes, stretches her hand, and softly intones in one of the many formulae current for these occasions.

(Carmichael 1994 [1928]: 234, cited in Kissling 1943)

REINTEGRATING FOLKLORE: TOWARDS A HISTORICAL ETHNOGRAPHY?

At the beginning of this chapter I called for a broadly based approach to the archaeology of the recent past, one that incorporates the evidence of folklore, in all of its manifestations, and is predicated upon a desire to create historical ethnographies. The potential for the application of anthropologically framed research to historical and archaeological evidence has been demonstrated by a number of authors (Ausenda 1995; Sahlins 1985; Yentsch 1994), but with some notable exceptions (e.g. Glassie 1982) has generally failed to integrate folklore in any substantial way.

In the case of the Outer Hebrides, any understanding of the structure of daily life and of events surrounding the social and economic upheavels of the past two hundred years is left wanting without a consideration of the rich and varied folklore. The predominance of oral tradition in Gaelic culture may have had the detrimental effect of limiting the range of written sources available for historical study – particularly those relating to the poorest members of society – but it also served to ensure that all aspects of life and work were woven into a communal web of words and meaning.

ACKNOWLEDGEMENTS

Research in South Uist has been funded by the Earthwatch Institute and Volunteer Corps, Boston University (International Programs), the Society of Antiquaries of Scotland, and Historic Scotland. In South Uist I have benefited from conversations with Paul MacCallum, Canon Galbraith, James MacDonald, William MacDonald, Angus and Isobel MacKenzie and family, and Neil MacMillan. My greatest debt is to Victoria Parsons, who suggested the idea of the 'fairy-eggs' and gave me her unfailing support during the writing of this paper.

REFERENCES

Ausenda, G. (1995) *After Empire: Towards an Ethnology of Europe's Barbarians.* Centre for Interdisciplinary Research on Social Stress. San Marino: The Boydell Press.

Bangor-Jones, M.(1993) 'The incorporation of documentary evidence and other historical sources into preservational and management strategies.' In R. Hingley (ed.) *Medieval or Later Rural Settlement in Scotland: Management and Preservation.* Edinburgh: Historic Scotland.

Basu, P . (1997) 'Narratives in a Landscape: Monuments and Memories of the Sutherland Clearances.' Unpublished MSc thesis, University College London.

Beaudry, M.C., Cook, L.J. and Morozowski, S. (1991) 'Artifacts as active voices: material culture as social discourse.' In R. McGuire and R. Paynter (eds) *The Archaeology of Inequality*, pp. 150–190. Oxford: Basil Blackwell.

Bender, B. (ed.) (1993) *Landscape, Politics and Perspectives*. Oxford: Berg; Providence: Bornish and Kilpheder.

Bourdieu, P. (1977) *Outline of a Theory of Practice*. Cambridge: Cambridge University Press.

Campbell, J.F.(1860) *Popular Tales of the West Highlands: Orally Collected*, Vol. 1. Edinburgh: Edmonston and Douglas.

Campbell, J.L. (1990) *Songs Remembered in Exile: Traditional Gaelic songs from Nova Scotia Recorded in Cape Breton and Antigonish County in 1937 with an account of the causes of Hebridean Emigration 1790–1835*. Aberdeen: Aberdeen University Press.

Carmichael, A. (1994) *Carmina Gadelica: Hymns and Incantations*. Edinburgh: Floris Books.

Chapman, M. (1978) *The Gaelic Vision in Scottish Culture*. London: Croom Helm; Montreal: McGill-Queen's University Press.

Cheape, H. (1993) 'Crogans and Barvas Ware: handmade pottery in the Hebrides.' *Scottish Studies* 31 (1993): 109–128.

Condry, E. (1980) 'Culture and Identity in the Scottish Highlands.' Unpublished DPhil. thesis, University of Oxford.

Connerton, P. (1989) *How Societies Remember*. Cambridge: Cambridge University Press.

Craig, D. [1990] (1997) *On the Crofters' Trail: In Search of the Clearance Highlander*. London: Pimlico.

Crawford, I. A. (1981) 'War or peace – Viking colonisation in the Northern and Western Isles of Scotland reviewed.' In H. Bekker-Nielson, P. Foote and O. Olsen (eds) *Proceedings of the Eighth Viking Congress, Arhus, 1977*, pp. 259–269. Odense.

Cregeen, E. (1974) 'Oral sources for the social history of the Scottish Highlands and Islands.' *Journal of the Oral History Society* 2(2): 23–36.

Crichton Smith, I. (1984) 'There is no sorrow.' In *The Exiles*. Manchester: Carcanet Press; Dublin.

Deetz, James (1994) 'Foreword.' In A.E. Yentsch, *A Chesapeake Family and their Slaves: A Study in Historical Archaeology,* pp. xvii–xx. Cambridge: Cambridge University Press.

Devine, T.M. (1988) *The Great Highland Famine*. Edinburgh: John Donald.

Devine, T.M. (1994) *Clanship to Crofters' War*. Manchester and New York: Manchester University Press.

Dodgshon, R.A. (1988) 'The Scottish farming township as metaphor.' In Leah Leneman (ed.) *Perspectives in Scottish Social History: Essays in Honour of Rosalind Mitchison*, pp. 68–82. Aberdeen: Aberdeen University Press.

Dorson, R.M. (1968) *The British Folklorists: A History*. London: Routledge and Kegan Paul.

Dorson, R.M. (1973) 'Sources for the traditional history of the Scottish Highlands and Western Isles.' In R. M. Dorson (ed.) *Folklore and Traditional History,* pp. 75–113. The Hague and Paris: Mouton.

Ennew, J. (1980) *The Western Isles Today*. Cambridge: Cambridge University Press.

Fay Shaw, M. (1986) *Folksongs and Folklore of South Uist,* third edition. Aberdeen: Aberdeen University Press.

Fenton, A. (1976) *Scottish Country Life.* Edinburgh: John Donald.

Fenton, A. (1978a) *The Northern Isles: Orkney and Shetland.* Edinburgh: John Donald.

Fenton, A. (1978b) *The Island Blackhouse.* HMSO.

Fenton, A. (1986) *The Shape of the Past.* 2 vols. Edinburgh: John Donald.

Fenton, A. (1993) 'Scottish ethnology: crossing the Rubicon.' Inaugural lecture for the chair of Scottish Ethnology, University of Edinburgh. *Scottish Studies* 31: 1–8.

Fleming, A. (1990) Landscape archaeology, prehistory and rural studies. *Rural History* 1: 5–15.

Geertz, C. (1986) 'Making experiences, authoring selves.' In V. Turner and E. Bruner (eds) *The Anthropology of Experience,* pp. 373–383. Urbana: University of Illinois Press.

Giddens, A. (1979) *Central Problems in Social Theory: Action, Structure and Contradiction in Social Analysis.* London: Macmillan.

Giddens, A. (1984) *The Constitution of Society.* Cambridge Polity Press.

Gillies, W. (ed.) (1985) *Ris A' Bhruthaich Criticism and Prose Writings of Sorley MacLean.* Stornoway: Acdir Press Ltd.

Glassie, H. (1982) *Passing the Time in Ballymenone.* Philadelphia: University of Pennsylvania Press.

Gray, M. (1957) *The Highland Economy, 1750–1850.* Edinburgh: Edinburgh University Press.

Gregory, D. and Urry, J. (eds) (1985) *Social Relations and Spatial Structures.* London: Macmillan.

Grele, R. [1975] (1985) *Envelopes of Sound: The Art of Oral History.* Chicago: Precedent Publishing.

Hunter, J. (1976) *The Making of the Crofting Community.* Edinburgh: John Donald.

Hutton, P.H. (1993) *History as an Art of Memory.* Hanover, NH and London: University Press of New England.

Ingold, T. (1993) 'The temporality of landscape.' *World Archaeology* 25: 152–174.

Kissling, W. (1943) 'The character and purpose of the Hebridean black house.' *Journal of the Royal Anthropological Institute* 73: 75–99.

Layton, R. (1997) *An Introduction to Theory in Anthropology.* Cambridge: Cambridge University Press.

Macdonald, S. (1997) *Reimagining Culture: Histories, Identities and the Gaelic Renaissance.* Oxford and New York: Berg.

Macinnes, A.I. (1988) 'Scottish Gaeldom: the first phase of clearance.' In T. Devine and R. Mitchison (eds) *People and Society in Scotland I, 1760–1830,* pp. 70–90. Edinburgh: John Donald.

MacInnes, J. (1994) 'Preface.' In Alexander Carmichael *Carmina Gadelica: Hymns and Incantations,* pp. 7–18. Edinburgh: Floris Books.

Martin, M. [1703] (1981) *A Description of the Western Islands of Scotland.* Facsimilie of the second edition [1716]. Edinburgh: The Mercat Press, James Thin.

Murray, A. (1936) *Father Allan's Island.* Edinburgh: The Moray Press.

Parman, S. (1990) *Scottish Crofters: A Historical Ethnography of a Celtic Village.* Fort Worth: Holt, Rinehart and Winston.

Portelli, A. (1998) 'What makes oral history different.' In R. Perks and A. Thomson (eds) *The Oral History Reader,* pp. 63–74. London and New York: Routledge.

Prebble, J. (1963) *The Highland Clearances*. Harmondsworth, London: Penguin.

Purser, M. (1992) 'Oral history and historical archaeology.' In B.J. Little (ed.) *Text-Aided Archaeology*, pp. 25–35. Boca Raton, Ann Arbor and London: CRC Press.

Richards, E. (1982) *A History of the Highland Clearances, Volume I: Agrarian Transformations and the Evictions 1746–1886*. London: Croom Helm.

Richards, E. (1985) *A History of the Highland Clearances, Volume 2: Emigration, Protest, Reasons*. London: Croom Helm.

Sahlins, M. (1985) *Islands of History*. Chicago: Chicago University Press.

Selkirk, A. (1977) 'Dun vulan.' In *Current Archaeology*, 152 (xiii) 8: 293–301.

Snell, K.D. (1989) 'Rural history and folklore studies: towards new forms of association.' *Folklore* 100(ii): 218–220.

Symonds, J. (1999a) 'Surveying the remains of a Highland myth: investigations at the birthplace of Flora MacDonald, Airigh Mhuillin, South Uist.' In M. Vance (ed.) *Myth Migration and the Making of Memory: Scotia and Nova Scotia c.1700–1900*, forthcoming.

Symonds, J. (1999b) 'Toiling in the vale of tears: everyday life and resistance in South Uist, the Outer Hebrides, 1760–1860.' *International Journal of Historical Archaeology*, forthcoming.

Thomas, J. (1993) 'The hermeneutics of megalithic space.' In C. Tilley (ed.) *Interpretative Archaeology*, pp. 73–97. Oxford and Providence: Berg.

Tilley, C. (1994) *A Phenomenology of Landscape*. Oxford and Providence: Berg.

Thompson, F. G. (1966) 'The folkloric elements in *Carmina Gadelica*.' *Transactions of the Gaelic Society of Inverness* 49(1964–1966): 226–255.

Turville-Petre, E.O.G. (1969) 'Fertility of beast and soil in old Norse literature.' In E.C. Polome (ed.) *Old Norse Literature and Mythology*, p. 245. Austin.

Urry, J. (1995) *Consuming Places*. London and New York: Routledge.

Vansina, J. (1955) 'Initiation rituals of the Bushong.' *Africa*, 25: 138–153.

Whiteley, D.S. (ed.) (1998) *Reader in Archaeological Theory: Post-Processual and Cognitive Approaches*. London and New York: Routledge.

Wyn Evan, D. (1964) 'John Francis Campbell, of Islay (1822–1885) and Norway.' In *Med Boken Som Bakrunn*, Festskrift til Harald L. Tveteras, pp. 52–64. Oslo.

Yamin, R. and Bescherer Metheny, K. (1996) Preface: reading the historical landscape. In R. Yamin and K. Bescherer Metheny (eds) *Landscape Archaeology: Reading and Interpreting the American Historical Landscape*, pp. xiii-xx. Knoxville: University of Tennessee Press.

Yentsch, A.E. (1994) *A Chesapeake Family and their Slaves: A Study in Historical Archaeology*. Cambridge: Cambridge University Press.

CHAPTER NINE

OF 'THE GREEN MAN' AND 'LITTLE GREEN MEN'

JOHN COLLIS

ABSTRACT

A consideration of the relationship of archaeology to popular culture raises the most fundamental questions of what we as archaeologists are trying to do, and our relationship to other sectors of society. Popular beliefs, including folklore, enter our subject at a number of different levels, either forming the basis of some of our paradigms, as parallel interpretations to our own, or as ideas which are completely antithetic to the whole practice of archaeology. Our reaction as archaeologists therefore needs to be varied – we cannot pretend we are some sort of neutral arbiter without our own cultural baggage and without our own ideology which we wish to impose on others, both in our own society and in other societies. There are some groups within all societies with whom dialogue is impossible, so should it worry us particularly if there is none, as often it is not we who are at fault? But we need to be aware of our own role in society as mythmakers, and also recognise areas where dialogue with those holding different views and approaches can enrich our presentations of the past. This chapter is illustrated with examples such as the Celts, showing how often we, as archaeologists, are unsure of where our own mythologies emanate.

I am not sure whether a concern for popular culture among archaeologists is a sign of self-confidence in the discipline, or of self-doubt. Are we so sure of our ground that we can take alternative views and interpretations of the past in our stride, or are we too aware that our own archaeological and 'scientific' approaches are subject to popular attitudes and fashions, and that there is no such thing as ultimate truth? Are we just one of a number of interest groups fighting for dominance in interpreting the past (and not necessarily winning)? I fear it may be the latter.

We may also be excessively concerned about the rights of other cultures, languages and lifestyles which are disappearing faster than the other species and life forms with which we share this planet. This gives us a guilt complex: we feel we must try to understand other cultures in their own terms; we must treat them as equals; and if possible we should try to preserve them. Alas, all cultures are not equal; some like that of the Tasmanians have been completely obliterated. Others like those of the Native Americans have been decimated; others in Africa and Asia have been modified to the point of no return. But often we are helpless bystanders in this process; the decisions are often made by members of these societies and not by ourselves. We may be able to explain and warn about the consequences of change; we may be able to restrict or attack the activities of governments intent on cultural destruction and genocide; but equally we cannot take a paternalistic approach to decide which societies or sets of belief should be preserved in aspic: why should Australian aborigines not communicate with one another on the Internet if they wish to do so?

Why, too, should we be concerned so much about destroying other people's belief systems when we are so busy destroying our own? We as archaeologists are continuously rewriting the past, both by making new discoveries and also by changing our perspective. Archaeological approaches are based on an assumption of change and the development of ideas and beliefs, whereas other views of the past, based upon folk-lore, religious manifestation or beings from outer space, usually assume a static interpretation, though the emphasis may change. We must also accept that the basic rules on which we operate are usually totally different from those of people who espouse these other approaches, to the extent that we as archaeologists are likely to be used when ideas seem to overlap, and abused when they don't. Our ideal of logical and self-critical analysis of ourselves, of our methodologies and of our data, is not usually shared by other groups.

FOLKLORE AND POPULAR CULTURE

The distinction between folklore and popular culture parallels that which existed for collectors of folk music in the earlier part of this century. Much of the music they were offered as part of the local traditions could in fact be documented as deriving from the popular music of the day, especially the music hall. It was only when its origin was unknown that it could be certified with the stamp of approval, as 'Trad.' or 'Anon.', even though that origin was likely in most cases to have been in the previous century or two.

Much of the oral history of the same period could similarly be documented as deriving from classical, biblical, historical or pseudo-historical sources, though this might be unknown to the person relating the story. Thus, one of my uncles told me that the British name of our home town of Winchester was 'Caer Gwent', the 'White City'. It in fact derives from medieval chroniclers such as Geoffrey of Monmouth who were providing often wildly imaginative rationalisations of classical sources – Venta Belgarum, meeting place or market of the Belgae, becomes Gwent – leading on to fanciful reconstruction of ancient history. The Winchester lodge of the Royal Antediluvian Order of Buffaloes (a poor man's version of the Masons), of which my grandfather was a prominent member, thus became the 'Caer Gwent Lodge', perpetuating the medieval myth. Place names of ancient sites in Britain, where they are not a corruption of descriptive terms in British or Anglo-Saxon, tend to be of such a rationalising nature – Caesar's Camp, Danes Graves, Oliver's Battery, the Gog-Magog Hills – though the precise origin of the names and the stories that developed around them may not be known.

The distinction between folklore and popular culture thus becomes muddled. Those transmitting the oral tradition may not be aware of the origin of what they are assuming to be some sort of 'accepted' truth, though this may be known to a small group of academics. Scholars themselves, though they may recognise or suspect recent rationalisations, may not be able to document the sources, or even be aware of the rationalisation. As one example of this I can quote my own particular interest in the Celts. Both in the popular and the academic tradition it is assumed that the original population of Britain and Ireland belonged to an ancient racial group of Celts, and that the inhabitants in the north and west of our islands are some sort of 'survivors' of a prehistoric tradition. This again is a recent rationalisation, starting in the sixteenth century. The broad outline of the development of this idea from scholastic conjecture to popular belief can be traced, but not in all its details, nor is it easy to fix a point in time when it did become accepted belief.

This raises the question of how much of the population, and which part of it, is the guardian or representative of popular culture. One of the original assumptions of collectors of 'folklore' was that it was the uneducated classes who might unwittingly preserve in their oral traditions some truths handed down from generation to generation, uncontaminated by the effects of education. As such, folklore is something which has disappeared from western European society (if it ever really existed), as all our belief systems have been affected by education. Not only is this 'education' of a scientific nature, but we are also influenced by classical and biblical sources, and increasingly by 'popular' books (i.e. books of a non-scientific nature) on topics such as leylines or beings from outer space, or by commercial sources such as Hollywood or tabloid newspapers.

EQUALITY OF TREATMENT

Do we need to treat all popular culture as of equal value, or is there a hierarchy of acceptability? First, there are several categories of 'we' – society as a whole, analysts of the psychology of modern society, or 'we' as archaeologists. I shall stick with this last, and here there is a clear hierarchy.

At the top are those popular beliefs and myths that are incorporated into historical or quasi-historical sources, though acceptance will depend on the quality of the individual sources and authors. In western European society the two main sources of this nature are the Bible and the writings of classical Greek and Roman authors. From the Bible only extreme religious fundamentalists would accept the stories of the Creation and of the Garden of Eden (fundamental though these stories are to the traditional treatment of women in Jewish, Christian and Muslim societies). The story of Samson would equally not be accepted in detail, but might be taken as a metaphor for the relationship between the Israelites and the Philistines. The delightful story of Ruth, however, though perhaps equally mythological, reflects more closely the norms of Jewish society at the end of the second millennium BC, and so is more likely to be accepted as 'true'.

Similarly, information given to us by classical authors tends to be graded. Thus the explanation given to us by Livy for the presence of Celts in northern Italy as being due to an invasion over the Alps is generally accepted, though his date of 600 BC is not. The Dorian invasions of Greece on the other hand are treated with greater scepticism. Caesar's explanation of the origin and the spread of the Belgae tends to be given considerable credence, but what do we make of his story of the hunting of the wild and ferocious elk? Did the people who told him the story believe it themselves? How gullible was Caesar, or did he just think it was a good one for the folks back home? And did the readers of his *Commentaries* actually believe it? We have no way of knowing.

Next in status come ethnographic myths preserved by oral tradition. Many stories are clearly simply stories like those in Genesis which explain the origin of the world, humans, the specific society and its institutions, but others such as genealogies are taken to reflect some historical truth, however conflated or corrupted for political expedience. In some cases there may be independent evidence, linguistic or archaeological, to support the stories, so that they become incorporated into the reconstructed history of that people.

The lowest level of acceptance is accorded those stories which are obviously recent rationalisations, like the writings of Geoffrey of Monmouth, graded into those explanations which are similarly rejected as belonging to the lunatic fringe. However, if we as archaeologists wish to reconstruct ancient societies, such sources need to be incorporated into our reconstructions as part of the ancient society's way of viewing the world and cosmology. We cannot completely ignore them, even in our own society.

LEVELS OF INCORPORATION

Parallel with these levels of acceptance are levels of incorporation into archaeological explanations. Thus the stories of Bantu or Celtic migrations have formed the basis for explanations of the spread of languages and material culture in Africa and Europe. In the latter case, however, it is interesting to note how the modern explanations go far beyond what the ancient sources tell us, and often do not critically evaluate the uses that have been made of those sources by earlier scholars. Thus the modern definition of Celts as speakers of a Celtic language derives from the Abbé Pezron at the beginning of the eighteenth century, who believed that 'Celtic' was one of the 'original' languages created at the time of the Tower of Babel; he also believed that the similarities between Breton and Latin and Greek were due to a period when the Celts were overlords of the Greeks and Romans, and that these Celtic kings had become incorporated into mythology under the names of Saturn, Zeus, etc! Likewise the assumption that there was an expansion of Celts into modern France derives largely from the ninteenth-century French scholar d'Arbois de Jubainville who equally believed that information on Palaeolithic cave dwellers was preserved in the story of Odysseus and the Cyclops Polyphemus, and that the Iberians originated from Atlantis in 6000 BC. Thus some of their ideas have been incorporated unquestioningly not only into modern popular belief but also into academic assumptions; others, were they known, would simply raise a smile.

More common, however, is to see archaeology and folklore/mythology as simply providing parallel explanations, which may relate to the archaeological interpretation, but more commonly do not. The non-archaeological explanations are thus seen as interesting or amusing non-scientific approaches which tell us about the progress that archaeology has provided in our understanding of the past: thus, for instance, the story of the bewitched army which was turned into the stones which now form the complex of monuments around the Rollright Stones in Oxfordshire. Here there is no conflict – the traditional story enlivens our narration of the history of the site, and the understanding of it by our ancestors. When we are dealing with landscape history, part of our description of the landscape of the past should try to incorporate the beliefs of those people who made the ancient landscape so that we can understand how they viewed it. In other cases there can only be a straight rejection of the alternatives. The ascribing of Zimbabwe to the Queen of Sheba, the official position of the white supremacist government of Rhodesia, supported its view that native Africans were incapable of building such a monumental site, and so of governing themselves; the views of professional archaeologists were simply overruled. Likewise archaeology is in direct conflict with religious fundamentalism. Religious fundamentalists make selective use of archaeological data; they reject our undermining of the story of the Creation as related in Genesis, but would accept our findings for the collapsed walls of Jericho. Are we happy to accommodate their views by allowing equal time to the Creationist version being taught in schools as is given to Evolutionist views, as is demanded in certain areas of the United States? We must simply accept that we are not on the same wavelength as leyline hunters, devotees of the Mother Goddess, religious fundamentalists, Neo-Druids or New Age travellers; nor do they play by the same rules.

ARCHAEOLOGISTS IN SOCIETY

Opposition between the terms 'archaeology' and 'folklore/popular culture' may imply that somehow we are outsiders to the mainstream of society. To a certain extent this is true in that we are a small interest or pressure group fighting for the preservation of the archaeological record, for funding for our research, and for the acceptance of our views within society at large. In this respect we need to recognise that we may be in direct conflict with other interest groups, some of whom will be using alternative views of the past to support their arguments. I have already mentioned the case of Creationists and the teaching of evolution in schools; there is also the matter of the New Age rituals carried out on ancient monuments in which there is often no concern for the long-term conservation of the site – witness the fate of the Nine Ladies stone circle on Stanton Moor in Derbyshire, where fires are lit up against the stones. In some cases 'education' may play a part, but in many cases there can be no compromise as there is simply no common ground.

So under what conditions can we accept a symbiosis? Can we simply accept the Neo-Druids as a harmless sect whose activities at Stonehenge are not in conflict with ours in the conservation of the site, and that we have no exclusive rights (or rites) over the monument? Is the contemporary view of the Celts equally harmless, indeed perhaps even positive as it brings the crowds into archaeological exhibitions and sells books? I have argued that this is not the case, as the methodology on which that interpretation is based is essentially racist, and can be used for political ends in other contexts. How do we deal with the von Dänikens whose books on intervention from outer space seem to sell so much better than 'boring' archaeological versions of the past; their data form a many-headed hydra, so that when we disprove one idea, many others spring up to take its place. Can we accept 'The Green Man' but not the 'little green men'? Can we speak to the unspeakable? For me the answer seems to be that yes, we should attempt a dialogue, and I can think of a few 'converts' to an archaeological way of thinking from fringe groups (for instance a Creationist who is now an eminent Palaeolithic archaeologist). But we must recognise that in most cases the gulf in thinking is just too great, and not allow ourselves and our data to be used for ideas of which we do not approve.

However, we must also ask ourselves if we have really been so unsuccessful in putting our message across. Fact and fiction will always live alongside one another. Tolstoy's *War and Peace* may have provided a reinterpretation for the defeat of Napoleon, Stevenson may have embroidered history to provide a good story line for *Kidnapped*, and Scott in *Rob Roy* may have romanticised Scottish history and culture. All of them were fiction writers, whose views may colour our view of the past, but none of them is treated as a historical source in school curricula, whereas archaeology is. We now have a public which is better informed than any previous generation, and though some individuals may shoot off into weird and wonderfully illogical fields of belief, we still provide the dominant, and most popular, view of the past. The average person may not know the details of what happened when (personally I still have problems with the geological sequence!), but the broad impression of social, technological and physical evolution (and not necessarily to the overall benefit of mankind) is that promulgated by archaeology. We need to be vigilant about how we deal with alternative views of the past — some aspects we can perhaps accommodate and others we must reject; but equally we should not underestimate our own achievements in forming modern popular culture.

PART II

INTERPRETING MONUMENTS IN ARCHAEOLOGY AND POPULAR CULTURE

CHAPTER TEN

INTEGRATING THE PAST

Folklore, mounds and people at Çatalhöyük

DAVID SHANKLAND

ABSTRACT

This paper examines a particular aspect of a research project aimed at investigating the interaction between the villagers at Küçükköy (the settlement next to the Neolithic site of Çatalhöyük, Konya, Turkey) and the excavators of the site itself. The overall remit of the investigation is to clarify the economic, social and cognitive pressures from outside on the local community, and to explore also the very diverse ways with which the archaeological landscape is imbued with meaning. Within this overall approach, we find that folk tales told by the villagers are a key way by which they link the mounds which surround their territory into their mental representation of the past of the area. The paper concludes by contrasting this type of representation with the overall, dominant Islamic cosmology within the villagers' lives.

Of the three subjects – anthropology, folklore and archaeology – that impinge on this paper, I can claim expertise in but one. Yet all three are in their different ways quite crucial for the study of Anatolia, and it would seem only beneficial if they could be brought together in a creative way. My attempt at this attractive but uncertain goal centres on research conducted during three short seasons' fieldwork at a village, Küçükköy, on the Konya plain. Küçükköy is not well known, but within its fields lies the renowned Neolithic mound of Çatalhöyük. First dug by Mellaart in the 1960s, the mound then remained untouched until a permit was granted to reopen the site in 1993. Now, under the auspices of Professor Ian Hodder and the British Institute of Archaeology at Ankara, there is a flourishing excavation in progress, incorporating a large, international team of researchers and a growing site complex of dig-house, laboratories, display centre and depots. It enjoys excellent relations with the local authorities and with the villagers themselves, some of whom work with the excavators.

Çatalhöyük is not the only evidence of the past in the villagers' territory: the plain is dotted with mounds from many periods and late classical remains such as ovens, roof tiles and shaped stones. There is also the occasional site now completely levelled (by natural or artificial means) and obvious only to those who know the land well. These too are the subject of extensive survey and analysis. In sum, this would seem to be an ideal opportunity to attempt a cross-disciplinary project: a peaceful combination of vibrant local community, a complex and visible past, and a long-term international initiative aimed at assessing and investigating the archaeology of the area.

BACKGROUND AND AIMS

My interest in such a project was initially stimulated by being the Assistant, then the Acting, Director of the British Institute of Archaeology at Ankara, yet trained as an anthropologist. There, I found myself curious as to the ways in which a practising anthropologist might contribute towards an archaeological endeavour. Not so much through ethno-archaeology, which usually takes one particular aspect of a community and draws specific comparisons with the archaeological material, but rather in the social anthropological sense whereby the investigator views the activities of a community within the context of its overall social life.

It seemed to me as if one way this could be done would be to clarify the 'voice' of the local people (cf. Shankland 1996). Archaeological research does not take place within a cultural vacuum. Except perhaps in those exceptional cases when members of a community have absolutely no idea of the existence of the site, they may have developed different and perhaps complex ways of integrating those same material remains into their own conceptions of history. This is relevant not just in the postmodern sense of an alternative and perhaps equally viable interpretation of the past to that of the archaeologists themselves, but also pragmatically. In any multi-period site the successive communities must have had some means of accommodating the remains of the past (even if only to ignore or destroy them) and looking at the way a living community examines these issues may be potentially useful for our understanding of these earlier inhabitants.

It also seemed to me that this would take the investigator into the realm of folklore simply because so much folklore centres around the past and its artefacts, though this is an area that most anthropological studies of Turkey have avoided. It is tempting to wonder whether this avoidance is partly due to reasons of temperament: the two outstanding anthropological studies of Turkey are undoubtedly Van Bruinessan's study of the tribes in the east (Van Bruinessan 1992), and Stirling's in-depth study of an

Anatolian village near Kayseri (Stirling 1965). Both these are highly serious, and one has the feeling that the quirky, often fantastic side to folk tales would fit uneasily with their purpose. This may be a poor speculation: what is certain is that anthropology since the days of Malinowski has developed a marked disinclination to use ethnographic data 'disembodied' from their setting. Whatever the enormous qualities of the folklore collections, they do fail to indicate the context in which they were collected. The religious beliefs, ethnic group, even the barest details of the life of the community in which they were engendered are rarely given, thus making it very difficult for anthropologists to create systematic links and connections with their own data. I was sure, then, that though the investigation might lead to folklore, it would have to retain that holism that is characteristic of social anthropology in order for the folklore to be given a specific setting in which to be understood.

Professor Hodder extremely generously gave me permission to explore these ideas further during the excavations at Çatalhöyük. He also suggested that I look at the conditions of the archaeological investigation itself, and at the potential effects on the local community. This turned out to be a fruitful area. Through several decades of self-criticism, anthropologists have become sensitive to the cultural and political context of their research. This movement is said by at least one writer today to have gone too far (cf. Barret 1996) but it has been extremely fruitful in exposing the interconnections between the researcher and the object of study.

Here, I found that there is a clear contrast between archaeology and anthropology as it is practised in Anatolia. Though often remarkably distinguished, successive generations of archaeologists have hardly remarked on the actual practice of the discipline in seminars or in their publications. Yet informal conversation reveals that there are a host of constraints on the political, national and administrative setting of the research which are extremely likely to influence and channel the academic direction of the project. Indeed, it is possible that this side of archaeological research has not yet been explored in Anatolian studies simply because of the extent of the area it opens up to questioning and doubt. Issues such as the difference between collective and individual representations of academic knowledge, the way that material data are pressed into different frameworks of meaning in dig reports, the composition of the dig team, the political context of the funding awarded, the international, national (and perhaps even nationalistic) motives behind permission and encouragement to dig, the way that the knowledge is disseminated from the site: all these and more become pressingly relevant.

To take only the question of the relationship between archaeology and the local community, where I was to concentrate part of my research: it might be reasonable to suppose that the presence of a large number of foreigners may have economic, social and ideological effects within a village setting, even if only because of the money that is provided to the workmen. Contemplating the great number of other archaeological sites being researched in Anatolia, some of them large and popular, it may also be assumed that the mass tourism attracted by them has potentially a profound effect on the surrounding communities (though the actual changes may be subtle and extremely difficult to describe accurately). However, whether difficult or not, there appears to have been no systematic investigation into these intrusions into the lives of communities all over Anatolia.

Turning to Çatalhöyük itself it is clear that it has had a large impact in the outside world. The existing popularity of the site means that images from it are refracted and interpreted within the wider world of Konya, Istanbul, Europe and even areas as far afield as America. There are also at the time of writing a flourishing number of web sites which discuss the site. As the new excavation grows and publicity mounts, interest groups as disparate as self-avowed radical feminists, diplomats, journalists and besuited international businessmen have visited the site, and as they develop longer term links their presence may influence the village, again in ways difficult to predict.

Further, it also may be noted that the site is absorbed into different layers of the Turkish state at the national, local and village level in a complex and interconnected way. For an example of this, we might take the fact that many villagers maintained to me that they learnt about the site from the mention it gains in elementary school textbooks rather than from the mound itself, even though it lies in their territory. The villagers may be mistaken in this recollection, or they may be minimising their own ideas and privileging the 'true' knowledge that is found in school textbooks, but even this initial, seemingly simple, enquiry indicates the complications inherent within any attempt to relate the villagers' changing world to the archaeological endeavour.

ÇATALHÖYÜK AND KÜÇÜKKÖY

These then were some of the preoccupations in mind when the research itself began in 1995, in the company of a government representative from the Konya Museum. The villagers kindly furnished us with a house within the village, and we were able to begin our research immediately. In sharp contrast to the enormous outside interest, it was surprising at the outset of the research to be told that the effect of the site on the local village appears to have been rather small. The villagers' most frequent comment when asked how they had been affected by it was a laconic '*Hiç Yok!*' (Not at all!) Even when they expanded more fully on this comment, they did not identify any specific effects.

From the economic point of view this may be comprehended. The site was closed down after four intense seasons. It is often stated that only 4 per cent of the mound has been dug. It was not at all developed for touristic purposes. Before the reopening occurred in 1993, the site was no more than a fenced mound with the occasional visitor. A watchman from the village was employed there by the local museum. He told me that he bought a little house in Konya on the strength of his regular wages. This, and fencing the site so that it could no longer be used as pasture for sheep, appeared to be the only specific economic influences that the archaeology had left behind.

Ideologically, given the way that certain finds from the site are frequently interpreted as being representative of a woman 'Goddess' religion it would seem that there is potential for disruption and clashes with the Islamic religion of the villagers. Yet, this was not at all apparent. Within the village itself, most of the people who knew Mellaart or his wife well have passed away. Those who remain were rather young at the time, and often recall only that the finds were exhibited at first in the village school house, where they were seen and admired. The villagers occasionally mentioned that they had learnt about the site from their school textbooks, and they were aware that it is sometimes claimed to be an early agricultural community, but, it seemed, no more than this. It is always possible to doubt one's own fieldwork, to assume that in such a short time (my total stay in the village amounts as yet to a little more than three months) nothing may be assumed, yet it seems that on this occasion the villagers' comments may be accepted, though very cautiously, as being broadly indicative of the comparatively small influence that the site has had on their lives.

The situation did not appear immediately to be greatly changed by the site's reopening. The mound of Çatalhöyük lies about half a mile from the village itself, which consists of about a hundred households. The houses are clustered in the centre of fields which are owned by the villagers, and most of the people in the village are engaged in intensive agricultural production. When I first began to work at Küçükköy, I was surprised to find that their agricultural production appeared to provide a degree of economic plenty far greater than in many other parts of central Anatolia. The fields are unusually fertile, a return in wheat may be as high as forty to one, whilst melons and sugar beet are grown as cash-crops. Not all families are wealthy by any means, but most have twenty or thirty *dönüm* (a *dönüm* being the amount of land traditionally ploughed by one pair of oxen in a day), and many much more. Animal husbandry is also extensively practised, for dairy produce, meat and for market. Of course, people do occasionally occur losses, particularly with delicate and risky crops such as melon, but it appears that overall many of the villagers are substantially better off than the great majority of civil servants in the town. Thus, it is certain that the money paid to the village from the site represents only a tiny proportion of its overall economy.

There may nevertheless be some highly specific effects. The villagers who have worked for the site are often those who have the least property. Just as did the first watchman, after a number of years (particularly if more than one person from the same family works there regularly) a family may succeed in moving up the village social hierarchy by buying a house or land. The money going into the community may be important in its selective influence on the village order, but much less so in its total economy (cf. Stirling 1974, 1993).

In the future, the situation is potentially very different. The success of the site's reopening is clearly attracting important people to the area. The ubiquity of tourism has made it clear to many that money can be made. Here, however, though the villagers are aware of the potential, they seem to assume that the people who will benefit from its economic development lie outside the village. They appear to be prepared, for example, to sell property which might be turned into a hotel or restaurant rather than exploit it themselves. One rather beautiful old house changed hands in 1997, bought by a person from Istanbul who was otherwise not known by the village. Though the purpose to which it is to be put is not yet clear, it appears at the time of writing (summer 1998) to have been purchased on behalf of a feminist organisation in order to provide a base from which to study Çatalhöyük.

Whilst the motives for this resigned reaction will only become clearer as the situation unfolds, it is possible to note one probable reason. The site at Çatalhöyük is actually owned by the treasury, not by one individual. Complex regulations govern the development of archaeological sites and their surrounding area. Academically, this raises questions of land tenure and archaeological heritage about which I hope to publish an account in the future. From the village point of view however, I think that first indications are that many people do not feel powerful enough to enter into a complicated procedural battle, one which would involve both the local authorities and various different government departments.

Further, the site lies about 10 kilometres from the local town, Çumra, which is also the sub-province centre. In contrast to the villagers, the mayor there is quite clear that Çatalhöyük is a resource to be developed for the town's greater benefit, and he is taking active steps to try to ensure that this comes about. Caught between so many interested parties, the villagers simply do not at present see where they might fit into the site's developmental pattern. Unless action is taken to embrace their interests, the villagers themselves may become aware of the impact of the site, both socially and economically, only when they have effectively been excluded from the decision-making process which will govern its future.

THE VILLAGE AND THE REMAINS OF THE PAST

I was at first concerned lest the site's comparative lack of importance (at least until very recently) to the villagers be reflected in their general conception of the material remains of the past. However, this does not seem the case. Indeed, my preliminary conclusion is that there is a complex but subtle and tolerant interaction between the villagers and the heritage that fills their landscape. Mounds, for example, may have a number of different roles in the life of the community. They may act variously as field boundaries, modern-day cemeteries, picnic places at festival times, repositories of water-proof earth, sources of buried treasure, the souls of those past or of the devil. Other remains may play an equally complex role, so that large classical period carved stones are often used as buffers to protect the corners of houses, or as simple decoration, but they are also often used to mark auspicious or holy places, or the graves of holy men.

Over the course of this initial fieldwork, we concentrated on mapping some of these various aspects of the heritage within the landscape (see Figure 10.1). The archaeological interpretation of the mounds and other sites within the village territory is progressing through a survey by Dr Douglas Baird. We concentrated therefore on the way that they are incorporated into the village cosmology.

It would be wrong to attribute any one fixed quality to any one mound, site or artefact. The process of investing the landscape with meaning is not uniform. Some objects do appear to hold a fairly constant position in the collective representations of the village: most villagers I spoke to, for example, were sure that Küçükköy was descended from the late classical remains known as 'Efeköy', near by to Çatalhöyük (cf. Shankland 1996). As well as this, however, people may interpret any one mound or stone in different ways, or attribute very different qualities to it. Overall it appears that the archaeological landscape acts as a number of mnemonic points for individual and collective representations, and it is not always certain which particular mound or artefact will spark a response, nor that it will always be the same response. The map therefore is a summation of the information that we have learnt, useful for the purposes of an overview, but it does not necessarily represent any one person's conception of the world.

Nor is it part of village life to periodicise the past into distinct historical and prehistoric ages. They are aware of course of the fact of the Ottoman Empire, and that various different peoples have lived on the same soil that they now inhabit, indeed their memory of the Anatolian Greek population (*Rum*), who only departed in 1923, is particularly clear. Most people do not, however, put the longer time frames into chronological or successive order, or seek even to make a very sharp distinction between the possibilities of a mound being Muslim or non-Muslim. Pragmatically, the villagers regard the mounds as being there for exploitation for treasure, for grazing or for earth unless impeded by the lie of the land, the government, the souls (*ruh*) of those who used to inhabit it and are now buried there, or other supernatural sanction.

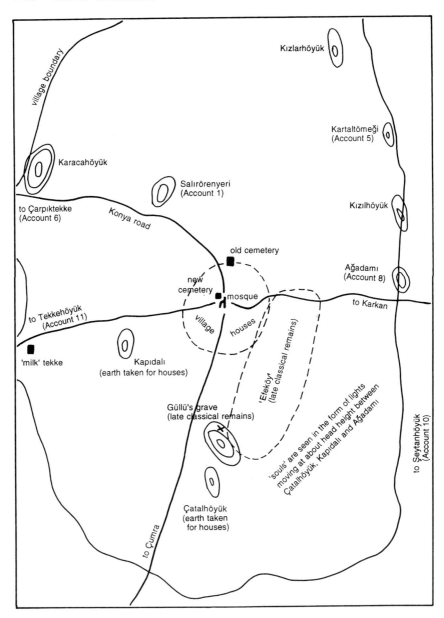

Figure 10.1   A preliminary archaeo-anthropological sketch map of Küçükköy.
Source: © D. Shankland 1998

PROTECTING THE HERITAGE

Once a mound is declared an archaeological site, a border is defined around it and it is then forbidden by law to plough or build on the land within that border. Nevertheless, archaeological sites are explored by treasure seekers, though at Çatalhöyük this is prevented by the presence of a guard. They may even be flattened entirely, particularly if they are not well known, by farmers who wish to turn the area into arable land, leaving behind no more than a few pot sherds in a freshly turned field. The Ministry of Culture is aware of these problems, and does its best to impede the destruction, but it is in the perennial situation of being unable to act until the damage has actually occurred.

Most mounds have within them skeletal material which becomes exposed as they are dug for soil or for treasure. Sometimes odd bones lie on the surface, mixing with the pot sherds. It is widely held that these mortal remains are guarded by their respective souls (*ruh*). The souls are usually inactive though they may on occasion haunt a particular location. Once the bones are disturbed, however, the consequences can be severe: it is said that the person responsible may suffer from trauma, misfortune, illness or even death. In spite of this prescription, if there is a particularly important reason, any bones in the location being dug may be simply ignored. However, the particular person who disturbed them may feel perturbed later. If they do so, it is held that reburying the remains may redress the grievance.

The following accounts, collected in 1996 and 1997, illustrate these preoccupations. They were gleaned in conversation from people in Küçükköy, and occasionally in the surrounding villages.

Account 1

A Küçükköy man told me that he took water-proof earth for his new roof from Salırörenyeri and placed it on his new house, exposing a skeleton as he did so. However, during the night he felt that the owner of the bones was strangling him. He woke up in a terrible sweat, and returned to the spot the next morning with an *imam* (mosque prayer-leader). Together, they read a burial service and he was not disturbed again.

Account 2

In a local village, I was told the following story: two men, looking for antiquities, opened up a tomb in a mound. It had a stone top, brick sides and a stone floor. Inside, they saw a little woman in an excellent state of preservation, eyes slightly slit. Her hair was jet black and went down to her feet, though it was by then very brittle. She had a white shroud, now falling into pieces. Whilst they were looking for gold in the tomb, they dislodged the skeleton and broke her hair. Both men gradually fell sick, and then died. Both of them complained that the woman came continuously to their dreams, demanding of them why they disturbed her bones.

Account 3

Two melon watchmen decided to build a little hut to shelter in whilst they watched over the melon field. As a joke, they used two skulls from the mound to support the roof of the hut. They emerged the next morning pale from fright and lack of sleep, complaining that the skulls did not let them rest for a moment. They put back the skulls, and never again returned to that place.

Account 4

In Küçükköy, there used to be a custom (common in this part of central Anatolia) known as *kadın oynatma* whereby a *danseuse* would be paid to perform a dance for a number of males. One man, who was too powerful to be opposed by the other villagers, moved one of these, Güllü, to the village, where she is said to have lived separately, organising such evenings for him. After her death, she was buried at Çatalhöyük, where her grave lies still. After some time had past, one night two men decided to steal her gold teeth. As they were doing so, her skeleton began to rattle and, terrified, they ran back to the village. The next day, they replaced those teeth that they had taken, and reburied her remains.

Souls are not necessarily harmful. It is sometimes said that during the night, particularly on Friday, it is possible to see little lights, moving slightly faster than walking pace, moving from one mound to another, Çatalhöyük, Ağadamı and Kapıdalı being the most frequently mentioned. Villagers variously say that these are the souls of holy men (*ermiş kişi*) who are buried in the mounds and now visiting each other. They add occasionally that only people who are themselves holy can see them. These auspicious figures can also appear during the night, or in dreams, to give aid or help. This story was told me by a local woman:

Account 5

At Kartaltömeği, my uncle was threshing grain. During this season, we used to sleep at the threshing ground. Whilst they were sleeping, a well-dressed man, as if a philosopher (*filosof*), woke up my uncle and told him that he would take him to a very good place. They began to walk. They walked until the cock began to crow, and at that point they arrived at Şeytanhöyük. As the sound of the cocks came, the man disappeared. My uncle went and told his wife about his experience, very excitedly. The next night, the man came to his side again, and said because you have told another about this, you have lost your chance of riches, I would have made you wealthy.

Provisionally, then, we can say that the mounds occupy a position in the village cosmology somewhere between what is usually regarded as the 'folklore' of the region (that is, the activities of supernatural, mythical or archetypical beings) and the Islamic faith. Indeed, the tales and the explanations that the villagers give of their reactions to the mounds are deeply imbued with religious motifs. Thus, while evil or misfortune may embody itself in different ways, it usually does so as *şeytan* (Satan) and evil *cin*. The villagers explain both these entities by reference to the wider cosmology of Islam as it is explained in the Koran. *Şeytan* is regarded as being an angel who refused to obey the word of God when instructed to bow before humanity. Thrown out of heaven, in revenge he has vowed to repay humanity for his humiliation. *Şeytan* has absolute powers at his disposal and should be feared at all costs. *Cin* (usually translated into English as 'spirits') may be either auspicious (*uğurlu*) or inauspicious (*uğursuz*). Inauspicious *cin* also can be extremely dangerous and to be struck by one can result in the face becoming paralysed. The evil *cin* strike most frequently when a person has failed to perform a ritual cleansing, *aptes*.

Account 6

One day, when I was a child, the side of my face tensed and froze. I went home and showed it to my mother, who immediately locked me inside the house, saying that I had been struck by *cin* for not performing the *aptes* properly. She forbade me to look at water or a mirror, saying that the devil would get me. The next day she took me to Çarpıktekke, 100 kilometres away. There, we said prayers and rubbed a shoe on the side of my face. It got better. It is said that the shoe belonged to one of two brothers who had once gone to winnow their grain there. Both were poor. As they shared the grain out, one said, 'My brother needs the grain, he has a large family', and tried to push more on to his side. The other brother said to himself likewise, 'My brother has little enough to get by on through the winter', and tried surreptitiously to give more to his brother. As they were thus trying to help each other, they were helped by God: the pile of grain grew and grew and became ample for both families. The spot is still holy today, and this explains its efficacy in making my face heal.

The *aptes* can be broken by passing wind, sexual intercourse, by suffering a cut or abrasion, by going to the toilet. It is mandatory to have performed the *aptes* before prayer. Usually, on encountering the devil, some protection would be afforded by calling the name of God, *Bismillah*, but it is a sin to invoke God or to worship in an impure state unless in the direst of circumstances, as the following account shows.

Account 7

A boy rode a tractor back to the village without having performed the cleansing *(aptes)* needed after sexual relations. As he was returning to the village, he saw that devils rode with him in the tractor. He was unable to say *Bismillah!* because of his impure state. However, at last, in desperation he did so. The devils vanished. When he got back to the village his face was stony white and he was quite terrified.

Between Küçükköy, and Karkan, the largest local village, there is a long flat mound known as 'Ağadamı'. The following two accounts are said to have taken place in its vicinity. In the first, there appears to be a general warning against interfering with the land, one which is heeded by the villager concerned. In the second, the devil appears to the man concerned, placing him in a very dangerous situation.

Account 8

A family who owned a field which lies next to Ağadamı sent the youngest son out to plough. He was just about to begin on a furrow adjoining the mound when he found himself unable to move the plough, because an old man was sitting on it.

Frightened, he went home saying that he was sick. He went to bed, not wanting to admit his fear. They sent out his brother, and the same thing happened. He too came home and said that he was sick, unable to confess to what he had seen. Finally the father went out to try, angry with his sons at their laziness, and the same thing happened to him. He went home, and said to his sons: 'Now I understand why you refused to work.' He drew a line around the area which had caused the trouble, and said, 'Henceforth nobody will plough here!'

Account 9

One day, a man from Küçükköy was returning from Karkan during the night past Ağadamı. In the darkness, he saw a woman on the path who raised her hand to stop his cart and ask for a lift. The woman was very beautiful and attractive. The man took her into the cart and continued on his journey towards the village. As he did so, he glanced behind and saw that her legs were elongated, stretching out behind the cart, impeding its progress. When the man saw this, he realised that this was Satan (*Şaytan*), and drove the cart immediately into a field of green shoots. The devil said, 'You recognised me for what I am straight away, and for this you will get off lightly', and floated away.

The following account is told in much of the region. Here it refers to a mound just upstream from Çatalhöyük, in the territory of Karkan village, and I give it as it was recited by one local man. Two words are clumsy to translate: the first is *helva*, used in spoken Turkish as a generic name for a sweet dish made from a variety of ingredients. The second is *bestlemesi* (adj.), literally 'without a *Bismillah*', a state wherein the name of God has not been intoned; in this case it refers to the food and the tray that the devils handle.

Account 10

Just below Şeytan mound, a man named Seyit made a *han* (inn), then about half a day's journey from the village itself. Both mounted and foot travellers used to come to the inn. One day, a man who had a caravan train of camels was arriving from his travels, and tied up his camels at the inn. It was a cold winter's day, and he sat in the corner near the fire wrapping his cloak around himself to warm up. Then, the door opened and a group of travellers entered the inn.

The whole group were devils in human shape. One of them said, 'Let each one of us take something from his bag and make a *helva* from the *bestlemesiz* goods that we have collected.'

They put together flour, sugar, oil, walnuts, hazelnuts, raisins to make a *helva*, all without a *bestleme*, that they had taken from other people's house. One of them had taken a tray which had been put away without a *bestleme*. They made the *helva* in this tray, and put it on the table.

The camel trainer was still sitting in the corner, and one of them invited him to come the table, claiming that it was shameful that he should not be invited to share the food. They argued whether it was right for a human being to join them, but eventually they agreed that it would be possible. Then, as the camel trainer was reaching out for the food, he said 'Bismillah!'

On his doing so, the *helva* turned to buffalo dung. The devils scattered themselves into the four corners of the inn. He looked at the dog, and it began to make wild movements as if it had become possessed. He shot it, thinking that the devil had taken the dog's soul.

When he finally arrived at his house, he showed the tray to the villagers for the years to come. Because of these events, and others like it, we changed the name of the mound to Devil's Mound. When coming to plough the fields with my father, we always heard the devils talking to each other.

THOSE WHO ARE CLOSER TO GOD

The villagers maintain that all people have a soul (*ruh*) which is ever-lasting and life (*can*) which ceases on their mortal death. All people are subject to Allah's commandments lest through their disobedience they suffer, either in this life or the next. However, it is also widely supposed that some individuals are closer to God than others. These individuals are known variously as possessing *keramet*, sometimes translated as 'charisma' but perhaps in the Turkish context better understood as a sign from God, usually the ability to perform miracles. Such holy figures and their teachings may also be the founding figure of a brotherhood, or *tarikat*, named after them. Thus, the Bektashi *Tarikat*, still active today, was founded by Hacc Bektar Veli.

Individuals may pass this ability through their patrilineage, or it may survive them after their death and benefit those who worship at their tomb. Throughout Anatolia there is a network of tombs, often known as *tekke*, some of which are appropriate to different illnesses or worldly afflictions, such as paralysis, malaria, failure in examinations or childless-ness. Some of these are accompanied by a saintly lineage living at the town of the tomb, in which case the leading members of the lineage may be credited with miraculous healing powers.

The people of Küçükköy, as do the other villagers in the area, attend a number of these in different locations. The tomb of the Mevlana in Konya is perhaps the most popular. Çarpiktekke, famous for curing people struck by *cin*, has been mentioned above. There is another, Avdan, about 130 km away, in the mountains, which is famous for the power to cure mental illness. During the summer, many coachloads of people visit each day, paying their respects to the lineage which lives at the tomb, and sacrificing at the tomb of the saint buried there. I visited in 1997, and there can be no doubt as to its flourishing.

Within the immediate area of Küçükköy, there are also areas where such holy people are supposed to be buried. The most important of these are two situated at mounds. A well, known as Süt (milk) Tekkesi, just at the border between the village named Tekkehöyük and Küçükköy, was visited by women who were unable to lactate. There also used to be a small mound there, held to be the burial place of a holy figure. It is now ploughed over, but this action is widely held to have been the source of misfortune and death to the brothers who did so. It is now rarely visited, though people remember it being so until very recently.

Just past Süt Tekkesi lies the large mound of Tekkehöyük itself, after which the village is named. At its foot is an enclosed cemetery and the grave of a holy figure. People still go to pray there today, some leaving little pieces of cloth in order to be cured of illness, or the clothing of those who are ill. The founding story of that tomb is known to all around the area, and is as follows:

Account 11

A man was tilling his fields, when the advance guard of the Sultan's army was passing by. They said that they were hungry. The man replied that he had enough food to feed all the troops, and placed a cauldron of rice and meat that never ended in front of them. Seeing this amazing feat, the Sultan said, 'We have need of men like you, come with us.' The man acquiesced, saying that he would do so.

Much later, when the army was returning to Istanbul they stopped again at the man's fields, and he repeated the same feat. The Sultan called him to his side and asked, 'Why were you not there?' The man replied, 'Do you recall the warrior at your side, who passed you his scarf to tie up your wounded arm at the height of the battle? That was me.' On his saying this, the Sultan realised that he was right, he had indeed been there, and recognised that he was favoured by God. In recognition of this, he awarded the man all the fields between the village and the Mevlana for him and his descendants in perpetuity. When the man died, he was buried at the spot where the cauldron was cooked, and people still visit there today.

VARIATIONS IN BELIEF AND PRACTICE

Looking at the village from above and plotting those parts of the landscape which may be said to play a part in the religious life of the village against the visible archaeological remains would reveal a high degree of correlation. This correlation can be traced in various ways, but one of the most important links derives from the fact that many of these remains are associated with the bones of human beings. Many villagers empathise with these bones, extending to them qualities, particularly a protective soul, whether or not they are from a Muslim culture or lived in a distant past. This leads on occasion to attributions of sanctity and, equally, recourse to Islamic means to ward off the unwished consequences when a grave is disturbed.

I do not wish to oversimplify this point. Individual villagers will have taken up different positions within this overall ideological concatenation of cultures in death. Taking the example of the *danseuse*, in Account 4 above, I do not know why she was buried at Çatalhöyük: it may have been coincidence, or it may have been that her past meant that they did not wish to bury her with other Muslims. It may have been because she was thought to have been of *Rum* ancestry: some of the villagers maintain that until the founding of the Republic there were *Rum* living in this area, and they occasionally associate them with Çatalhöyük. Certainly, the villagers affirm that she was a controversial figure, and it is likely that she remained so after death.

Whatever the debates then, the potency of people after their death is one of the single most contested areas of the Islamic faith as it moves into the modern world. Summing up a much wider debate, Gellner (1981), in his work in North Africa, stressed the fact that there is a point of fission within Islam between those who accept the possibility of individual sanctity and who are comfortable with the idea of saintly influence, whether alive or dead, and those who have recourse to a different style of worship: one more based on mosque and on the requirements of the daily religious practice. He argued that people tend to be against the brotherhoods, and do not approve of worshipping at tombs or religious foundations based on the supposed sanctity of a particular figure.

At one level, Turkey appears to have been exempt from the drastic consequences that such doctrinal difference can provoke (Tapper 1991 gives an overview). In particular, the brotherhoods have not gone through the process of vilification at the hands of orthodoxy that Gellner might have supposed. However, there is an emerging political Islamic movement which, at its grass-roots level, has adopted a seemingly puritanical, mosque-based worship which is strikingly similar to that which he outlines. Something of this movement can be seen in Küçükköy and the surrounding villages, where the most popular political religious party, the *Refah Partisi* (now, in 1998, renamed the Virtue Party, *Fazilet Partisi*), is active. Its members, often supported by the mosque *imam*, actively discourage villagers from sacrificing at tombs and are contemptuous when they leave pieces of clothing in the hope that this may aid healing. In general, it seems that such politically active Islamic villagers are more aware of the periodicisation of the past than the villagers are as a whole, and are much more concerned as to whether an archaeological site is Islamic, Christian or from one of the prehistoric periods.

This area of Islamic practice is also relevant to gender differences. There is less research published about women's worship than about men's and to be a male foreigner in a village is a far from ideal base from which to attempt to fill in the gaps. However, it is indisputably the case that all believing Sunni men with whom I spoke regard women as being in some way qualitatively different in the eyes of God (cf. Tapper and Tapper 1987). Women are not necessarily formally less significant as believers, in that they too may have a place in heaven, but the men were adamant that special rules apply. Among these rules are the necessity for women to wear their headscarves in public, to avoid being seen by men who are praying (and in general to avoid mixing with men during any public collective ritual, whether sacred or not), to avoid the public places of worship in the village, that is, the mosque and the cemetery, and the insistence on the utter impossibility of their becoming mosque *imam*.

Perhaps because of this exclusion, women are much more prominent in just those areas of the faith which the believing politically active men regard as being unacceptable and far from central orthodoxy. Though men visit tombs, women do so even more (cf. Nicolas 1972). They are also more likely to practise 'alternative' healing methods. There is a term *ocak,* for example, which applies to a tree, stream or stone which appears to have special healing properties. When asked, villagers usually explain this quality by assuming that there is the grave of a holy person (*yatır*) beneath. However, the term *ocak* is also used to denote a person who has the personal quality of curing people's illness. *Ocak* cater for specific ills, just as do the *tekke*, such as the evil eye (*nazar*), a fractious child or illness. *Ocak* are usually women, and they may pass their power to their daughters-in-law as they grow older. They themselves certainly would claim that they are part of the Islamic faith – during the healing consultation they usually use a combination of prayer and object (often a bone or a stick) held over the afflicted part – but they are not publicly approved of by the Islamic movement that I identify above.

I use the word 'publicly' advisedly, because people can take up more than one position. One man who was working very hard to try to prevent women from going to alternative healers or to the tombs of saints, said to me, 'It's absurd that they should go to Tekkehöyük to cure malaria, ridiculous that holy power can go through a man after he is dead.' Then he paused, and said in a hopeful manner, 'They do say, though, that the saint chucks stones at people if they pass his tomb when they are drunk!'

In spite of any private weaknesses one small consequence of this public disapproval is already discernible. Within Anatolian Islam, there is an annual festival *Hıdrellez*, which takes place in the spring. During the night before the festival, it is supposed that a holy figure, *Hızır*, sometimes referred to by folklorists as 'green man', may appear in the guise of a beggar requesting alms (cf. Walker and Uysal 1966). If his wish is granted, then it is said that the household will enjoy plenty. If ignored, they may suffer terrible misfortune. It has long been noted that the day itself is the occasion for excursions to tombs and for picnics. At Küçükköy, I was told that Çatalhöyük itself used to be the site of such excursions, when women alone would go, taking their children and picnicking to celebrate the spring. Now Çatalhöyük is cordoned off. However, the villagers have not sought a direct replacement. Rather, those families who are not politically religious go together to a nearby municipal picnic spot, where, though men and women may sit apart, they are still within sight of one another, whilst other more religious families do not go. Men from these latter families are said to deplore the interaction between the sexes that might result and the potential jollity of the occasion. Thus what was once a women's preserve through exploiting an alternative 'folk' Islam within the village community as a whole has now become the object of scepticism and disapproval and led to a polarisation of gender practices.

The enormous complexities of social change caution against making any generalisation. However, on the basis of the research so far, I think that it is likely that this process of codification, of increasing orthodoxy will continue. The quiet, confident belief which seems characteristic of the area suggests that the religious differences will be unlikely to develop into a sharp confrontation, in spite of the split which appears to have emerged at the *Hıdrellez*. Rather, it is likely that there will be gradual change whereby the unorthodox aspects of the faith will decline; certainly they will become less obvious. As this shift occurs, there is a possibility that the mounds will become increasingly viewed as archaeological sites, with a distinct place in the past, and perhaps excluded from the incorporation into the sacred that the lack of periodicisation currently permits. They may then become part of an overall, national debate as to the place of prehistoric archaeology in a predominantly Islamic nation. At this point indeed, village conflicts and debates may become indistinguishable from wider issues of national policy. Both ideologically and economically, Çatalhöyük, far from being unimportant in the lives of the villagers, may then become extremely significant indeed.

CONCLUSION

I opened this chapter by expressing the tentative hope that folklore, archaeology and anthropology can be brought together. Though this research is still very much in progress, I feel that there has been some partial success at achieving this goal, particularly that the incorporation of folklore into the project has led the research into areas that are not usually examined by anthropologists working in Anatolia. Whether this endeavour will be creative for archaeology too, and perhaps play a small, but wider part in helping an interdisciplinary synthesis of two disciplines which (in the United Kingdom at least) have grown sadly apart, it is far too soon to tell. I would like to imagine that, ultimately, the body of material gathered on the villagers' conception of the material remains of the past will prove helpful to those working on the excavation. If this does occur, that the topsy-turvy world of folklore should play a key role in brokering a reunion between anthropology and archaeology is a stimulating concluding thought.

ACKNOWLEDGEMENTS

This research has been funded by the British Institute of Archaeology at Ankara, by the Pantyfedwyn Fund, University of Wales, Lampeter, and by the Anthropology Unit, University of Wales, Lampeter. I am extremely grateful for their support. Permission to undertake the research was granted by the Directorate-General of Antiquities and Museums, Ankara, to whom I would also like to express my thanks. I was fortunate indeed to be helped in 1996 by Mr Lütfi Önal, and in 1996 and 1997 by Mr Nürettin Özkan. I would like to extend my deepest thanks to them both. I am grateful to Professor Ahmet Edip Uysal, himself a master of folkloric researches in Anatolia, for sharing so generously the fruits of his research with me and welcoming me so splendidly in 1986, right at the beginning of my research. I am also grateful to David Barchard, Ian Hodder, Stephen Mitchell and to the late Paul Stirling for comments on earlier drafts of this paper, and to Douglas Baird for most helpful discussions of the issues involved.

REFERENCES

Barret, S. (1996) *Anthropology: A Student's Guide to Theory and Method.* Toronto: University of Toronto Press.
Gellner, E. (1981) *Muslim Society.* Cambridge: Cambridge University Press.
Hasluck, F. (1929) *Christianity and Islam Among the Sultans*, 2 vols. Oxford: Clarendon.
Hodder, I. (1997) 'Always momentary, fluid and flexible: towards a reflexive excavation methodology.' *Antiquity* 71: 691–700.
Hodder, I. (ed.) (1996) *On the Surface: The Re-opening of Çatalhöyük.* MacDonald Institute, Cambridge.
Nicolas, M. (1972) *Croyances et Practiques Populaires Turques Concernant les Nissances.* Paris: P.O.F.
Shankland, D. (1993) 'Diverse paths of change: Alevi and Sunni in rural Turkey.'

In P. Stirling (ed.) *Culture and Society: Changes in Turkish Villages*, pp. 46–64. Huntingdon: Eothen Press.

Shankland, D. (1996) 'The anthropology of an archaeological presence.' In I. Hodder (ed.) *On the Surface: The Re-opening of Çatalhöyük*, pp. 349–357. MacDonald Institute, Cambridge.

Shankland, D. (1999) 'Integrating the rural: Gellner and the study of Anatolia.' *Middle Eastern Studies*, in press.

Stirling, P. (1965) *Turkish Village*. London: Weidenfeld and Nicholson.

Stirling, P. (1974) 'Cause, knowledge and change: Turkish village revisited.' In J. David (ed.) *Choice and Change: Essays in Honour of Lucy Mair*, pp. 191–229. London: Athlone.

Stirling, P. (ed.) (1993) 'Introduction.' *Culture and Economy: Changes in Turkish Villages*. Huntingdon: Eothen Press.

Tapper, N. and Tapper, R. (1987) 'The birth of the prophet: ritual and gender in Turkish Islam.' *Man* (N.S.) 22: 69–92.

Tapper, R. (ed.) (1991) *Religion in Modern Turkey*. London: Taurus.

Van Bruinessan, M. (1992) *Agha, Shaikh, and State*. London: Z Books.

Walker, W. and Uysal, A. (1966) *Tales Alive in Turkey*. Harvard: Harvard University Press.

CHAPTER ELEVEN

ON THE FOLKLORE OF THE EXTERNSTEINE

Or a centre for Germanomaniacs

MARTIN SCHMIDT AND UTA HALLE

ABSTRACT

Since the nineteenth century, the natural and cultural monument Externsteine near Horn, Kreis Lippe, Germany has been a meeting place for all sorts of researchers studying the Teutons, Gods and Ghosts. During the Third Reich the research work at the rocks escalated to a climax when the National Socialists redeveloped the site into a 'Teutonic cult site'. This Germanenforschung was initiated by the völkisch-orientated 'Friends of Teutonic Prehistory' around the former Reverend Wilhelm Teudt. The ideas of this group were similar to National Socialist ideology and it was hence supported by the Nazis. In this context archaeological fieldwork was carried out at the site, initially by the Amt Rosenberg (Bollmus 1970) and from 1935 onwards by the SS Ahnenerbe (Kater 1974). The objective of the excavations was to find evidence for a 'Teutonic cult site'. Although no evidence for any use of the rocks by the Teutons was found, the archaeologists supported the ideological interpretation. Himmler, however, stopped the publication of the excavation report. Since 1993 the material found at the excavations in 1934/35, has been studied anew by Uta Halle. In this paper an overview will be presented of the excavations at the Externsteine as well as of the contemporary use of the rocks, which are frequented by ordinary tourists but are also used as a meeting place by neo-pagans and neo-nazis.

This paper demonstrates how a single monument can be perceived and understood in many different ways by different people, including archaeologists. We argue that the most successful story in society is not necessarily the one that is academically correct. Instead, those stories which appeal most to the public imagination dominate the social significance of a monument. Even though recent theoretical arguments advocate multiple interpretations of the past, a position from which this situation may seem desirable, it can be argued that archaeologists have a duty to serve the public with the facts and argue vehemently against misinterpretations of the evidence. But is this really possible?

Our case-study is the Externsteine in north-west Germany (Figure 11.1). In the following we will discuss some of the main interpretations of this assemblage of rocks over the past hundred years and briefly outline how different groups of people understand this natural and cultural monument in the present.

The Externsteine is a unique and very bizarre natural sandstone formation near the little town Horn, Kreis Lippe in north-west Germany. Since the sixteenth century this part of Germany has been called the 'Teutoburger Wald' after Tacitus' 'saltus teutoburgienisbus'. Because of its various prehistoric monuments, and the construction of the Arminius-Monument (1875), this region has been seen as the 'cradle of Germania' since the nineteenth century. Here researchers, teachers, priests and officers looked for the battlefield of the war between Romans and Germans in 9 BC. Today there are some 800 dots on maps indicating where the battle should have been. There is a high statistical agreement between the locations of the battlefield and the home towns of the different researchers. In this region also one of the first open-air archaeological museums was founded, in Oerlinghausen in 1936 (Griepentrog 1998: 387–399; Schmidt 1998; Ströbel 1936).

Today at the Externsteine you can see four so-called 'columns'. The first column (column I) contains a cave which was used as a hermitage

Figure 11.1 The Externsteine in the year 1948

in the Middle Ages and served in the sixteenth century as a prison for the town of Horn. On the outside of column I is a famous carving, showing how Jesus was lifted from the cross. Several dates have been proposed for the formation of the carving: the early ninth century (Matthes 1982; Matthes and Speckner 1997); the early twelfth century (Fuchs 1934); approximately the year 1250 (Großmann 1993: 157). Some people and groups see one part of the carving as a picture of the Irminsul, the most important sanctuary of the pagan Saxons. In front of column I, on the north-east side, is a smaller stone called *Felsengrab* (rock tomb), which contains a body-shaped so-called arcosol-grave. Column II is called *Turmfelsen* (tower rock). High above the ground is an open room inside the column, with a round window in the eastern wall. Many researchers believe this window was built by prehistoric people to observe the midsummer sunrise on 21 June (Teudt 1926). Others date the room and the window to the twelfth century. One can visit the room only by crossing a 150-year-old bridge between column III and column II. On column III there is only a seventeenth-century rock-carved staircase used to reach the iron bridge. Column IV is separated by a gap from the other columns. This column is the *Wackelstein,* so-called because there is a balancing stone on top of the column. The only way to reach the top of column IV is by climbing. The gap between columns III and IV allows the passage of a major road, built in 1836; before that the main road passed the stones beside column I. The picturesque lake beside the stones was also constructed in 1836. From the beginning of the twentieth century until the 1950s a trolley track passed between columns III and IV.

THE HISTORY OF RESEARCH AT THE EXTERNSTEINE

The record of historical and archaeological research on the stones begins in the sixteenth century. At first the site was interpreted as a prehistoric sanctuary. From this time discussion about such a use has not ceased. The first climax in the research was in the nineteenth century, when, due to public discussion, two excavations took place, in 1881 and 1888 (Halle 1997). The first excavation attempted to find the battlefield of the *clades Variana* as mentioned by Tacitus. This excavation was financed and directed by Gustav Schierenberg, the former mayor of Horn. He did a very good job for that time. Schierenberg discovered the foundations of a small hunting lodge, erected in 1660, that had started to fall to ruins after only three years of use. Schierenberg also found that some layers were 'modern' fill. The small finds were only partly preserved in the Lippisches Landesmuseum at Detmold. The 'pagan' pottery fragments (as prehistoric sherds were called in those days) were interpreted as not belonging to the stones because they could have been introduced with fill brought in during the nineteenth century.

The object of the second excavation, in 1888, was to prove that the Externsteine had been a Christian pilgrimage centre. This excavation was conducted by the head of the Paderborner Altertumsverein, Mr Mertens. Paderborn is the seat of the Catholic archbishop, so religious questions were the main interest.

In 1926 the former evangelical parson Wilhelm Teudt and his fellows, the Society of Friends of German Prehistory, claimed to have identified the Externsteine as an astronomical site of the 'old Germans'. In a letter to the Historical Society of Lippe and to the government of Lippe Teudt wrote, 'Now we have the German Stonehenge!' (Schockenhoff 1990: 113). Teudt contacted Gustaf Kossinna and Carl Schuchhard, the two most eminent archaeologists of the time. Kossinna was the editor of the journal *Mannus*, and Schuchhard of *Prähistorische Zeitschrift*, and the two did not like each other. Only Kossinna gave Teudt the opportunity to publish a report, in *Mannus* (Teudt 1926). Because of Teudt's activities the government of Lippe decided to undertake an excavation at the Externsteine in 1932. This excavation was directed by August Stieren, famous for his research on Roman Haltern. Stieren's excavation brought no new results. After 1933 Teudt gained considerable influence with the National Socialist leaders, without being a member of the party himself. He planned a new excavation of the site, the main aims of which were to prove:

1   The astronomical significance of the site.
2   The destruction of the site by Charlemagne in 772, during the *Sachsenkriege*. Teudt's interpretation of the rock as the Irminsul made him think that this was the location of the holy tree of the world, the most eminent Saxon/Germanic idol, which was destroyed by Charlemagne.

The excavation began in 1934 under the supervision of Julius Andree, professor of geology from Münster (Trier 1997: 23) (Figure 11.2). Despite National Socialist organisation and *Gleichschaltung* (bringing into line) of German archaeology, only local government officials took any interest in the excavations. The *Reichsbund für deutsche Vorgeschichte im Amt Rosenberg*, which should have overseen the project, took no notice.

Public interest in the discussion, interpretation and excavation was immense. On Whitsuntide 1934, a short time after the beginning of the excavation, 34,000 people visited the site (Franssen 1934: 1).

After the first excavations in 1934 Teudt feared that, for complex political reasons, some other researchers would control Andree's results, so he went to Heinrich Himmler (Halle 1998). Teudt's influence at the time was such that from 1935 control over the excavations, and indeed over the Externsteine itself, was seized by Himmler's SS. In April 1935, as the *Reichsbund* began to lose control over the excavations at the Externsteine, it made an effort to regain some authority by building

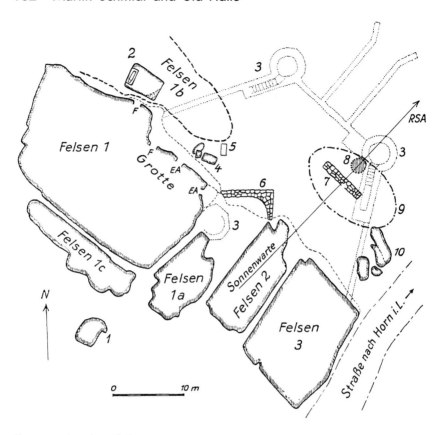

Figure 11.2 Plan of the excavation in 1934–1935

open-air archaeological museums, such as the *Germanengehöft* in Oerlinghausen mentioned previously, which is only 20 km away from the Externsteine.

Teudt and his fellows were not concerned about state censorship. Although Himmler had prohibited it, Andree published the 'results' of both excavations. He wrote that he had found pottery from the period before AD 772. In front of the rock carving Andree found two large stones, one on top of the other. These stones were reconstructed by Andree as a 'Germanic stone table' (Figure 11.3) with two supporting stones and a table-plate. To some people this looks like an altar or a small megalithic grave (Focke 1943: 31–33). Andree claimed that this stone table was destroyed by Charlemagne in AD 772. Andree also thought that he had found the original location of the Irminsul on the top of column II. However a copperplate from 1662 portrays a large balancing stone on top of the column. This balancing stone must have fallen down shortly after the copperplate was created.

Figure 11.3   The 'Germanic stone table' during the excavation, 1934

With the date 772 and with his cultic interpretations Andree provided 'scientific evidence' for Teudt's theory: the stones formed a prehistoric sanctuary with astronomic cultic function, destroyed by Charlemagne (Andree 1936). But the details of the excavation and finds were never published by Andree. What was really found there? Sixty years after the excavations, Uta Halle evaluated the ceramics and other finds for the first time. The material evidence includes:

1   Some late Palaeolithic artefacts (Ahrensburger culture).
2   Medieval pottery from the tenth to fourteenth century.
3   Pottery from the seventeenth to the nineteenth century.
4   Some iron artefacts from the twelfth to the seventeenth century.

There was not a single find of anything that could be called 'Germanic' or dated to later pre-Christian times. Before Halle's evaluation nobody knew what really had been found during the excavations in 1934/5. The cultic interpretations of Teudt and Andree have been widely accepted and embellished during the past sixty years. The result is that today there are at least ten main theories, with many different variations, communicated in more than a thousand publications, to explain the Externsteine:

- a sanctuary of late Palaeolithic nomadic reindeer hunters (Michell 1977: 58);
- a megalithic meditation centre of the Neolithic (Neumann-Gundrum 1981; Niedhorn 1993);
- a Celtic cave sanctuary of about 700 BC (Schlosser and Cierny 1996);
- the location of the battlefield of the *clades Variana* (Schierenberg 1882);
- a Germanic sanctuary with astronomic function (Teudt 1929) (Figure 11.4);
- the Saxon sanctuary with the Irminsul, destroyed by Charlemagne in 772 (Teudt 1929; Andree 1936);
- the location of the Hethis monastery in the ninth century (Matthes 1982; Matthes and Speckner 1997);
- a tenth-century nobleman's fortified palace (Gaul 1955; Meiners 1791: 160);
- a Christian pilgrimage centre with imitations of the holy grave of Jerusalem in the eleventh century (Focke 1943; Fuchs 1934);
- a hermitage of the late Middle Ages (Mundhenk 1980–83).

FROM 1945 TO THE PRESENT

A brief account will show how the Externsteine has been used by different groups since the Second World War.

Ordinary tourism

The Externsteine has been developed for tourists for nearly 200 years. Today, during the summer, daily, up to 50,000 visitors spend anything from one hour to an entire day at the Externsteine. There is a large carpark, for both cars and buses, a restaurant, a fast-food outlet, and a small souvenir shop. Both individual tourists and coach parties visit the site. Classes from schools in the region and abroad make trips to the Externsteine, usually combined with a visit to the huge *Hermannsdenkmal*, the memorial to Arminius, which was erected in 1875. Other tourists are groups staying for a few days in the youth hostel in Horn and guests from the rehabilitation hospitals in Bad Meinberg or the hotels and guest houses in Holzhausen, a little village nearby. The Externsteine is a classic tourist site everybody 'must' visit, and it is extensively advertised in travel

Figure 11.4 An idea for the reconstruction of the 'Germanic sanctuary', and the reality of the reconstruction in 1939

guides and brochures. Most people want to climb to the top of columns I and II to view the region and the bizarre stone setting. Most of them have little interest in the history of the site.

Neo-pagans

At the winter solstice in 1935 the National Socialist party (NSDAP) held a great celebration, with fire and music, at the Externsteine. Solstice fires were traditions among *völkisch* groups, and were adopted by the NSDAP for their own propaganda purposes during the 1930s. During the war these celebrations stopped, but they were revived on a small scale in the 1970s. The big boom in these fire celebrations began in the 1980s. In 1988, G. Graichen published her *Kultplatzbuch* ('Book of Cult Places'). This book was very successful, and has had several new editions since 1988. It was accompanied by a two-part television programme. The first 45-minute programme, on a Sunday at prime time, had an audience of about 4.95 million households (15 per cent), and the second on a weekday after 10 pm reached 2.22 million households (7 per cent). Undoubtedly the book and TV programmes increased public interest, especially for members of esoteric and other fringe groups. The book was published at a time when there was a great boom in New Age ideas. There are some critical words hidden in her book, but generally Graichen's descriptions allow people to find whatever they would like to find at these places.

The archaeological community has mixed views on Graichen's work. She has good connections to important and influential archaeologists, but the archaeology in her reports is often very close to treasure hunting. As bad as some of her work may seem, many archaeologists appreciate that her successful TV reports and books on archaeological themes contribute a great deal towards the acceptance of archaeology by the public.

One chapter of Graichen's book describes the Externsteine (Graichen 1991: 261–263). After its publication the number of visitors at the summer solstice increased from a few dozen to nearly 2,000 in 1997. These visitors have few political interests and just want to spend a nice evening drumming, drinking, smoking joints and playing on their Australian didgeridoos that are very *en vogue* these days in Germany. Most of these visitors are seeking a 'Woodstock' kind of experience (Burghoff 1990).

Neo-Nazi groups

The Externsteine is also a very important place for all kinds of neo-Nazis. One example is the Armanen-Orden which, on 1 November at the rocks, holds its annual celebration of the Autumn Thing, a gathering imitating the old Germanic public meetings at which laws were dispersed, disputes settled and public affairs conducted (Monrath-Hold 1994). The

Armanen-Orden seems to be a religious group with a hidden political agenda (von Schnurbein 1993: 25). One of the most important members is Meinolf Schönborn, who was the leader of the now forbidden Nationalist Front (NF), although other NF leaders have also had contacts with the Armanen-Orden (Asta Antifa Referat: 22).

The Externsteine is also a meeting place for Gylfiliten, a 'German pagan group for which Adolf Hitler was a Germanic god' (Asta Antifa Referat: 25). Like the Armanen-Orden, the Gylfiliten have personal connections with the Nationalist Front (ibid.).

Officials generally do next to nothing against the meeting of these right-wing or neo-Nazi groups. It is obvious that the police regularly observe left-wing or communist groups, but pay less attention to right-wing groups.

Other esoteric groups

Esoterics cannot always be divided from neo-pagan or neo-Nazi groups because sometimes the esoteric groups have the same interests in cultic behaviour. However, there are some groups without overt political interest: for example, women's groups meet at the Externsteine once a month during the high moon to celebrate their menstruation and to demonstrate the influence of the moon on female bodies. Other groups feel the leylines and the energy from the stones at the Externsteine. You can join seminars or travelling groups who visit the Externsteine to feel the energy on the rocks. According to these groups, if you lean your back on the stone you can feel the vibrations and the power and fill yourself up with the energy you will need for the next phase of your life. These seminars or magic journeys are very 'cheap', about DM200–300 for a few hours. There is a great market for these esoteric groups in Germany today. Offers for such seminars are found not only in esoteric journals, but also over the Internet. For example, the *Arbeitskreis Geobiologie Ostwestfalen* (www.fakt.com/argo/index.html) offers seminars and books on 'energy and light centers like Stonehenge or the Externsteine that can open the door to deep secrets of the human psyche'. A second example of esoterics' use of the Internet in connection with the Externsteine is the project 'Vision'. The inventor of the project wanted to use the energy of many human thoughts to form a crop circle near the Externsteine (www.fgk.org/vision.html).

Pseudo-scientific groups

There are many pseudo-scientific groups working at the Externsteine that use or misuse modern dating methods like thermoluminescence (TL) dating to prove their ideas. The core group of these researchers consists of about a dozen, mostly elderly people who have worked continuously for many years. Sometimes the leaders or members of the groups are also members of neo-Nazi groups. For example, the 'Walter-Machalett-Arbeitskreis for the prehistory of the Externsteine' held its twenty-ninth annual meeting at the Externsteine in 1995 (Rückschau 95 1995). Walter Machalett, the founder of this group who died in 1983, was a member of the Armanen-Orden and was involved in the *Guido von List-Gesellschaft* (Goodrick-Clarke 1985; von Schnurbein 1993: 55). Other 'researchers' take this misuse of the Externsteine worldwide. Jacques de Mahieu, for example, believed he had found another Externsteine in Brasilia, where, he argues, it was formed as a sanctuary by Vikings from Haithabu, who visited the Externsteine at Horn before starting their journey across the Atlantic to Brazil (Mahieu 1975: 139). This book uses the Externsteine to make arguments about racial theories and apply them worldwide.

Some people believe also that the rocks are human constructions, and that they contain amazing mummies. This interpretation has been spread by the tabloids under the title 'Magic Places' (Fiebag 1996).

The work of the serious researcher Wolfram Schlosser is difficult to comment upon. Schlosser ordered three samples of the burning visible on the ceiling of the cave in column I to be taken for thermoluminescence dating. The samples date to between 1,000 and 0 BC. However, older inhabitants of Horn and Holzhausen remembered that in the 1950s parties and bonfires were often held in the cave.

In lectures Schlosser and some of his fellows claim that this TL date of about 700 BC is scientific proof of the cave of the Externsteine being used as a Celtic sanctuary for burning the dead. Among some groups in the 1990s, Germans are replaced by Celts as the focus of esoteric beliefs (cf. Dietler 1994). While we were writing this chapter, a new 'professional meeting' in Horn with a visit to the Externsteine was announced. The theme of this meeting is 'Mystery of the Externsteine', and speakers include W. Schlosser and U. Niedhorn. The title of one typical report is 'Siegfrid and Beowulf, two dragon-killers at the Externsteine' (*Lippische Landeszeitung* 1997).

Among these pseudo-scientific groups is also 'EFODON', the European Society for Prehistoric Technology and Marginal Lines of Science. In 1992, during their meeting in Horn, a member of the group found a rock carving on one of the lesser-known rocks (Riemer 1992; Tiggelkamp 1992) (Figure 11. 5). The carving shows the Externsteine with a number of runes, which seem to have been carved shortly after 1930, following a book from R.J. Gorsleben (1930; personal communication, A. Pesch, Paderborn). The 'EFODON Specialists' translated the runes as a Germanic form of the Christian Lord's Prayer. And because of this, the EFODON members believe that Jesus visited the Externsteine and that he learned the Lord's Prayer there. This also proves for EFODON that Christianity is an 'Aryan' religion. But these are questions – so EFODON say – that normal historians would never ask (Riemer 1992: 18).

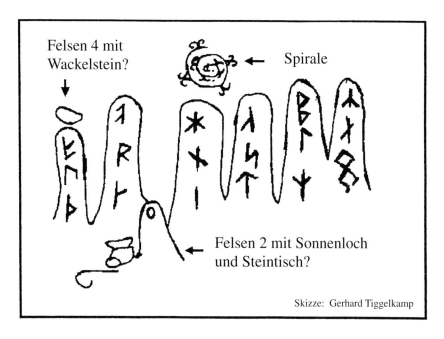

Figure 11.5   Drawing of the rock-carving with the runes and the original from 1930

In their interpretations of the Externsteine, many pseudo-scientific groups refer to supposedly ancient oral traditions which they assume have been transmitted in unbroken continuity since prehistory. Studies of oral traditions generally show, however, that their content is much more recent and does not reflect prehistoric conditions (Seidenspinner 1993). Similarly, the relief of Jesus' descent from the cross is taken in scientific discussions as an indication that Christians preferred prehistoric sacred sites as locations for their sanctuaries. But continuity cannot be assumed in this respect either.

For a long time the different groups mentioned above did not work together. But this is changing. For example, on the mailing lists of the pseudo-scientists one can find some of the most important neo-Nazi groups, neo-Nazi publishers and other groups with political and esoteric interests. Information from the anti-fascist groups couldn't say whether these people and groups accept the invitations or not. In the past few years neo-Nazis have made intensive attempts to infiltrate the esoteric and neo-pagan scenes. They have been very successful; today one can hear such comments as 'Get foreigners out of the Externsteine, because they are disrupting the ley lines'. That is nearly the same as in 1935, when Himmler forbade visits to the Externsteine by Jewish people, because they did not have the 'right feeling for a Germanic sanctuary' (Halle: in preparation).

Reasons for the current situation at the Externsteine are:

1   There is an almost 400-year-old tradition that the rock formation was a prehistoric sanctuary.
2   Between 1933 and 1945 most archaeologists supported the political system, either to benefit their own careers or from real belief. Accordingly the interpretations of Wilhelm Teudt were influential. But the actual situation at the Externsteine, even at the beginning of the Third Reich, was not very oppressive, because Hitler had a preference for ancient Greek and classical archaeology. In Hitler's mind the *Germanentümelei* were insignificant and embarrassing. Himmler and Rosenberg thought positively about *Germanentümelei* but they clashed with each other. Critical scholars, like the geologist and archaeologist Fritz Wiegers, a member of the NSDAP (the German Nazi party), were afraid to publish their critical remarks about the excavation at the Externsteine. After a meeting where the results of the excavation were discussed by archaeologists, but under the supervision of high SS officers, Wiegers wrote a letter to Karl-Hermann Jacob-Friesen noting that, 'If I had given my honest opinion about the excavations, I would have lost my job that very evening or something worse would have happened.' With these words Wiegers hints at his fear of being imprisoned in a concentration camp. Wiegers also wrote, 'from now on the Externsteine will be Germanic!' (Halle: in preparation).
3   After 1945 researchers excused their behaviour during the NS dictatorship as the result of their fear during this time. But none of the scholars who had taken notice of the false excavation results would touch the question of the Externsteine again. Therefore the NS interpretation of the place, forced by Wilhelm Teudt, survived and could spread.

Up to 1997 more than a thousand books, brochures, articles, videos and CD-ROMs, have been published by crackpots, old and new Nazis, pagans, esoterics, etc. They are mostly built on Teudt's interpretation of seventy years ago, without consideration of its ideological content. There are many activities around or at the Externsteine, most of which draw no attention from officials and some of which even have the consent of the keepers, who are mainly interested in tourist numbers and sometimes are somewhat resigned, because everybody believes whatever he or she wants. So, for example, esoteric groups get the key for the cave in column I, although, in the interests of preservation, visits to the cave are normally forbidden. With institutional permission, the groups are very sure that officials will not protest.

One example from 1996 clearly demonstrates official reaction. In late November of that year unknown people erected the rudal rune on the top of one of the rocks (Klute 1996). This rune is one symbol of the forbidden 'Viking Youth' (*Wiking-Jugend*). The officials didn't respond very strongly. They only gave the order to remove the rune, without informing the police about the incident. This behaviour reveals the officals' desire to avoid negative press, in order not to jeopardise the future volume of tourist traffic to the site. However, the Police Union in its February 1997 issue of *Deutsche Polizei* published a long article dealing with the Externsteine, neo-pagans and esoterics, and how they are infiltrated by different right-wing and/or neo-Nazi groups.

CONCLUSION

At the end of our brief survey of the activities around the Externsteine we reach the conclusion that everybody creates his or her own story about the site. For these stories, the results of archaeology are not normally very important and perhaps without any significance whatsoever. It has been argued that archaeologists have a great responsibility to serve the public with the provision of the facts and to argue against certain misinterpretations of the evidence. But how realistic is it to hope that archaeologists can really make a difference and educate the rest of society about the results of their work?

The natural and cultural monument Externsteine is one of those archaeological-historical objects whose ideational or emotional value is more important than their actual historical value. Such monuments are not appreciated purely for their academic significance but receive their social meaning from the way they are perceived by different members of society. This assemblage of rocks, like Stonehenge, belongs to the group of monuments whose actual archaeological-historical significance cannot easily be conveyed to a larger public. As the discussion of the various activities at the Externsteine has shown, alternative perceptions are much easier to convey and to market. They provide compelling explanations that draw on people's desires for mystery, identity and connection to unseen power, and are far more fascinating than the sometime very dull and pragmatic result of the scientists.

REFERENCES

Andree, J. (1934–1935) 'Zu den Grabungen und Untersuchungen an den Externsteinen bei Horn i.L.' *Aus der Vorzeit* 2(H3/4): 25–29.

Andree, J. (1936) *Die Externsteine. Eine germanische Kultstätte.* Münster: Verlag der Universitätsbuchhandlung, Franz Coppenrath.

Asta Antifa Referat (Hrsg.) (n.d.) *Von Karma bis Lebensschutz. Über Ökofaschismus, New Age und Heidentum.* Gütersloh: O.J. Selbstverlag Bielefeld.

Arnold, B. (1990) The past as propaganda: totalitarian archaeology in Nazi Germany. *Antiquity* 64: 464–478.

Arnold, B. (1992) 'The past as propaganda: how Hitler's archaeologists distorted European prehistory to justify racist and territorial goals.' *Archaeology* 45(4): 30–37.

Arnold, B. and Hassmann, H. (1995) 'Archaeology in Nazi Germany: the legacy of the Faustian bargain.' In Philip L. Kohl and Clare Fawcett (eds) *Nationalism, Politics, and the Pratice of Archaeology*, pp. 70–81. Cambridge: Cambridge University Press.

Bertram, M. (1991) 'Zur Situation der deutschen Ur- und Frühgeschichtsforschung während der Zeit der faschistischen Diktatur.' *Forschungen und Berichte* 31: 23–42.

Bollmus, R. (1970) *Das Amt Rosenberg und seine Gegner. Studien zum Machtkampf im nationalsozialistischen Herrschaftssystem.* Stuttgart: Deutsche Verlags-Anstalt.

Bollmus, R. (1989) 'Alfred Rosenberg – "Chefideologe" des Nationalsozialismus?' In Ronald Schmelser and Rainer Zitelman (eds) *Die braune Elite: 22 biographische Skizzen*, pp. 223–235. Darmstadt: Wissenschaftliche Buchgesellschaft.

Burghoff, C. (1990) 'Voodoo im Teutoburger Wald. Sonnenwendfeier an den Externsteinen: Nationalsozialistische Mystik als Bodensatz kultischer Treffen.' *Die Tageszeitung* 22 December: 17.

Deutsche Polizei (1997) 'Neuheidnische Gruppen zwischen Esoterik und Rechtsexremismus. Alte Kameraden und junge Heiden vereinigen sich.' *Deutsche Polizei* 2: 13.

Dietler, M. (1994) ' "Our Ancestors the Gauls": archaeology, ethnic nationalism, and the manipulation of Celtic identity in modern Europe.' *American Anthropologist* 96(3): 584–605.

Dorow, W. (1823) *Die Denkmale germanischer und römischer Zeit in den rheinisch-westphälischen Provinzen.* Stuttgart: Untersucht und Dargestellt.

Fiebag, J. (1996) 'Magische Orte 3. Folge: Wunderbare Kräfte aus dem Götterfelsen.' *Das Goldene Blatt* 48, 20 November: S23.

Focke, F. (1943) *Beiträge zur Geschichte der Externsteine.* Berlin and Stuttgart: W. Kohlhamer Verlag.

Franssen, Arendt (Franz Breitholz) (1934) 'Grundsätzliches zur Frage der Externsteine. Die neuesten Untersuchungen und Entdeckungen am Turmfelsen.' *Germanien* 8: 1–15.

Fuchs, A. (1934) *Im Streit um die Externsteine. Ihre Bedeutung als christliche Kultstätte.* Paderborn: Verlag der Bonifatius-Druckerei.

Gaul, O. (1955) 'Neue Forschungen zum Problem der Externsteine.' *Westfalen* 32: 141–164.

Goodrick-Clarke, N. (1985) *The Occult Roots of Nazism. Secret Aryan Cults and their Influence on Nazi Archaeology.* London and New York: Tauris & Co.

Gorsleben, R.J. (1930) *Hoch-Zeit der Menschheit*. Leipzig: Koehler und Amelang Verlag.

Graichen, G. (1991) *Das Kultplatzbuch*. Third edition. Munich: Knaur.

Griepentrog, M. (1998) *Kulturhistorische Museen in Westfalen (1900–1945). Geschichtsbilder, Kulturströmungen, Bildungskonzepte*. Paderborn: Ferdinand Schöningh.

Großmann, U. (1993) 'Kunstgeschichte.' In Wilhelm W. Rinne (ed.) *Landeskunde Nordrhein-Westfalen Lippe*, pp. 157–232. Paderborn: Ferdinand Schöningh.

Halle, U. (1997) 'Im Spiegel archäologischer Quellen: Das Mittelalter und die frühe Neuzeit.' In J. Buchner (ed.) *Stadtgeschichte Horn 1248–1998*, pp. 32–61. Horn-Bad Meinberg: Hütte-Verlag.

Halle, U. (1998) 'Detmold und die deutsche Vorgeschichtsforschung.' In H. Niebuhr and A. Ruppert (eds) *Nationalsozialismus in Detmold. Dokumentation eines stadtgeschichtlichen Projekts*, pp. 528–555. Bielefeld: Aisthesis Verlag.

Halle, U. (in preparation) 'Die Externsteine sind bis auf weiteresgermanisch!' – eine dokumentarische Studie zur prähistorischen Archäologie in spannungsfeld Völkisch-nationalsozialistischer Ideologie und Propaganda. Manuskript.

Haßmann, H. (forthcoming) 'Prähistorische Archäologie im "Dritten Reich".' German manuscript of the English essay 'Prehistoric Archaeology and the "Third Reich"'. In H. Härke (ed.) *Archaeology, Ideology and Society: The German Experience*. Cambridge: Cambridge University Press.

Hinter Schloß und Riegel. Burgen und Befestigungen in Westfalen (1997). Edited by Landschaftsverband Westfalen-Lippe. Münster: Aschendorff-Verlag.

Hohenschwert, F. (1985) 'Externsteine bei Horn.' *Führer zu archäologischen Denkmälern in Deutschland* 11: 220–230.

Hohenschwert, F. (1991–1995) 'Externsteine.' *Reallexikon der Germanischen Altertumskunde* 8: 37–49.

Kater, M. (1974) *Das 'Ahnenerbe' der SS. 1935–1945. Ein Beitrag zur Kulturpolitik des Dritten Reiches*. Stuttgart: Deutsche Verlags-Anstalt.

Kittel, E. (1969) *Die Externsteine. Ein kritischer Bericht zu ihrer Forschung und Deutung*. Sonderveröffentlichungen des Naturwissenschaftlichen und Historischen Vereins für das Land Lippe 18. Detmold.

Klute, O. (1996) 'Bericht über rechtsradikale Aktionen an den Externsteinen.' *Horner Stadtanzeiger* 27 November.

Lippische Landeszeitung (1994) '2500 Jahre alte Feuerspuren. Geschichte der Externsteine reicht weiter zurück als angenommen.' 31 August.

Lippische Landeszeitung (1997) 'Fachtagung über "Geheimnis Externsteine".' 12 September.

Mahieu, J. de (1975) *Des Sonnengottes heilige Steine. Die Wikinger in Brasilien*. Tübingen: Grabert-Verlag.

Matthes, W. (1982) *Corvey und die Externsteine. Schicksal eines vorchristlichen Heiligtums in karolingischer Zeit*. Stuttgart: Urachhaus.

Matthes, W. and Speckner, R. (1997) *Das Relief an den Externsteinen. Ein karolingisches Kunstwerk und sein spiritueller Hintergrund*. Ostfildern: Ed. Tertium.

McCann, W.J. (1990) ' "Volk und Germanentum": the presentation of the past in Nazi Germany.' In P. Gathercole and D. Lowenthal (eds) *The Politics of the Past*, pp. 74–88. London: Unwin Hyman.

Meiners, C. (1791) *Kleine Länder und Reisebeschreibung*. Berlin: Spener-Verlag.

Michell, J. (1977) *A Little History of Astro-Archaeology*. London: Thames and Hudson.

Monrath-Hold, M. (1994) 'Brauner Kult um ein lippisches Naturdenkmal.' *Lippische Landeszeitung* 3 November.

Mosse, G.L. (1991) *Die völkische Revolution. Über die geistigen Wurzeln des Nationalsozialismus.* Frankfurt am Main: Anton Hain Verlag.

Mundhenk, J. (1980–1983) *Forschungen zur Geschichte der Externsteine*, 4 vols. Lippische Studien vol. 5–8. Lemgo: F.L. Wagener.

Neumann-Gundrum, E. (1981) *Europas Kultur der Groß-Skulpturen. Urbilder/ Urwissen einer europäischen Geistesstruktur.* Gießen: Schmitz-Verlag.

Niedhorn, U. (1993) *Vorgeschichtliche Anlagen an den Externstein-Felsen.* Isernhägener Studien zur Frühen Skulptur 5. Frankfurt am Main: Haag und Herchen.

Obmann, J. and Wirtz, D. (1994) 'Orte der Kraft? Bodendenkmale im Spannungsfeld zwischen Archäologie und Esoterik.' *Kölner Jahrbuch* 27: 565–594.

Riemer, T. (1992) 'Vorläufige Lesung der Runen an Fels 11 der Externsteine.' *EFODON News* 2: 14–18.

Rückschau 95 (1995) 'Zur 29ten Arbeitstagung des Arbeits – und Forschungskreis Walther Machalett in Horn-Bad Meinberg 1995.'

Schierenberg, A. (1882) 'Ausgrabungen an den Externsteinen.' *Lippische Landeszeitung* 25 and 26 February.

Schlosser, W. and Cierny, J. (1996) *Sterne und Steine Eine praktische Astronomie der Vorzeit.* Darmstadt: Wissenschaftliche Buchgesellschaft.

Schmidt, M. (1998) 'Reconstruction as ideology.' In P. Stone and P. Planel (eds) *Title*, London: Routledge.

Schockenhoff, V. (1990) ' "Stonehenge" contra "Störrische Kuh". Die Externsteine im Spannungsfeld der NS-Germanenkunde.' In *Wir zeigen Profil. Aus den Sammlungen des Staatsarchivs Detmold* (Ausstellungskatalog), pp. 97–115. Detmold: Selbstverlag des Staatsarchivs.

Seidenspinner, W. (1993) 'Archäologie, Volksüberlieferung, Denkmalideologie. Anmerkungen zum Denkmalverständnis der Öffentlichkeit in Vergangenheit und Gegenwart.' *Fundberichte aus Baden-Württemberg* 18: 1–15.

Smolla, G. (1991) 'Archäologie und Nationalbewußtsein.' *Zwischen Walhall und Paradies*, pp. 11–15. Berlin: DHM.

Springhorn, R. (1989) 'Geologische Grundlagen der Externsteine-Gruppe.' In D. Kestermann (ed.) *Berichte der ersten Horner Fachtagung*, pp. 1–8. Dortmund.

Ströbel, R. (1936) 'Ein germanischer Hof um die Zeitenwende. Wiedererstellt in Oerlinghausen im Teutoburger Wald.' *Germanen-Erbe* 1: 50–53.

Teudt, W. (1926) 'Altgermanischer Gestirndienst. I Das Zerstörungswerk an den Externsteinen.' *Mannus* 18: 349–357. Reprinted in *Volksblatt* 7(188) (14 August 1926); *Lippische Landeszeitung* 160(190) (15 September 1926); *Lippische Tageszeitung* 31(190) (15 September 1926).

Teudt, W. (1929) *Germanische Heiligtümer. Beiträge zur Aufdeckung der Vorgeschichte, ausgehend von den Externsteinen, den Lippe-Quellen und der Teutoburg.* Jena: Diedrichs-Verlag.

Tiggelkamp, G. (1992) 'Runeninschrift an den Externsteinen.' *EFODON News* 2: 13–14.

Trier, B. (1997) 'Zur Geschichte der Altertumskommission für Westfalen.' In *Hinter Schloß und Riegel. Burgen und Befestigungen in Westfalen*, edited by Landschaftsverband Westfalen-Lippe. pp. 11–31. Westfälisches Museum für Archäologie. Münster.

von Schnurbein, S. (1993) *Göttertrost in Wendezeiten. Neugermanisches Heidentum zwischen New Age und Rechtsradikalismus.* Munich: Claudius-Verlag.

CHAPTER TWELVE

THE CONTINUING REINVENTION OF THE ETRUSCAN MYTH

DIURA THODEN VAN VELZEN

ABSTRACT

The Etruscans provide a powerful source of inspiration to the popular imagination. Present-day Tuscans claim to have Etruscan eyes or fingers, or to speak with Etruscan accents. Tomb robbers even assert that they communicate with their forebears. This article opens a new perspective on such modern Etruscan myths by undertaking a historical investigation. The results show that these tales are by no means merely a commercial modern invention, but are rooted in long-standing traditions in the area and often inspired by academic findings. Some modern Etruscan myths find their origins in Renaissance concepts, passed on in a local oral tradition. Although not always recognisibly so, academic findings, including those from the archaeological discipline, have often shaped popular beliefs. Whereas academic interpretations were modified, popular perceptions formed an independent, unchanging tradition; they became 'archaeo-folklore'.

INTRODUCTION

Etruscan civilisation faces a surge of popularity. In the former Etruscan area (modern Tuscany and northern Lazio) 'Etruscan' hotels, bars and restaurants have mushroomed and Etruscan merchandise fills the streets. Many inhabitants of the area are convinced of the crucial importance of their past. Disregarding scientific historical findings, they assert that the Etruscans laid the cultural foundations for modern central Italy, and that the Romans and the Roman Catholic Church had very little impact on the region. Numerous Roman practices, it is thought, such as religious customs and the use of the chariot, were originally Etruscan. The Etruscan influence is also claimed to be apparent, for example, in the

Figure 12.1 Sovana's baker inspects Etruscan-inspired paintings

iconography of the Roman Catholic devil and angel, which is modelled on Etruscan Charun and Lasa figures, depicted in wall paintings.

Many emphasise the similarities between themselves and the Etruscans. It is said, for example, that the aspirate used in the pronunciation of Italian in the Florence area is directly derived from the Etruscan language. Some people believe themselves to be physically related to the Etruscans and claim to possess Etruscan eyes and fingers. Others see their lives affected in other ways by their illustrious ancestors. A potter selling souvenir fake vases on the market of Tarquinia, for example, assumes his artistic talent was a gift from the Etruscans.

Tomb robbers claim the most direct bond with their ancestors. A number of tomb robbers' biographies have appeared in print, and in them it is asserted that the Etruscans inspired them to take up looting and have guided them in their illegal expeditions through dreams, intuitions and apparitions (Thoden van Velzen 1996).

Although the Etruscans seem firmly embedded in contemporary Tuscan and Lazian identity, some feel that the Etruscans continue to be appropriated by the wealthy and the educated. An artist, trained in Rome, is now working in his native Sovana, to 'return the past to the people', as he puts it. The inhabitants of this sleepy town are given the privilege of visiting his exhibitions free of charge, while he makes a living from selling Etruscan inspired paintings to tourists.

The appeal of this ancient culture is felt beyond the villages of the Etruscan heartland. Just outside Milan the ex-president and television magnate Berlusconi has constructed a mausoleum for himself and his close allies, to whom he refers as his 'gens', i.e. the Roman extended family (Willey 1994). The structure of the chamber closely resembles that of an Etruscan tomb. Carved in the wall are the objects Berlusconi has chosen to take to the afterlife: a fruit bowl, car keys and a mobile phone. This is a gesture of which an Etruscan would approve. One of the deceased in the Tomba dei Rilievi in Cerveteri, for example, had his armour, slippers and dinner plate carved in the space around his funerary bed. Both inside and outside Tuscany and northern Lazio, many who are fascinated with the Etruscans perceive them as a mysterious people, whose origins and language remain unknown. No matter what professional archaeologists do to shatter this illusion, the general public on the whole stick to their belief (Pallottino [1986] 1994).

The revived interest in the Etruscans, or contemporary Etruscan myths, as we could call them, clearly covers a wide range of phenomena. For some the Etruscans merely provide the adventure and excitement of an unknown past. Others feel a more personal bond with the Etruscans, who to them represent the core of a distinct central Italian identity. Tomb robbers particularly emphasise the link with their ancestors, in an attempt to justify an illegal activity. In this chapter I will further investigate the roots of the contemporary Etruscan myths to show that these are often far from modern inventions. The notion of a centrally important Etruscan past was initially invented by a Renaissance elite and has been passed on ever since. Popular perceptions of the Etruscans were influenced by those of the educated, yet often retain outdated notions long abolished by the upper classes. Archaeology, it will be shown, has had a considerable impact on the creation of popular Etruscan myths.

THE DAWN OF THE RENAISSANCE ETRUSCAN REVIVAL

Whereas the texts of Greek and Roman authors guaranteed a continued familiarity with classical antiquity throughout the Middle Ages, a renewed interest in the Etruscans did not surface until the thirteenth century. Initially the reacquaintance came about through Dionysios of Halicarnassus' and Livy's historical accounts of pre-Roman Italy. At the same time an awareness of the physical remains of this culture surfaced. Ristoro d'Arezzo in his 1282 *Libro della composizione del Mondo* describes encounters with Etruscan black and red vases in the Arezzo area (Chastel 1959: 165, 170; Vickers 1986: 156). Remarkably he and interested contemporaries, such as potters and painters, realised that these vases belonged to a different time and place from their own. Some were so impressed with the quality of this pottery that they wondered whether it had been made by human hands. Maybe, they speculated, they had fallen from the sky.

The work of late thirteenth-century artists provides indirect evidence of the growing familiarity with the Etruscan remains. Nicola Pisano, Arnolfo di Cambio and Giotto, for example, seem to have been inspired by Etruscan models (Thomson de Grummond 1986: 21–4). In his fresco 'Justice Enthroned' in the Arena chapel of Padua (*c.* 1300), Giotto painted a landscape strongly reminiscent of those found in Etruscan wall paintings. The movements of his dancers seem to mimic those in the Tomb of the Lionesses and the Tomb of the Jugglers in the Monterozzi cemetery of Tarquinia. Also his Satan and Judas in the Arena chapel closely resemble the Etruscan death deity Charun in the Tomba dell'Orco in Tarquinia.

During the fifteenth century the interest in the Etruscans surged to such an extent that the French art historian Chastel (1959) speaks of an 'Etruscan revival'. The work of the most famous artists of this time, such as Masaccio, Donatello, Pallaiuolo, Leonardo and Alberti, displays Etruscan influence and written sources of the fifteenth and sixteenth centuries testify to an expanding knowledge of Etruscan sites and monuments (Thomson de Grummond 1986: 25–22). It is known, for example, that some sculptors, such as Ghiberti, kept their own collections of antique portraits (Weiss 1969: 180). The architect Leone Battista Alberti in his *Ten Books on Architecture* (*c.* 1472) discusses his visits to ancient sites and cemeteries, which greatly influenced his architectural style. The arches and masonry of the Palazzo Rucellai in Florence, for example, closely resemble those found on some Etruscan urns. The famous art historian and architect Giorgio Vasari dedicated a passage in his *Lives of the Artists* to the many recent discoveries in the Arezzo area, such as the well-known bronze Chimaera statue, found in 1554.

THE POLITICAL DIMENSION

The rediscovery of the Etruscans was of great political significance. At the beginning of the fifteenth century early humanists found in the Etruscan and pre-Imperial Roman political system a model for Florence (Cipriani 1980: 1–13). Both cultures were perceived as republics, like Florence, and free of despotic rulers. Florence had its connections with both Etruria and Rome. Fiesole, a small town just outside Florence, was an old Etruscan settlement, whereas the Roman Republican general Sulla founded the first settlement at Florence. The Etruscans, according to the early humanists' interpretation, lived in autonomous and independent city-states. Their supreme rulers, the *lucumones*, it was thought, did not rule as monarchs but as magistrates, always in consultation with the people. Particularly interesting to the Florentines were the accounts of Livy, according to whom the Etruscans ruled over the seas and land of central Italy before the Romans, and of Dionysios of Halicarnassus, who claims they had indigenous roots. Together these accounts provided the basis for a tradition in which the Etruscans were hailed as a paragon of successful self-government.

Encouraged by the pre-Imperial Roman and Etruscan examples the Florentines found the strength to stand up against the dictators, who at the time rose to power in large parts of central and northern Italy. These so-called *signori* were often descended from aristocratic families and started their careers as military leaders. Through clever negotiating between powerful factions, such as noble and merchant families, they acquired personal power enabling them to overrule communal institutions. One of the most notorious autocracies was that of the Visconti family from Milan. During the late fourteenth century Gian Galeazzo Visconti seized large parts of northern Italy. Powerful cities, such as Genoa, Verona, Bologna and temporarily Siena, came under his control. He reduced the Florentine territory significantly and threatened to occupy the city. His plans may even have included bringing the rest of Italy under his rule, but in 1402 he suddenly died of fever. Florence survived as a republic and continued under oligarchic rule.

The Florentine political scene underwent a dramatic change in 1434, when Cosimo de' Medici came to power (Cipriani 1980: 15–36). The Medici family made a fortune as bankers and established a loyal clientele amongst merchants and industrialists. Gradually they came to dominate the affairs of the city, although officially Florence was still ruled by the executive body called the *signoria*. Cosimo, also called the elder, and his successors were keenly interested in the Etruscans, yet their view of this past differed significantly from that of the early humanists. The Etruscan *lucumones* were no longer portrayed as first citizens within a liberal city-state, but as kings ruling over their rightful territory. Of particular interest at the time was King Porsenna who, according to the literary sources, had led a united Etruscan army in an attempt to restore the Etruscan King Tarquinius Superbus to power in Rome. Throughout the next centuries the Medici family sought recognition as the successors of the *lucumones*.

The Etruscan past held an equal fascination for the citizens of other former Etruscan cities, such as Arezzo and Viterbo. The Dominican friar, Annio da Viterbo, claimed that Viterbo was one of the first places to be inhabited after the Flood. According to his *Commentaria* of 1498, the Etruscans were descendants of Noah, who settled in Italy with the help of Hercules. Viterbo, he asserts, became one of the prime Etruscan settlements. The evidence on which he based his theories was Etruscan inscriptions, which he could barely read, and manuscripts, some of which are now known to be false.

The sixteenth century brought political upheaval to Florence, as foreign powers seized large parts of Italy. After Emperor Charles of Habsburg had removed the French from Milan in 1521, he reinstated Florence as a republic under Allessandro de' Medici. His successor Cosimo I (1537–1574) was determined to restore the city as a strong, independent state ruling over an even larger territory. Clever propaganda was one of his main weapons (Cipriani 1980: 71–112; Vickers 1986: 158–159). Cosimo, as his predecessors had done, turned to the Etruscans. He became a keen collector of antiquities and founded the Florentine academy to promote historical research. Many of the treatises, produced by the academy, were influenced by the work of Annio da Viterbo. In his *Origine di Firenze* (1545) Giambattista Gelli, for example, describes how Hercules and Noah founded the city of Florence. In 1555 Cosimo annexed Siena and Chiusi, which he saw as rightfully his, as they were part of the Etruscan territory. In 1569 Cosimo's newly crafted status was officially recognised when Pope Pius V awarded him the title of Grand Duke of Etruria: *Dux Magnus Etruscus*. The Etruscan myth was now a political reality; Cosimo had become the Etruscan, not the Tuscan Grand Duke. At the time of his inauguration anonymous verses circulated, hailing him as the new Porsenna (Cipriani 1980: 108).

In 1616 one of his successors, Cosimo II, further consolidated the Medici position as rulers of Etruria. He employed Thomas Dempster, at the time professor of law at Pisa, to write the first comprehensive study of Etruscan civilisation. The book entitled *De Etruria Regali* was written between 1616 and 1619, but not published until a century later under the direction of Thomas Coke. Dempster wrote seven books, based on classical sources, humanists and Renaissance authors, on the language, origins, customs and history of the Etruscans. According to Dempster, the Etruscans were the only autochthonous people in central Italy, who had laid the foundations for later civilisations, including the Roman Empire. Following Livy, he named all the institutions that Romans copied from the Etruscans: the use of the toga, chariot, fasces and war trumpet, gladiatorial games and cultivation of vines. On the basis of manuscripts, rather than visits to the countryside, he described the geography of Etruria, which he argued closely resembled that of seventeenth-century Tuscany. Drawing on false documents and spurious linguistic analysis, his next step was to present a genealogical overview showing that the Medici were in fact direct descendants of the Etruscans. According to Dempster the name 'Medici' was directly derived from the Etruscan word for supreme magistrate: *Meddix* (Cristofani 1983: 18–23).

THE ETRUSCANS IN THE ORAL TRADITION OF THE LOWER CLASSES

The Renaissance Etruscan revival, in conclusion, was initially an upper-class affair. The early humanists who discovered the Etruscans in classical literature formed a small elite capable of reading Latin. The well-to-do further promoted the study of the Etruscans by collecting antiquities. On this basis the rulers of Florence defined their identity as the successors of the Etruscan rulers or *lucumones*. Territorial expansion, along the same lines of reasoning, was presented as an attempt to restore the former Etruscan empire. The Etruscan identity, however, as will be shown in the following paragraphs, was as readily welcomed by the lower classes and appropriated to serve their distinct political aims. The widespread acceptance of the Etruscan identity highlights the close cultural integration between different strata in society. Burke in his *Popular Culture of Early Modern Europe* ([1978] 1994) emphasises the need to analyse the cultures of sub-groups in early modern Europe in relation to one another. In his analysis of popular culture Burke builds on the definitions of Redfield ([1956] 1963: 41–42) who speaks of the 'little tradition' of those with very little education, and the 'great tradition', promoted, for example, by schools and religious institutions. Redfield compared the two traditions to currents that occasionally entwine, yet keep their independent course. The little and the great tradition draw from one another, yet exist independently and maintain their own individual course (ibid.: 42–43). A good example Redfield provides is that of the great epics. The courtly epics are often initially based on the oral traditions of the lower classes, yet in their turn influence the tales of lower-class culture. The adoption of elements from another cultural tradition, Redfield stresses, is never a straight copying but a process of adaptation to suit the needs and existing conventions of the receiving group.

This complex process of cultural interaction and mutual dependency is well documented for the case of Italian literary traditions (Burke [1978] 1994: 59–64). Both Italian and foreign sources mention that people in the streets sang stanzas from the poet Tasso and that Dante's work was fully integrated in popular culture between the fourteenth and sixteenth centuries. A verse called the octave was invented in the 1300s probably by Tuscan bench singers and minstrels, and was adopted by court poets as the vehicle for chivalric subjects (Kezich 1986: 35–36). A famous example of an octave poem is *Orlando Furioso* by Ariosto, written for the courts, yet largely inspired by traditional oral epics. At the peak of the popularity of the octave between 1350 and 1500 the printing press was invented, which further contributed to the distribution of these verses and their transmission through the centuries. The farmers of Tuscany and northern Lazio became acquainted with these texts and renditions by travelling bench singers and minstrels. They memorised octave verses and this was the start of a new tradition, which was partly oral, based on memory, and partly literary, based on texts which circulated amongst their communities and were read by some of its semi-literate members. Scarce documentary evidence testifies to the performances of the octave by local farmers, the so-called 'peasant poets' through the centuries. The fascinating research of the anthropologist Giovanni Kezich reveals that this tradition remains alive today. Contemporary peasant poets were found to possess great knowledge of the work of their predecessors in the octave and classical and Renaissance authors, such as Homer's and Virgil's epics, Ovid's *Metamorphoses*, Ariosto's *Orlando Furioso* (1516), Cartari's *Imagine de li Dei degli Antichi* (1647) and Torsellino's *Storia del Mondo* (1606). Copies of these Renaissance books still circulate amongst farmers today.

Giovanni Kezich began his study of the peasant poets in the 1960s, when there was very little interest in this tradition. Peasant poetry was considered of little folkloristic or cultural value and no documentation was kept. Kezich studied the communities of peasant poets at various locations in northern Lazio. He describes how farmers and shepherds during the quiet hours study mythology and chivalric sagas, if they are capable of reading, and compose new verses. Farmer Riccardo Colotti, from Tarquinia, keeps his books, the ones he saved from the hands of his wife, in the stable, where he used to keep his mules (Kezich 1986: 49–50). He possesses torn and thumbed copies of Homer, Virgil, Torsellino's *Storia del Mondo* and Cartari's *Imagine de li Dei degli Antichi*. He wears a woollen cap, from which his long ears stick out, which according to some is a sign of longevity or even Etruscan ancestry. He has led an extremely productive life as a poet and his work *Storia di Tarquinia*, a historical account starting from Etruscan times, has become a classic amongst other poets. Two of his verses have appeared in print at a local publishers. In Tuscania lives the renowned peasant poet Omero Quarantotti who after a divorce withdrew into a cave, a despoiled Etruscan tomb (ibid.: 97). Living by himself he eked a living out of looking after cattle, collecting mushrooms, fishing or plundering Etruscan tombs.

On Sunday afternoons the peasant poets, like Colotti and Quarantotti, come together, for example, in a shed, violated Etruscan tomb or local bar. Anywhere so long as it is far away from their wives! They sing hits from the 1950s and tell tales of mythology, tomb plundering and the brigand called the *cignale*, or the wild boar of medieval Tolfa, who stole from the rich to give to the poor. In these settings they sing their verses as a dialogue, a type of contest in which each side defends one side of an argument. A wide range of topics is covered, such as a dispute between Penelope and Odysseus, or the Russians and the Americans. Although the subject matter is drawn from the classics, the poets improvise on the spot, demonstrating wit, knowledge of the classics and agility in the handling of the verse form. Sometimes these performances take a more formal shape in the form of competitions before a larger audience, in which prizes are to be won. Although for a long time the performances of the peasant poets were held in low esteem, during the past two decades the situation has changed dramatically. The media and the tourist industry have become greatly interested and suddenly these poetic competitions have become a major attraction. Expensive prizes and large sums of money are awarded and the poetic events have become a scene for fierce rivalry and competition.

Figure 12.2 There's no business like 'Etrusco-business'!

The octave verses offer us a glimpse into the peasants' perceptions of their past, an image which is rooted in the tradition of centuries. The influence of the classics is especially notable. Inspired by Homer and Virgil, Greek and Trojan heroes play a substantial role in the creation of modern central Italy. Equally important, however, is the contribution of an older or even indigenous element in the area: the Etruscans. The builder and poet, Pietro Morani, for example, explains it as follows. The Pelasgi, a Greek tribe from Thessaly, invaded Italy and founded Agillina, which is now Cerveteri. The Tyrrenians, or Etruscans, who had originally come from Lydia, felt threatened by their presence and declared war on them. They won and the two tribes amalgamated. Next the

Trojans arrived in central Italy. When Aeneas landed on the shores of Italy, he met with the opposition of King Turnus. Pallas, son of the Arcadian Evander who founded the first settlement on the future site of Rome, decided to help Aeneas in his fight against the Latins and asked the Etruscan *lucumon* at Cerveteri for help. This request was granted and the Trojans joined the existing Greek–Etruscan alliance. According to the peasant poets, therefore, the modern inhabitants of central Italy share a particularly glorious past, as the descendants of the illustrious Greeks and Trojans, who found their destiny in central Italy under the wings of the Etruscans (Kezich 1986: 98).

Although the form and subject matter of the octaves are based on Renaissance models, the political reality evoked in these poems is that of the beginning of the present century (Kezich 1986: 123–148). More than 60 per cent of the contemporary peasant poets reside is northern Lazio, a region which remained under the dominion of the Papal States until 1871. During this period its economic and political history diverged from that of Tuscany. In both regions landed property had been organised into large estates, the so-called *latifundia*. While during the eighteenth century in Tuscany the situation of small farmers improved with the introduction of share cropping, in northern Lazio relations remained unaltered. The *latifundia* were owned by Roman nobility and managed by local middlemen. The peasantry cultivated the land in exchange for certain compensations, but was never allowed to settle within the estates. Poverty was high and literacy levels low. Finally, with the emergence of the new united state of Italy, a programme of reform was set in motion. The state confiscated the estates of the nobility, but as a consequence deprived the farmers of their traditional rights to work the land. A state of anarchy was the result. Desperate farmers revolted and invaded the former estates with varying degrees of success. Brigands terrorised the countryside often with full support from the farmers. It was 1950 before a new package of agricultural reforms was launched, which included the large-scale redistribution of land to the small farmers. Although these measures to a large extent solved the prevalent social injustice, the rhetoric of the peasant poets remained unchanged. Up to today their poems rage against wealthy landowners, cruel middlemen and authoritative institutions, such as the Italian state and the Roman Catholic Church. Their songs glorify the deeds of brigands, tomb robbers and poachers, who in their eyes fight the establishment and have rightful claim to the land. The octave, founded on the traditions of the upper classes, became the voice of discontent of the farmers: a true counter culture, kept alive to the present day.

POPULAR PERCEPTIONS OF THE ETRUSCANS
FROM THE RENAISSANCE TO MODERN TIMES

The verses of the peasant poets illuminate how, drawing on the literature of the upper classes, the farmers of former Etruria created their own historical framework. According to this view the Etruscans laid the cultural foundations for central Italy. Unfortunately, many other dimensions of the popular response to the Etruscans remain obscure. It could be asked, for example, whether the Etruscans played a role in other realms of popular culture. Equally important is the question regarding how excavations, which were undertaken since the Renaissance but greatly increased during the eighteenth and nineteenth centuries, affected local perceptions of the past. Little information is available on any of these topics. Although the involvement of the lower classes in excavations was probably considerable, as they provided labour and the information on where to dig, archaeologists on the whole remain silent on the local involvement with the rediscovery of the Etruscans. Exceptional references are, for example, local names for Etruscan sites, which helped to identify sites of potential interest. It is known, for example, that at least since 1840 the inhabitants of Populonia called one of their Etruscan cemeteries *Buche delle Fate*, 'pits of the fairies' (Fedeli 1983: 325).

The study of folklore reveals little more. Major folklore reference works, such as Thompson's (1936) *Motif Index of Folk Literature*, D'Aronco's (1953) *Indice delle Fiabe Toscane* and Rotunda's (1942) *Motif Index of the Italian Novella in Prose* include only occasionally references to the Etruscans in central Italian folklore. The leading character of one tale, for example, is called 'Queen of the Etruscans'. Apart from her name, however, she displays no Etruscan characteristics and closely resembles the heroines of other tales. This absence of information does not necessarily imply that the Etruscans played an insignificant role in the folklore of the region. It could equally indicate that the tales of the Etruscans had no place within research interests. The study of early modern popular culture at large is affected by the absence of evidence or at least its partiality (Burke [1978] 1994: 65–77). The educated classes, who produced historical documents, were on the whole not interested in popular culture, until the late eighteenth and nineteenth centuries, when the recording of tales, songs and stories began. Stories were often recorded with the help of mediators and the selection often depended on the tastes of the editors.

Some evidence does suggest that the Etruscans featured in local folklore. In his 1934 collection of Tuscan folk tales Idilio dell' Era speaks of the many tales of the Etruscans that his grandmother used to tell him. Unfortunately he recounts only one of them: the tale of Porsenna's tomb. The theme is an old one; both Varro and Pliny describe this spectacular structure. According to their accounts it was 50 feet high and 300 feet wide. The chamber was built on top of a labyrinth and crowned by five pyramid-shaped structures. These towers were adorned by bells which could be heard for miles around. Dell' Era's story tells how King Porsenna, when he knew death drew near, ordered his craftsmen to produce a golden chariot on which his sarcophagus would lie, and twelve golden horses. Pleased with the results he also asked for a hen with 5,000 golden chicks and begged the gods to bring them alive so that their chirping would cheer him up in the underworld. After his death his servants placed the corpse on the chariot, pulled by the horses and followed by 5,000 chicks. Immediately a cloud arose from lake Chiusi, enclosing the wagon and its following. The next morning not a trace of the royal cortege was found, except for the footprints of the 5,000 golden chicks. The splendid tomb had disappeared under the ground and was never found (dell' Era 1934: 10–13).

MODERN ETRUSCAN MYTHS: THE TALES THAT JUSTIFY TOMB ROBBING

The resentment of the social and economic inequality northern Lazian farmers faced up until the 1950s, which is so vividly described in the verses of the peasant poets, is shared by many. The aversion to political and religious authorities is easily transferred to archaeologists who, it is thought, make yet another claim to the disputed land. As a result some inhabitants of the former Etruscan towns favour the illegal excavations of local tomb robbers to those of professional archaeologists. Although this phenomenon is of great archaeological concern, it is rarely discussed in the literature. An exception is Cambi's introduction to an Italian edition of George Dennis' *Cities and Cemeteries* of 1848. He describes how people in the Maremma, the former marshes along the coast, are not really interested in archaeological progress (Cambi 1993: xxiii–xxiv). Instead they prefer to cling to their image of their past, which seems frozen in the years just after the unification of Italy, a period of deep economic and social crisis. The Italian government is blamed for any type of social injustice since then, although it is precisely the central government which set in motion the long-awaited reforms. The brigands of the nineteenth century are heralded as heroes and local bars are filled with their photographs and hunting trophies. The Etruscans are embraced as their ancestors, lovers of nature and the arts, who were obliterated under the Roman domination. Tomb robbers are portrayed as the defenders of this heritage, rather than those who destroy it.

This negative image of archaeologists and support for tomb robbers is one of the greatest difficulties facing Etruscan archaeology today. Large-scale sites disappear at a vast rate, while archaeologists stand powerless in the face of the vast number of illegal diggers as well as the sheer size of the areas threatened. Locally it is known that in most of the former Etruscan towns, one or more groups of tomb robbers go out at night

Figure 12.3 'Who are you to disturb the slumber of someone who has slept for 3,000 years?', she heard a voice cry after she had fallen into the tomb. (From Copponi 1992.)

to rob, on average, five tombs a night. Although such numbers can hardly be verified, the devastated cemeteries have a tale to tell. During the excavations in the Laghetto area of Cerveteri's Banditaccia necropolis, the archaeologist Linington (1980: 11), for example, discovered that only four of eighty-seven chamber tombs still contained some of their grave goods. In the Monte Abbatone cemetery in Cerveteri 400 of 550 tombs were found empty in 1962 (Lerici 1962: 19–20). These had probably been robbed after the Second World War, as fresh breaks in the pottery suggested. In Tarquinia the situation was similar. When the Lerici foundation investigated the Fondo Scataglini necropolis in the 1960s and 1970s, they discovered that all 146 chamber tombs had been robbed (Serra Ridgway 1986: 255–6). The only exceptions were two or three chambers hidden beneath the upper chambers of the same tomb.

Tomb robbers justify the devastation they cause with a rhetoric linked to that of the deprived farmers. In their autobiographies they place great emphasis on the poverty they endured as children and how tomb robbing presented the only possible escape. Omero Bordo described this turning point in his life dramatically as the moment when, left outside by his parents for a night, he saw a sudden light (Cecchelin 1987: 17). Shaking from the cold in his shabby clothes, he felt the presence of a power which would protect him through life; he knew it was the influence of the Etruscans. The moments of greatest triumph in the lives of tomb robbers are those in which they play tricks on the authorities. Luigi Perticarari takes great pride in the fact that he managed to steal a painting from a tomb which was to be opened the next day by the highest archaeological authorities, accompanied by a television crew (Perticarari and Giuntani 1986: 116–33). Omero Bordo particularly enjoyed the time he sold a priest a fake vase for the price of the genuine object. He was proud as he felt he had avenged the injustice committed by the Church through the centuries (Cecchelin 1987: 112).

In many aspects the stories of the tomb robbers resemble traditional tales of treasure (Hoffmann-Krayer 1935–6: 1002–1015). These usually follow the same pattern. The protagonist in the story wants to free a treasure, which is guarded by a spirit, sometimes disguised as an animal, a snake, for example, or a more fantastic creature like a dragon. The hero needs to overcome this obstacle in order to gain access. Sometimes he is helped by a supernatural occurrence, such as a light which guides the way, or a vision or dream in which the deceased owner of the riches explains what to do. Treasures are often predestined for a particular person. Such tales have been popular all over the world, as much in Tuscany as in India or the USA. They have existed probably since at least the Middle Ages and remain current to the present day.

The authors of the 'Storie di Magia' from the Bergamo area name the discovery of unexpected fortune as one of the most popular themes amongst the lower classes (Anesa and Rondi 1986: 145–146). One of the ways in which such stories distinguish themselves from other fairy tales is that they betray the deeply felt fear of some unknown presence. People with long working hours who spent a great deal of time outside are especially prone to such feelings. They allay their fear by telling a story, a cultural projection of the fear they wish to dispel.

Tomb robbers are no different. They spend many lonely hours outside at night, with the possibility of being captured by the police. As no other they know the lure of treasure, as well as the price they may have to pay. Not surprisingly some of them are extremely superstitious. Luigi Perticarari describes this sensation clearly. The Etruscans, he claims, have always determined whether he would find a tomb or not and have sheltered him from danger. They guided him through dreams, visions or signs, such as the flickering of a candle. When he was most desperate, they have always led him to tombs. One night, when he was totally broke, he felt an urge to go out (Perticarari and Giuntani 1986: 87). He stumbled along, as it was extremely dark, until he fell into a pit. When he had a better look he discovered this was in fact an extremely rich grave. In other cases the Etruscans gave warnings not to open certain tombs. A snake in a tomb would not deter him, yet a pile of vipers was a clear sign the tomb was not to be touched (ibid.: 106). Certain times of the year, such as the transition from spring to summer, are known to be unlucky amongst tomb robbers (ibid.: 34–35). During this period it could be extremely dangerous to disturb the abodes of the dead.

THE GENERAL PUBLIC AND THE ETRUSCANS: MYSTERY AND IDENTITY

The tales of the tomb robbers are amongst the most fantastic modern Etruscan myths. Other groups, although on a more modest scale, maintain their own Etruscan legends. Many inhabitants of the former Etruscan area, as was maintained in the introduction to this chapter, feel that their identity is directly linked to the Etruscans. Inside and outside Etruria the interested lay public cherishes the notion of the mysterious Etruscans. Pallottino ([1986] 1994), looking back on a long career as the so-called 'Father of Etruscan Studies', is astounded at the tenacity with which the public holds on to outdated concepts of the Etruscan past: the unknown origins and a language which cannot be deciphered. Although great progress has been made in the study of the Etruscans, for example in the field of language, the public at large refuses to abandon the idea of a mystery. After lectures on the new developments in the study of Etruscan language, people would come up to Pallottino to express their disbelief or disillusionment (Pallottino 1994: 13). What surprised Pallottino even more was that journalists, in their coverage of such an event, totally ignored the information given and instead chose to perpetuate the old view.

Pallottino concludes that two divergent traditions exist. On the one hand, scientists continuously strive to increase a rational understanding of Etruscan culture; on the other, the more irrational, romantic vision of this culture persists. The two, according to Pallottino, do not communicate. In an analysis of this phenomenon, however, it should not be forgotten that Etruscan origins and language have been key issues in academic archaeology at least until the 1970s and even up till today are considered central issues in semi-popular publications. It is therefore likely that the popular view of the Etruscans drew initially from academic interpretations, which were never abandoned. Semi-popular publications further encouraged the popular perspective. This process of the popularisation of academic findings and its consequences has been studied in other disciplines, such as folklore studies.

In the early 1960s Moser detected a dramatic change in the status of folklore studies; they were no longer the domain of an elite, a small group of scholars, but enjoyed great popularity in different strata of society. Popular folklore publications suddenly sold like hot cakes and traditional dance and music performances became major attractions. Commercial stakes in the popularised folklore studies became considerable, and accuracy was compromised to suit the tastes of a large audience, including tourists. So-called 'traditions' were re-enacted outside their original geographical and social context (Moser 1962: 179). Moser named

Figure 12.4 Vino Nobile from the estate 'Sanguineto', probably named after the bloodshed in a battle between Romans and Etruscans in the third century BC

this trend 'folklorismus'. Although popular approaches to folklore were originally based on the academic study of the topic, the popularised version came to lead its own life, further reinforced by semi-popular publications. The existence of an independent popularised folk culture imposes considerable difficulties on the researcher. Moser (ibid.: 9) recounts how during the years before the Second World War a renowned Germanist visited Bavaria. Interested in the meaning of a local festival, he addressed one of the elderly people. His informant was astonished by the ignorance of the researcher and explained: 'You have to take a folk-loristic view you know.' He proceeded to lecture the researcher on the meaning and vitality of primitive cultic traditions, in a style which was reminiscent of local newspaper articles and popular folklore publications. The researcher asked no further questions.

Other contemporary Etruscan myths, such as the historical significance of this culture and its affinity with the modern population, are equally the outcome of a process of popularisation, or 'archaeo-folklorismus', as we could call it. Academic and literary interpretations have been equally influential. The literary tradition, which predominantly promoted the idea of direct continuity from Etruscan times onwards, was first repre-sented by Thomas Dempster in the seventeenth century and remained particularly strong in Britain (Kezich [1986] 1994; Pallottino 1994). Dempster saw in central Italy and its inhabitants a direct continuation of former Etruria. The arguments he used to support Etruscan superiority, such as the use of the chariot and other examples derived from Livy, are still current in the area today.

The Etruscan-inspired literary movement reached its peak during the nineteenth and early twentieth centuries, with representatives such as George Dennis, Mrs Hamilton Gray, Frederick Seymour and of course D.H. Lawrence. On Etruscan civilisation these writers could project their view of an ideal society, unhindered by written sources to contradict them (Kezich 1994: 163). In the contemporary population they saw modern Etruscans untouched by the imperialism of the Romans or the morals of the Catholic Church. Mary Cameron Lovett (1909), for example, describes how in the local peasants' faces she recognised the traits of the age of Perugino. After visiting the tomb of the Volumnii close to Perugia, the connection with an even more remote Etruscan past became clear to her (Cameron Lovett 1909: 296–298). She continues to list the similarities between ancient Etruria and modern Tuscany: the shape and the size of towns, the love of horse racing, the icon-ographical resemblance between the Etruscan Charun and Lasa deities and the Roman Catholic devil and angel, and the strong aspirate in the pronunciation of Italian in the Florentine area. She concludes that the Etruscans have played a far greater role in the shaping of European history than has so far been recognised. Many modern Tuscans would agree with her.

Some of the most up to date scientific investigations continue to promote the romantic view of the Etruscans, such as, for example, that of Professor Piazza from Turin University and Cavalli-Sforza from Stanford University. As part of their work on an ethnic map of Italy, Piazza and Cavalli-Sforza took blood samples of 150 people in the former Etruscan town of Murlo. The researchers selected Murlo as the base of their central Italian DNA analysis because of the excellent state of its civic archives. These go back to the sixteenth century and show that little migration to and from Murlo has taken place since. The results of the DNA analysis of the blood samples reveals that the population of Murlo is a genetically homogeneous group, distinct from other parts of Italy. The researchers conclude that the cause of this discrepancy lies in the Etruscan origins of the Murlo population. Although the results are still tenuous, as so far it has not been possible to extract DNA from Etruscan bones and positively identify modern Murlo DNA as related to the Etruscan, the press immediately responded by reporting that Tuscany has remained Etruscan and in Murlo the Etruscan genes were best preserved (D'Amico 1991). It is clear that such coverage is welcomed by those who like to feel that a special link exists between them and the Etruscans.

CONCLUSION

The Etruscans are subject to the creation of a rich and diverse modern mythology. People perceive them as a mysterious culture, as ancestors with whom they share a direct blood link, or even as ghosts who support illegal digging. At first such stories may seem a commercial invention designed to please tourists or justify an illegal activity. The historical investigation undertaken in this paper, however, reveals a far more intriguing background. Modern Etruscan myths are firmly rooted in older traditions, some of them going back to the Renaissance. Peasant poets, for example, use the form and content of Renaissance verses to tell the story of their past. A larger public elaborates on Renaissance theories, when, for example, they profess the superior historical importance of the Etruscans. Such ideas were for the first time given a definite shape by Thomas Dempster in the early seventeenth century and became key ingredients in a romantic literary tradition, which persisted until the first half of the present century. The building stones of modern Etruscan myths were, therefore, sometimes passed on within the groups who use them today, sometimes reinforced by a continuing tradition outside.

The influence of older traditions on modern Etruscan myths by no means implies that they are straight copies from Renaissance concepts. On the contrary, they are reshaped to serve contemporary purposes. Today they provide escapism in the form of adventure and mystery, in a world which is increasingly perceived as lacking in these qualities (Lowenthal 1985); a sense of regional identity within a more and more globalised world view (Featherstone 1990); and the justification for claiming the material benefits of this past by tomb robbing. Modern Etruscan myths, in conclusion, are a reinvention of tradition, rather than an 'invention of tradition' (Hobsbawm and Ranger 1983).

Class concerns have played a dominant role in the creation of modern Etruscan myths, which came to function as an independent, 'other', history (Hastrup 1992), reserved to promote the interests of the lower classes of central Italy. The need for such a distinct past was particularly acute in the farmers' struggle for social and economic equality in northern Lazio until the 1950s. Although such marked forms of inequality no longer exist, the ideology of the deprived farmers remains firmly in place.

Although modern Etruscan myths function partly as counter-culture against the upper classes, their roots lie precisely in the academic and literary culture of the well-to-do. Interestingly, in the popular realm concepts from the academic realm were not modified to reflect the outcome of new findings. This is apparent in the now outdated ideas of the mystery of the Etruscan language and origins. Although such concepts are no longer tenable in scientific archaeology, they still thrive in the popular domain. Such beliefs have been subject to a process of 'archaeo-folklorismus': archaeological findings were popularised and came to form an independent tradition. The only scientific findings which seem to trigger a public response are those that tie in with existing ideas. The genetic analysis suggesting a direct blood link between those illustrious Etruscans and the modern population is a good example of the type of scientific research, that has met with great public interest. Archaeological research, in conclusion, still provides a great source of inspiration for the continuing reinvention of the Etruscan myth.

ACKNOWLEDGEMENTS

I am extremely grateful to the Warburg Institute for providing the opportunity to research this theme, as part of a Crawford fellowship. Giovanni Kezich introduced me to the long-standing traditions of northern Lazio, and I would like to thank him for his inspiration and practical help.

REFERENCES

Anesa, M. and Rondi, M. (1986) 'Storie di Magia.' In *Quaderni dell'archivio della cultura di base*. Bergamo: Sistema Bibliotecario Urbano.

Burke, P. [1978] (1994) *Popular Culture in Early Modern Europe*. Reprint. Aldershot: Scolar Press.

Cambi, F. (1993) 'Introduction.' In George Dennis (1848) *Città e Necropoli d'Etruria. Vulci. Canino. Ischia. Farnese*, trans. and edited by F. Cambi. Siena: Nuova immagine.

Cameron Lovett, M. (1909) *Old Etruria and Modern Tuscany*. London: Methuen.

Cecchelin, R. (1987) *Omero: La mia vita con gli Etruschi*. Rome: Edizioni Mediterranee.
Chastel, A. (1959) 'L'"Etruscan Revival" du XV siecle.' *Revue Archéologique* 1: 165–180.
Cipriani, G. (1980) *Il mito etrusco nel rinascimento fiorentino*. Florence: Leo S. Olschki Editore.
Copponi, G. (1992) *Il Segreto degli Etruschi*. Cerveteri: Edizioni La Goccia.
Cristofani, M.(1983) *La Scoperta degli Etruschi. Archeologia e Antiquaria nel '700*. Rome: Consiglio Nazionale delle Ricerche.
D'Aranco, G. (1953) *Indice delle Toscana*. Florence: Leo S. Olscki.
Dell' Era, I. (1934) *Leggende Toscane*. Milan: Pro Familia.
D'Amico, A. (1991) 'Etruschi, greci e celti regnano ancora nel Dna.' *La Republica* 3/4 November: 13.
Featherstone, M. (ed.) (1990) *Global Culture: Nationalism, Globalisation and Modernity*. London: Sage.
Fedeli, F. (1983) *Populonia: Storia e Territorio*. Florence: All' Insegna del Giglio.
Hastrup, K. (ed.) (1992) *Other Histories*. London: Routledge.
Hobsbawm, E. and Ranger, T. (eds) (1983) *The Invention of Tradition*. Cambridge: Cambridge University Press.
Hoffmann-Krayer, E. (1936–6) *Handwörterbuch des Deutschen Aberglaubens*, Band VII. Berlin and Leipzig: Walter de Gruyter.
Kezich, G. (1986) *I Poeti Contadini. Introduzione all'ottava rima popolare: immaginario poetico e paesaggio sociale*. Rome: Bulzoni.
Kezich, G. [1986] (1994) 'Lawrence in Etruria: "Etruscan Places" in context.' In D.H. Lawrence, *Etruscan Places*, edited by G. Kezich and M. Lorenzini, pp. 157–171. Siena: Nuove Immagine.
Lerici, C. (1962) *Italia Sepolta*. Milan: Lerici editori.
Linington, R. (1980) 'Lo scavo nella zona Laghetto della necropoli della Banditaccia a Cerveteri.' *Rassegna di studi del civico museo archeologico e del civico gabinetto numismatico di Milano*, vol xxv–xxvi.
Lowenthal, D. (1985) *The Past is a Foreign Country*. Cambridge: Cambridge University Press.
Moser, H. (1962) 'Vom Folklorismus in unserer Zeit.' *Zeitschrift für Volkskunde* 58(2): 177–209.
Moser, H. (1964) 'Der Folklorismus als Forschungsproblem der Volkskunde.' *Hessische Blätter für Volkskunde* 55: 9–57.
Pallottino, M. [1986] (1994) 'In search of Etruria: science and imagination.' In D.H. Lawrence, *Etruscan Places*, edited by G. Kezich and M. Lorenzini, pp. 9–27. Siena: Nuove Immagine.
Perticarari, L. and Giuntani, A. (1986) *I segreti di un tombarolo*. Milan: Rusconi.
Redfield, R. [1956] (1963) *Peasant Society and Culture*. Chicago: University of Chicago Press.
Rotunda, D. (1942) *Motif-Index of the Italian Novelle in Prose*. Bloomington, IN: Indiana University Publications.
Serra Ridgway, F. (1986) 'Aspetti della necropoli ellenistica nel Fondo Scataglini ai Monterozzi.' In M. Bonghi Jovino and C. Chiaramonte (eds) *Tarquinia: Ricerche, Scavi e Prospettive*, pp. 255–259. Roma: Bretschneider.
Thoden van Velzen, D. (1996) 'The world of Tuscan tomb robbers: living with the local community and the ancestors.' *Cultural Property* 5(1): 111–126.

Thomson de Grummond, N. (1986) 'Rediscovery.' In L. Bonfante (ed.) *Etruscan Life and Afterlife*, pp. 18–46. Warminster: Aris & Phillips.

Thompson, S. (1932–1936) *Motif-Index of Folk-Literature*. Indiana: Indiana University Press.

Vickers, M. (1986) 'Imaginary Etruscans: changing perceptions of Etruria since the fifteenth century.' *Hephaistos* 7/8: 153–168.

Weiss, R. (1969) *The Renaissance of Classical Antiquity*. Oxford: Blackwell.

Willey, D. (1994) 'The tomb that Berlusconi built.' *Observer* 10 July: 16–17.

CHAPTER THIRTEEN

NAMING THE PLACES, NAMING THE STONES

SARA CHAMPION AND GABRIEL COONEY

ABSTRACT

This paper begins by examining the folkloric/mythohistoric elements associated with Irish prehistoric and early historic monuments as evidenced by their given names, e.g. Labbacallee, Labbanasigha, Caheraphuca, or 'generic' names such as 'Finn's Fingers' and 'Diarmaid and Gráinne's Bed', tracing their earliest manifestations in text and/or map and the history of their usage. We then look at the related question of stories associated with such monuments and their direct effect on the preservation of sites, using examples from our own (separate) work in Ireland to show two very different outcomes which may be linked to social and economic changes in the past twenty-five years. We explore the idea of polyvocality raised by folkloric interpretations of the meanings of monuments (and the possibility of its cynical endorsement by archaeologists in the interests of cost-free preservation); the nature of archaeologists' own storytelling (and its relevance for the 'users' of monuments); and the use of monuments, particularly megaliths, as media images in the promotion of Irish identity, and the relation of this practice to polyvocality.

> There are legends one can't argue with:
> The agent Blaney ordered help
> to break the stones to ease the plough
> and was refused, 'It's poor fate
> will befall the man . . . '
> Peter Fallon, 'The Speaking Stones'

INTRODUCTION

Perhaps the best-known aspect of the relationship between archaeological sites and folklore in Ireland is what could be referred to as the deterrent effect: the very many stories of the ill-luck and/or physical damage that befell people (predominantly men!) who dared to break the taboo surrounding sites such as ringforts (enclosed settlements dating mainly to the early historic period) and prehistoric megalithic monuments, including tombs and stone circles, which were recognised by oral tradition and naming as part of the Otherworld. For example, in Maria Edgeworth's novel *Castle Rackrent* (1800) 'honest Thady', the steward of the Rackrent family, relates how a member of the family dug up a fairy mound against his advice and had no luck afterwards. One of us (Champion) had difficulty recruiting local labour for emergency work on a ringfort in Co. Galway in 1972 because the owner was said to have suffered the withering of his arm after cutting down a tree on the monument. From a heritage management perspective it is perhaps not surprising that this deterrent effect has long been recognised as showing the potential power of folklore to act as a tool for preservation (e.g. Ó Ríordáin 1979). The presence of this form of protection has undoubtedly been actively used by archaeologists and the state authorities in helping to protect the archaeological heritage. The recognition of the importance of folk beliefs in monument protection is an interesting example of how polyvocality can be seen as a legitimate approach to speaking about the past when it is perceived as helping to preserve the past. It also forms an interesting contrast with archaeological narratives interpreting the past which have in general tended to ignore folklore or to relegate it to an anecdotal status (but for a different view see Raftery 1976).

The reality, however, is that this traditional deterrent effect based on folklore has now largely disappeared amongst the Irish farming community and other active agents in the Irish rural landscape, who are more in tune with the latest twists in the Common Agricultural Policy of the European Union than with stories associated with the land that would be seen as relating to outmoded ideas about life. Now the folklore itself has become part of the history of sites and it has by and large lost its active meaning. It is also clear that despite the deterrent effect of folklore the destruction of sites has been going on on a large scale in Ireland for hundreds of years (e.g. O'Flanagan 1981). Evans (1966: 1) quotes T.J. Westropp writing in 1897 deploring the way in which sites were being destroyed or damaged. In some of these acts of destruction there may in fact also have been an attempt to harness the other major aspect of the folklore embedded into archaeological sites, that is the power incorporated into them, as reflected in the frequent tales of buried treasure. On the other hand there are instances where sites have continued to be actively used and venerated up to the present day, such as in the case of holy wells or hilltop cairns.

So these contrasting attitudes raise a number of important questions. What was the actual efficacy of folkloric protection? Was it associated with particular types of monuments? Were monuments with names associated with myth and folklore actually more protected than those without? To what extent is the naming of sites related to the past perceptions of their meaning in the landscape and does this remain static or unchanging? How does the meaning of monuments change over time as oral tradition is passed on from one generation to the next? How are the folkloric/mythic views of monuments reflected in the presentation of monuments to the public? To what extent are landscape histories constructed and informed by local inhabitants using and identifying with their environment, and how far can outside bodies transform such histories for their different purposes? In relation to this last question one avenue of research is the way in which the recognition and renaming of monuments by map surveyors and archaeologists changes local perceptions of those sites.

In this paper we would like to focus on some of these topics and to look first at the basis of the folklore associated with archaeological sites. Second, we wish to discuss the way in which the meaning of monuments can be changed, from the extreme of physical removal to the subjection of the site to new meanings. Third, the paper considers the importance of the continuity of place, and fourth, examines present attitudes to monument preservation in the rural landscape. We conclude with a look at Loughcrew, Co. Meath as an example of a landscape charged with many overlapping and changing meanings.

NAMING THE PLACES

Many of Ireland's monuments now have names which associate them with general folkloric categories of spirit being known as the *sí*, or with specific mythic individuals who appear in mythohistories, such as the *Lebor Gabála Erenn* or the Book of Invasions, first written down in the eleventh or twelfth century (e.g. see Welch 1996: 304). The associations serve to preserve the memory of these figures in the landscape, and on the other hand offer an explanation of the presence of sometimes very ancient monuments in a landscape where they had no obvious function. To early Christian writers the *sí* were the pagan gods of earth, over whom Christianity had triumphed. But in Gaelic tradition they were the Tuatha Dé Danann, the ancient gods of Ireland who live on in a parallel world or Otherworld to which one could gain access through archaeological sites such as ringforts or various kinds of mounds. So these places were seen as being the visible expression of the Otherworld, liminal places which had the linked properties of danger and power. The danger was of an encounter with the Otherworld and its alternative reality; the power lay in the belief that this contact with the spirit world could bring its own reward in the form of treasure or a change in fortune.

The fairies were seen as either a collective entity, a host or singular figures. They were especially active at critical times in the annual cycle of the seasons and festivities, such as Beltane (May Day), marking the beginning of summer, and Samhain (Hallowe'en), the beginning of winter. They also were seen as intervening at critical times in personal lives, foretelling good or bad fortune, and this intervention also offered an explanation of extreme behaviour by people – they had been 'touched' by the fairies.

The fairies feature frequently in their various guises in the names given to archaeological sites, for example, names incorporating the *sí* element, such as in the case of the passage tombs at Sheemore and Sheebeg in Co. Leitrim (Cooney 1979) or just the general and very common 'fairy fort'. Interestingly in the latter case one is also dealing with the very complex question of the translation of oral tradition from Irish into English, a feature that was central to the growth of cultural nationalism from the late eighteenth century (Cronin 1996: 91–130). Ó Súilleabháin's *Handbook of Irish Folklore* (1942) records some of the dire consequences supposedly attendant on the disturbance of such sites, including the case of the man who was turned into a dwarf as a consequence of levelling a ringfort. Ó Súilleabháin also relates the various revenges that were exacted on people who cut trees, particularly the whitethorn, or bushes in ringforts or other sites. These included having a growing flax crop plaited by the fairies or damage to farm animals. Fairies are associated with particular types of archaeological sites such as megalithic tombs and ringforts. They are often said to guard gold in the former, perhaps a very distant oral echo of the placement of material with human bone deposits in the tombs in the Neolithic and Bronze Age. There are many examples of stories like the one associated with the portal tomb at Aghavas, Co. Leitrim of a man who was half-way through the demolition of the tomb chamber looking for the 'crock of gold' when he was struck with lockjaw and never recovered (Cooney 1985).

Alongside a general lore about fairy folk, the chief figures of the Tuatha Dé Danann became deities in Irish mythology and play a central role in the various tales or epics such as the Ulster cycle and the Fionn cycle (Welch 1996: 523). The names of these figures are as well known from their association with monuments as through the texts, such as the *Lebor Gabála*, where these oral traditions were first recorded. Maeve's Cairn (Figure 13.1), for example, a passage tomb on the very prominent hill known as Knocknarea in Co. Sligo (see Bergh 1995) or the hilltop cairn at Knockmaa in Co. Galway (e.g. Evans 1966: 122), is where most visitors first encounter Maeve, the mythic queen of Connacht. Queen Maeve was famous for setting out on a bull quest, in an attempt to catch up on her husband's possessions, which brought her and her army into conflict with the kingdom of Ulster and its hero Cú Chulainn, and all these dramatic events are recorded in the *Táin Bó Cuailnge* (see Kinsella 1969). The hero of the Fionn cycle of tales, Fionn Mac Cumhaill, is met at places such as at Fin McCool's Fingers, at Shantemon, Co. Cavan (O'Donovan 1995: 15).

Figure 13.1 Maeve's Cairn, Knocknarea, Co. Sligo, with one of the Carrowmore passage tombs in the foreground
Source: Photograph courtesy of Dúchas, The Heritage Service

Much more widespread are monuments, most commonly the type of megalithic tombs known as portal tombs, named after Fionn's wife Gráinne and her lover Diarmaid. Examples of 'Diarmaid and Gráinne's Bed' are found all over Ireland (Figure 13.2), reflecting the tale of the daily movement of the lovers as they attempted to escape Fionn's wrath (Cooney 1994). Again the power of contact with this tradition was reflected in the folk belief that if a childless woman sleeps on the top of one of these tombs she will, as Gráinne did, conceive (Ó hÓgáin 1990: 162). The concentration of monuments called Diarmaid and Gráinne's Bed in Co. Clare (e.g. Borlase 1897; de Valera and Ó Nualláin 1961) suggests that the story had a particular strength there. By contrast in Co. Cork some megalithic tombs, mostly wedge tombs, are referred to as the bed of the hag or witch: 'labbacallee' or 'labbanacally'. This suggests that there is some degree of regionality in folk traditions about megalithic tombs. This is borne out by the strength of tradition about the hag or the witch in west Munster, and she is specifically referred to as the *Cailleach Bhéarra*, the hag or witch of the Beare peninsula in west Cork.

The complex strands tied up in folk beliefs and their absorption of different influences over time can be seen in these two folkloric themes also. North of Munster, for example, the *Cailleach Bhéarra* became fused with

Figure 13.2 Cleenrah, Co. Longford, portal tomb, an example of a tomb known as 'Diarmaid and Gráinne's Bed'

the idea of a harvest witch, whereas in Scotland she came to be represented as a female spirit of the wilderness (Ó hÓgáin 1990: 68). The early medieval composer of the Diarmaid and Gráinne tale incorporated classical mythology into the story, as reflected in the parallels between Diarmaid and Adonis, particularly their deaths fighting boars (ibid.: 162). On the other hand in Cork, Borlase (1897) also records a version of the story as being about Gráinne and Shearla (Charles). A proverb emerges from the story when, after a lovers' tiff, Gráinne says, 'Bad as Shearla is, I might be worse without him'. This saying was used by the Irish about Charles I in the seventeenth century and perhaps demonstrates a linkage between an existing story and an early modern political reality, a hint of how narratives and folk tradition can shift and adapt through time.

REMOVING THE STONES, CHANGING MEANINGS

Despite the strength of tradition and respect for monuments, it is clear that many sites and monuments were destroyed, even before the introduction of the conventional baseline used to measure rates of monument destruction, namely the first edition of Ordnance Survey 6-inch maps compiled in the 1830s and 1840s. Rising population in the late eighteenth and early nineteenth centuries, allied to the reorganisation of the landscape (Aalen *et al.* 1997: 67–89), would have been a general process bringing about a greater impact on archaeological sites at this time. The spread of people into areas of marginal ground may have led to a disturbance of landscapes that had been by and large intact since their abandonment in prehistoric or earlier historic periods (e.g. Whelan 1994: 61–63).

More specifically, the growing interest in antiquities and the amassing of private collections (e.g. Mitchell 1985; Woodman 1993) with the consequent market for objects may have led to a more deliberate search for objects. Cahill (1994) has made a detailed study of the collection of Redmond Anthony (1768–1848), an innkeeper, collector and antiquarian who lived at Piltdown, Co. Kilkenny and kept his collection of gold objects of Late Bronze Age to medieval date in a specially made bog oak case with trays. Anthony's correspondence gives an insight into the complex world of nineteenth-century Ireland and the web of people involved in the antiquities trade. Anthony relates how it was difficult to get details of find locations because 'countrymen . . . did not like to be questioned on account of their landlords'. Anthony's most important contacts were jewellers to whom the finders brought objects to see what their bullion value was. While some finds of such objects may not have been on recognisable sites, it seems clear that there were circumstances in which people were prepared to overlook the taboos that were designed to protect sites. Indeed the traditions themselves often contain an inducement in referring to 'crocks of gold' to be obtained by the person brave or foolhardy enough to ignore the 'legends that could not be argued with'. Again in the world of the late eighteenth-century Irish midlands depicted in Maria Edgeworth's *Castle Rackrent* we see that landlords were often prepared to take on these taboos for the sake of demesne improvements ([1800] 1964: 16).

Apart from physically removing the stones themselves, there was a variety of ways in which the power of monuments and their names could be subjugated or appropriated. It is clear that since early Christian times there has been a deliberate desire to incorporate the power of pre-existing sacred sites (e.g. Aitchison 1994; Pochin Mould 1955). At its simplest this might consist of a cross inscribed on a standing stone, but it also extended to the renaming of sites and the reshaping of traditions. In relation to the many holy wells dedicated to St Brigit (Figure 13.3) it can be argued that they and the saint herself represent a Christianisation of the earlier Irish mother goddess Brigid or Brigit. She was the daughter/lover/wife of the Dagda, one of the Otherworld lords (Brenneman and Brenneman 1995).

Subjugation may have also taken a more prosaic, secular form as monuments became incorporated into the evolving agricultural landscape. Earthworks or stone monuments that became part of field boundaries were more likely to have been removed with that field boundary if it became redundant. Other kinds of incorporation were recorded in the nineteenth century. Borlase (1897) records a tomb at Kilnaboy, Co. Clare,

Figure 13.3   St Brigit's well at the monastic site at Faughart Upper, Co. Louth, reputedly the birthplace of the saint

which in the mid-nineteenth century the Ordnance Survey had noted as being used as a bedchamber to an attached hut 'inhabited by a poor man of the name of Michael Coneen', in use in the late nineteenth century as a cowhouse.

The destruction, appropriation, incorporation and continuing use of monuments embodies both changing meanings and changing narratives and is echoed in the more strictly archaeological record of the long-term re-use of sites. For example, there is the frequent re-use of megalithic tombs as Bronze Age cemetery mounds, as at Fourknocks or the Mound of the Hostages, Tara, both in Co. Meath (e.g. see Waddell 1990) or for Iron Age activity as in the case of one of the tombs (site 26) at Carrowmore passage tomb cemetery, Co. Sligo (Burenhult 1984) and cairn H, Loughcrew (Raftery 1994: 167–168). Eogan (1991) has detailed the prehistoric and historic sequences of activity at the main passage tomb (site 1) at Knowth in the Boyne Valley. This offers a fascinating example of how people must have come face to face with a past to be explained as they exploited the same location for different purposes on a number of occasions over a period of more than four millennia.

Recent work by O'Brien (1993) at the Altar and Toormore wedge tombs in Co. Cork also shows long-term use of relatively small sites after their formal use ended. At Altar, for example, the original construction date is unknown, but there are deposits including cremated human bones of final Neolithic/Early Bronze Age date. There was a small pit of Late Bronze Age date within the chamber. There appears to have been some activity in Iron Age and early historic times with the deposition of shell and fish-bone. The tomb was used as a shelter in medieval/post-medieval times. It was used as a Mass-rock in Penal times. Fires were lit in the tomb chamber, and this was followed by the dumping of field stones during nineteenth-century potato cultivation around the tomb (O'Brien 1993: 68).

In both the more recent and more distant activity on some of these sites there is scant evidence for any concern about disturbance. Again this suggests that where tales of bad luck and retribution existed they did not apply to all sites. It seems likely too that the attribution of a name to a site may in some cases have happened quite late, and that some types of sites were much more susceptible to destruction than others. In the case of megalithic tombs with substantial cairns or mounds, it may well have been the case that it was only after a phase of removal of cairn stones or mound material that the more impressive structural stones became exposed and led to the need to explain the function and nature of such monumental constructions.

The continued reshaping of narratives and traditions, often reflected in a reinterpretation of the meanings of place names, underlines the fact that continuity of place may be the essential ingredient in understanding and interpreting the long-term history of sites. The very fact that structures survive from one era or cultural context to another may lead to their meaning being transformed (Horne 1986: 154).

SAME PLACES, DIFFERENT STORIES

The assertion that continuity of place was of vital importance is borne out by remembering that we are dealing with a world where narrative tradition was dominant in many areas up until the mid-nineteenth century. In this world connections with the landscape are regarded as history. This can operate both at the mundane, everyday level and at the level of the larger events and places that influenced the development of society. As an example of the former, Tim Robinson (1994: 27–29) has explored the changing meaning of a white quartz standing stone at Garraunbaun, in Connemara, Co. Galway (Figure 13.4), which has now been captured as the front cover of the archaeological inventory of the

Figure 13.4   Standing stone at Garraunbaun, Co. Galway

region (Gosling 1993). Archaeologically the standing stone is important as one of a number of megalithic monuments in this area, also including megalithic tombs and stone rows or alignments. The site is marked as a standing stone on the recent 1:50,000 Ordnance Survey map of the area (Discovery Series 37).

The name of the local area or townland where the standing stone is located is Garraunbaun – said to be an anglicisation of the Irish *An Garrán Bán*, the white or fallow thicket. But Robinson's research indicates that the Irish name is *An Gearrán Ban* – the white horse (a lake to the south of the standing stone is known as *Loch an Ghearráin Bháin*, the lake of the white horse). It is clear that the sound of both Irish names is very similar, and as Robinson puts it 'the difference between them would be lost, like so much else, in anglicisation'. A note in the Ordnance Survey notebooks, compiled when the area was first mapped in 1839, said that the place was named after a rock of the same name, but they did not say where the rock was. The quartz standing stone is set in a prominent hilltop location in the area; the hill occupies most of the townland, and Robinson describes how on approaching the hilltop the stone looks like the rump of a white horse. The story he was told by a local to explain the name is that the stone represents (and looks like the rear of) a mythical white horse that had come from the nearby lake. A man had saddled it, then taken the saddle off and put it on a rock; the horse then ran back into the lake and the rock became the horse. In this story we see a very complex interweaving of the topography of the area with the prehistoric human addition, all blended together over time in oral tradition to make and inhabit a landscape which was very much alive and real to the inhabitants of Garraunbaun.

FROM MEGALITH TO NON-PLACE

The complex story with its varied meanings built around the standing stone at Garraunbaun would have been known and familiar to the older residents in the locality, like the man who told Robinson that the mark of the saddle could still be seen on the rock. Most of the younger people, however, would either not know of the location of the stone or its stories, or their knowledge would be derived from Robinson's publications. This reflects changes in attitude to both folklore and archaeological monuments over the past twenty-five years. For older farmers in general respect for archaeological sites was based on folk tradition. Sites which were not named or were difficult to distinguish, such as low burial barrows or *fulachta fiadh*, sites where hot-stone technology was used for cooking purposes leading to a build-up of a horse-shoe shaped mound of burnt stones (e.g. Buckley 1990), were often removed. In the case of younger farmers – particularly those who are progressive – folklore, and very often the monuments associated with it, was often seen as part of a past to be escaped, forgotten, removed without regret, and in some cases the act of removal was perceived as part of the process of looking forward. This can be linked to the disdain in which traditional architecture, most prominently thatched cottages, came to be held and why Ireland has seen the rise of bungalow bliss and/or bungalow blight in the rural landscape.

Now with the changed emphasis in the European Agricultural Policy towards diversification of land-use, rural tourism and the establishment of the Rural Environmental Protection Scheme whereby farmers are rewarded for preserving/managing sites (e.g. Aalen *et al.* 1997: 255–259; O'Sullivan 1996), archaeology and folklore are again being seen in a more positive light. But it would be fair to say that this respect is at least in part based on economics. The basis of the knowledge which informs farm plans under the Rural Environmental Protection Scheme is *archaeological* information derived from the county Sites and Monuments Records compiled by the Archaeological Survey of Ireland, National Monuments and Historic Properties Service of the Department of Arts, Heritage, Gaeltacht and the Islands. The names associated with sites, their folklore/mythology, have in many cases now become just part of the story; they are part of the national archaeological inventory and no longer serve as the local justification for the preservation of archaeological sites.

So while some of the traditional respect for sites based on folklore survives at a local level, particularly amongst the older members of rural communities, now the basis for preservation depends primarily on archaeological criteria and the legislative framework centred on the National Monuments Act in the Republic of Ireland. Given the very rapid rate of social change in Ireland since the 1970s and the gathering pace of change in the landscape (see Aalen *et al.* 1997) these changing attitudes are not surprising. The belief that sustained folklore has by and large disappeared. There are important implications for archaeological resource management in these changes in that it can no longer be assumed that folk tradition offers any significant protection for archaeological sites. It is now imperative that the archaeologically-based stories of sites and their importance for understanding the past become embedded in the population in the same way that folk belief was in the past. This could be seen as probably one of the most important challenges facing archaeologists in Ireland now and in the future.

One of the other trends that has been gathering pace in recent years is the concept of the past that is not tied to place but is an image commodity, a movable feast and a selling point for a mythic, Celtic Ireland. Megalithic art motifs, such as the triple spiral from the interior of the Newgrange passage tomb, and images of portal tombs (Figure 13.5), particularly Poulnabrone in Co. Clare, are used to sell beer, microchips, perfume, insurance (through companies such as the Celtic Insurance Company!), hotels, as well as Ireland itself. As Gibbons (1996: 89) has argued, this is not really done so much out of respect for the past. Rather

Figure 13.5 Advertisement for the new European (golf) Club at Brittas Bay, Co. Wicklow, using a portal tomb motif

it represents a blatant recourse to the material remains of the past in an attempt to confer its mystique and aura of permanence and stability on an information-based present which increasingly blurs the lines between different places and times. Image is everything in a world where it is possible to commute on a daily basis between Ireland, Britain and continental Europe.

O'Connor (1993) has argued that the historic colonial image of Ireland as an empty landscape awaiting development has strong resonances in the present-day tourist image of Ireland as an uncrowded, green and pleasant land. Postcards, tourist literature and videos focus on the image of a timeless land where visitors from more frenetic lifestyles and landscapes can come for rest and relaxation. You might even encounter the 'little people' (although as Welch (1996: 524) has noted the fairies were rarely small in authentic folklore, and the 'little people' are a representation influenced by the colonial encounter with the English tradition of imps and elves).

A linked concept is contained in the idea that the Irish rural landscape can be seen as the epitome of a timeless continuity of the past and the way in which the past and present can be viewed as contemporaneous (Leerssen 1994; McDonagh 1983). This slippage between past and present which was so important in providing a cultural basis for nationalism is now at the centre of Ireland's current image-making on the international scene. There is the inherent danger here that we are losing the sense of place that we have argued above is a central characteristic of Ireland's past, and the recognition that this past is not constant or unchanging but was a country where the meaning of monuments was contested and changed as new stories were developed to explain the past.

SPEAKING FROM THE HILLS

As archaeologists we have the challenge of trying to understand and present the record of this complex past from the palimpsest of evidence left behind, and our standard analytic device is to peel off the sediments of activity and experience one by one. The reality is that a number of images of the past may be contemporaneously drawn on and narrated by people to give it meaning. It is important to remember that the past would have been explained in mythic terms through oral history and folklore by people living and creating the archaeological record.

Looking at the landscape at Loughcrew, Co. Meath, the terrain is dominated by a striking elongated ridge orientated south-west to north-east. This ridge lies on the interface between the catchment areas of the Boyne/ Blackwater and Shannon river systems. The most prominent archaeological feature is the passage tomb cemetery with large focal hilltop cairns along the ridge with smaller sites clustered around them (Figure 13.6). The Irish name of the place, *Sliabh na Caillighe*, the hill of the witch or hag, directly refers to the tales of the harvest hag referred to on page 201

Figure 13.6 Loughcrew, Co. Meath. Photograph taken from Cairn D on Carnbane West looking to Cairn T on Carnbane East, the focal tomb in the cemetery. Some of the smaller tombs on Carnbane West are visible to the left in mid-ground

and to these cairns. They are seen in oral tradition as stones dropped from her apron as she hopped from west to east across the flat summits on the ridge before falling and dying as she jumped towards another hill. We can regard this story as an origin myth to explain very prominent features in the landscape visible from a great distance and also as a mnemonic device to aid the passing on of information on place names.

When Loughcrew was documented by Eugene Conwell (1866) as an archaeological complex in the 1860s he thought that it could be equated with the pagan cemetery of Tailteann mentioned in the early Irish literature, and he proposed that Cairn T was the tomb of Ollamh Fodhla, a legendary king and law-giver. Now we know that Loughcrew is much older than this mythohistorical connection, but Conwell's view has to be set in the state of knowledge in the 1860s and in the context of the importance of Ollamh Fodhla as an iconographic figure of great importance for Irish nationalism in the nineteenth century (Hutchinson 1987: 58). He was regarded as the founder of the nation in ancient antiquity and, for example, he was one of the heroic figures shown on the banners and membership cards of the Repeal movement in the 1840s (see e.g. Owens 1994).

Archaeologically Loughcrew is best known as a passage tomb cemetery, but in order to put that cemetery in context we have to bring into focus other aspects of the archaeological record. In the lithic material collected from the area in the late nineteenth and early twentieth century by Edward Crofton Rotherham, a local landowner and antiquarian who also investigated several of the tombs on Loughcrew, there is both Mesolithic and a substantial quantity of Neolithic material. Loughcrew would have been known as a striking range of hills in the Mesolithic and its significance would have been enhanced and more widely known because of its position on the interface between the catchment areas of the Boyne and Shannon river systems. With the development of the cemetery the human perception of the place would have varied depending on location in relation to the site, from distant landmark with the major cairns as distinctive features, to close encounters where the interplay between the landscape and the siting of the cairns created a range of different settings for the ceremonies that would have been carried out at and around the tombs (Cooney 1990; McMann 1994; Thomas 1992). It would appear that there was significant settlement activity in the vicinity of the cemetery. In the Bronze Age it seems that there was both a continued use and veneration of what were now ancient monuments with the insertion of pottery and presumably burials into the tombs, but there was also the further development of a ceremonial focus on a lower shoulder of ground to the north at Ballinvalley, where a cursus, stone circle, standing stones, cairns and a few examples of rock art, including the capstone of a cist (see Moore 1987; Newman 1995), lie within sight of the ridge and its cairns to the south. The tombs, if we can judge by much more recent oral and literary tradition, became mythic and ambiguous, places where the real world and the other world collided. Their continuing or renewed power in late prehistory is illustrated by the very large deposit of bone plaques with La Tène decoration in Cairn H referred to on page 203. To move forward to today, Loughcrew is recognised as an internationally important archaeological landscape. It has retained a special atmosphere which allows people to experience the past in a very real way (e.g. Kearney 1996; O'Brien 1992). Loughcrew, as Jean McMann (1993: 14) has put it, is a place with many histories. The challenge is to respect those histories into the future without detrimentally altering the places where it all happened.

> Ancient Ireland, indeed! I was reared by her bedside
> The rune and the chant, evil eye and averted head
> Fomorian fierceness of family and local feud.
> Gaunt figures of fear and of friendliness,
> For years they trespassed on my dreams,
> Until once, in a standing circle of stones,
> I felt their shadows pass
>
> Into that dark permanence of ancient forms.
>
> John Montague,
> 'Like dolmens round my childhood . . .'

REFERENCES

Aalen, F.H.A, Whelan, K. and Stout, M. (1997) *Atlas of the Irish Rural Landscape.* Cork: Cork University Press.

Aitchison, N.B. (1994) *Armagh and the Royal Centres in Early Medieval Ireland.* Woodbridge: Cruithne Press/Boydell and Brewer.

Bergh, S. (1995) *Landscape of the Monuments: A Study of the Passage Tombs in the Cúil Irra Region, Co. Sligo, Ireland.* Stockholm: Riksantikvarieämbetet.

Borlase, W.C. (1897) *The Dolmens of Ireland.* London: Chapman and Hall.

Brenneman, W.L. and Brenneman, M.G. (1995) *Crossing the Circle at the Holy Wells of Ireland.* Charlottesville: University Press of Virginia.

Buckley, V. (ed.) (1990) *Burnt Offerings.* Dublin: Wordwell.

Burenhult, G. (1984) *The Archaeology of Carrowmore.* Theses and papers in North European Archaeology Vol. 14. Stockholm: Institute of Archaeology, University of Stockholm.

Cahill, M. (1994) 'Mr Anthony's bog oak case of gold antiquities.' *Proceedings of the Royal Irish Academy* 94C: 53–109.

Conwell, E.A. (1866) 'On ancient sepulchral cairns on the Loughcrew hills.' *Proceedings of the Royal Irish Academy* 9: 355–379.

Cooney, G. (1979) 'Some aspects of the siting of megalithic tombs in county Leitrim.' *Journal of the Royal Society of Antiquaries of Ireland* 109: 74–91.

Cooney, G. (1985) 'An unrecorded portal tomb at Aghavas, county Leitrim.' *Journal of the Royal Society of Antiquaries of Ireland* 115: 156–158.

Cooney, G. (1990) 'The place of megalithic tomb cemeteries in Ireland.' *Antiquity* 64: 741–753.

Cooney, G. (1994) 'Sacred and secular Neolithic landscapes in Ireland.' In D.L. Carmichael, J. Hubert, B. Reeves and A. Schanche (eds) *Sacred Sites, Sacred Places*, pp. 32–43. London: Routledge.

Cronin, M. (1996) *Translating Ireland.* Cork: Cork University Press.

de Valera, R. and Ó Nualláin, S. (1961) *Survey of the Megalithic Tombs of Ireland, Vol. 1, Co. Clare.* Dublin: Stationery Office.

Edgeworth, M. [1800] (1964) *Castle Rackrent.* Oxford: Oxford University Press.

Eogan, G. (1991) 'Prehistoric and early historic culture change at Brugh na Bóinne.' *Proceedings of the Royal Irish Academy* 91C: 105–121.

Evans, E.E. (1966) *Prehistoric and Early Christian Ireland: A Guide.* London: Batsford.

Fallon, P. (1978) *The Speaking Stones.* Dublin: Gallery Press.

Gibbons, L. (1996) 'Coming out of hibernation? The myth of modernisation in Irish culture.' In L. Gibbons (ed.) *Transformations in Irish Culture*, pp. 82–93. Cork: Cork University Press.

Gosling, P. (1993) *Archaeological Inventory of County Galway: Volume I, West Galway.* Dublin: Stationery Office.

Horne, D. (1986) *The Public Culture.* London: Pluto Press.

Hutchinson, J. (1987) *The Dynamics of Cultural Nationalism.* London: Allen and Unwin.

Kearney, M. (1996) *Mortally Wounded; Stories of Soul Pain, Death and Healing.* Dublin: Marino.

Kinsella, T. (1969) *The Táin.* Oxford: Oxford University Press/Dolmen Press.

Leerssen, J. (1994) The western mirage: on the Celtic chronotope in the European imagination. In T. Collins (ed.) *Decoding the Landscape*, pp. 1–11. Galway: Centre for Landscape Studies, University College Galway.

McDonagh, O. (1983) *States of Mind: A Study of Anglo-Irish Conflict, 1780–1980.* London: Allen and Unwin.

McMann, J. (1993) *Loughcrew: The Cairns.* Oldcastle: After Hour Books.

McMann, J. (1994) 'Forms of power: dimensions of an Irish megalithic landscape.' *Antiquity* 68: 525–544.

Mitchell, G.F. (1985) 'Antiquities.' In T.O. Raifeartaigh (ed.) *The Royal Irish Academy, a Bicentennial History 1785–1985*, pp. 93–165. Dublin: Royal Irish Academy.

Montague, J. (1995) *Collected Poems.* Loughcrew: Gallery Press.

Moore, M.J. (1987) *Archaeological Inventory of County Meath.* Dublin: Stationery Office.

Newman, C. (1995) 'A cursus at Loughcrew, Co. Meath.' *Archaeology Ireland* 34: 19–21.

O'Brien, T. (1992) *Light Years Ago: A Study of the Cairns of Newgrange and Cairn T Loughcrew, Co. Meath, Ireland.* Dublin: The Black Cat Press.

O'Brien, W.F. (1993) 'Aspects of wedge tomb chronology.' In E. Shee Twohig and M. Ronayne (eds) *Past Perceptions: The Prehistoric Archaeology of South-West Ireland*, pp. 63–74. Cork: Cork University Press.

O'Connor, B. (1993) 'Myths and mirrors: tourist images and national identity.' In B. O'Connor and M. Cronin (eds) *Tourism in Ireland: A Critical Analysis*, pp. 68–85. Cork: Cork University Press.

O'Donovan, P.F. (1995) *Archaeological Inventory of County Cavan.* Dublin: Stationery Office.

O'Flanagan, P. (1981) Survey, maps and the study of rural settlement development. In D. Ó Corráin (ed.) *Irish Antiquity*, pp. 320–326. Cork: Tower Books.

Ó hÓgáin, D. (1990) *Myth, Legend and Romance: An Encyclopaedia of the Irish Folk Tradition.* London: Ryan Publishing.

Ó Ríordáin, S.P. (1979) *Antiquities of the Irish Countryside*, fifth edition, revised by R. de Valera. London: Methuen.

O'Sullivan, M. (1996) 'REPS, farming and archaeology.' *Archaeology Ireland* 37: 8.

Ó Suílleabháin, S. (1942) *Handbook of Irish Folklore.* Dublin: Irish Folklore Commission.

Owens, G. (1994) 'Hedge school of politics, O'Connell's monster meetings.' *History Ireland* 2(1): 35–40.

Pochin Mould, D.D.C. (1955) *Irish Pilgrimage.* Dublin: Gill.

Raftery, B. (1994) *Pagan Celtic Ireland: The Enigma of the Irish Iron Age.* London: Thames and Hudson.

Raftery, J. (1976) 'Things and people.' In C. Ó Danachair (ed.) *Folk and Farm*, pp. 235–238. Dublin: Royal Society of Antiquaries of Ireland.

Robinson, T. (1994) 'A Connemara fractal.' In T. Collins (ed.) *Decoding the Landscape*, pp. 12–29. Galway: Centre for Landscape Studies, University College Galway.

Thomas, J. (1992) 'Monuments, movement and the context of megalithic art.' In N. Sharples and A. Sheridan (eds) *Vessels for the Ancestors*, pp. 143–155. Edinburgh: Edinburgh University Press.

Waddell, J. (1990) *Irish Bronze Age Burials*. Galway: Galway University Press.

Welch, R. (ed.) (1996) *The Oxford Companion to Irish Literature*. Oxford: Clarendon Press.

Whelan, K. (1994) 'Settlement patterns in the west of Ireland in the pre-famine period.' In T. Collins (ed.) *Decoding the Landscape*, pp. 60–78. Galway: Centre for Landscape Studies, University College Galway.

Woodman, P.C. (1993) 'The prehistory of south-west Ireland: an archaeological region or a state of mind?' In E. Shee Twohig and M. Ronayne (eds) *Past Perceptions: The Prehistoric Archaeology of South-West Ireland*, pp. 6–15. Cork: Cork University Press.

CHAPTER FOURTEEN

CLEARANCE CAIRNS

The farmers' and the archaeologists' views

INGUNN HOLM

ABSTRACT

In this paper I will present a case study from eastern Norway concerning the relation between the archaeologists' opinion about a certain group of ancient monuments and the local population's oral tradition. The ancient monuments under study are a type of cairn field. In this case the local oral tradition was giving the right explanation of the cairn fields. The archaeologists had either considered these cairn fields as nineteenth-century clearings for grass production or as Iron Age cemeteries. The local tradition explained them as deserted fields for cereals, used prior to the Black Death. Archaeological studies during the past ten years have shown that the cairn fields are fossil fields representing an agricultural system that has been in use from 800 BC to AD 1600. This system is not described in any written sources, but has survived in the folk tradition in certain parts of Norway and Sweden. After the desertion of the cairn fields the local tradition tells that the huldrefolket *moved in. These were a subterranean people living a life parallel to ordinary people in deserted farms and fields. The young men of the* huldrefolket *came courting the young girls who stayed in the summer dairies during the season. This case shows that archaeologists can learn much from listening to the local oral tradition concerning ancient monuments.*

The landscape that surrounds us is full of history. As archaeologists we are trained to survey and interpret the concrete, physical antiquities we find. From this we create a history that begins with the landscape we study. But there are others who occupy the same landscape and interpret the remains they see from their own traditions. The antiquities and local knowledge and tradition combine to create histories that interpret and explain the landscape people move around in on a daily basis. In this chapter I will show how such local histories and the knowledge of inhabitants can be an important part of the archaeological research process.

THE ANTIQUITIES

The example comes from the parish of Vardal, in the town of Gjøvik, county Oppland, in the inland region of eastern Norway. The parish is rural, with agricultural areas and large forested tracts. It lies above the post-glacial shore lines and contains wide areas of well-drained moraine with a low content of limestone. Prehistoric remains in the parish include grave mounds and large and small groups of clearance cairns, which I refer to as cairn fields. Both grave mounds and clearance cairns are located in areas near modern agricultural fields and also in forest areas which were commonly utilised for summer grazing – the Norwegian summer farms. Cairn fields are largely preserved in the forested areas, where agricultural activities and modern expansion have been limited.

Such cairn fields can be found over large parts of southern Norway and southern and central Sweden (Pedersen 1990a; Widgren 1997), as large areas (up to 200 ha) of small clearance cairns (Figure 14.1). Normally there are fifty to sixty clearance cairns per hectare. The cairns have diameters of 2–6 m, and are 0.1–0.5 m high, and the stones in them have diameters of 0.1–0.3 m. The cairns were created by hand. In sloping terrain they often have an elongated form, while in flatter areas they are usually round. It is possible to see that the area between the cairns is cleared and tilled, but there are usually no lynchets or stone fences. Cairn fields are usually situated on moraine above the post-glacial shore lines. Burial mounds are sometimes found among the clearance cairns, on high points or other similar locations in the terrain, and they are much more prominent than the clearance cairns (Figure 14.2) (Holm 1995).

Different Norwegian archaeologists have interpreted these clearance cairns in very different ways. Interpretations have varied over time, and from museum district to museum district. In the 1800s archaeologists interpreted clearance cairns as graves (Nicolaysen 1879; Pedersen 1990a). In south-western Norway they have been regarded as traces of agricultural activity dating to the first centuries after the birth of Christ (Møllerop 1957). In the 1950s and 1960s in eastern Norway the cairn fields were interpreted as the remains of hayfields from the middle 1800s (Pedersen 1990a). Since I have done my research in eastern Norway, I will focus on this interpretation.

In the 1980s archaeologists Ellen Anne Pedersen and Christian Keller investigated a group of clearance cairns in eastern Norway as the subject of an interdisciplinary research project, including detailed mapping, pollen analyses, radiocarbon dating and intensive interpretation of the profiles of the cairns under investigation (Pedersen 1990a; Pedersen 1990b). The cairns were interpreted as traces of agricultural activity from the Early Iron Age. This interpretation led to the classification of clearance cairns as prehistoric remains, and consequently their inclusion in archaeological surveys in eastern Norway.

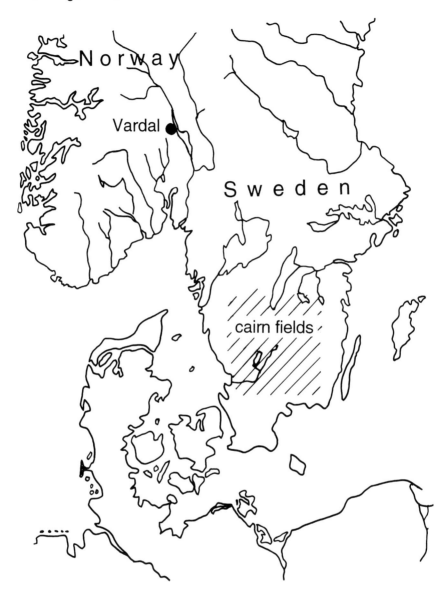

Figure 14.1 Southern Norway and Sweden, showing the research area at Vardal and the area with cairn fields in south and central Sweden

I started my research on clearance cairns in 1989 as part of my master's (*magistergrad*) thesis. My premise was that the clearance cairns were traces of agricultural activity, probably from the Iron Age and the Viking Period. During the research process, this premise was confirmed, when I found

Figure 14.2 Typical clearance cairn

layers of cultivated soil in connection with the clearance cairns. According to radiocarbon dates the cairns were in use in the Iron Age and in the medieval period. I chose to concentrate my research on a single church parish, Vardal (Holm 1995).

THE TRADITION

I will now discuss the traditions associated with the cairn fields. There are two related traditions, the first explaining their origin and the second explaining their continued use. According to these traditions, the cairn fields under study are deserted farms from the time of the hoe farmers, in Norwegian, *hakkebøndene*. As *hakkebøndene* died out, the cairn fields were said to be inhabited by *huldrefolket*, the underground folk.

In my efforts to acquire a better understanding of this parish, I read all the available historical literature on it. Four books on the history of the parish, written by a local sexton, were published in the 1930s (Lauvdal 1930–41). He recorded many legends from the area. During the sixty years between the collection of these oral traditions and my research, traditions regarding antiquities have become poorer. Few of these legends are alive today, and most likely they would have disappeared if they hadn't been collected by Lauvdal. Torun Zachrisson has reported a similar situation in Sweden, with a significant reduction in the oral traditions regarding antiquities from the turn of the century to the modern era (Burström *et al.* 1996). There may be several reasons why these traditions are declining. People do not believe in the legends about *huldrefolket* any more, and have hardly done so for almost a hundred years. Therefore these stories are considered less important and are forgotten. In Vardal these stories were connected to the use of summer farms and the herding of cattle in areas where the cairn fields were situated. These practices declined at the beginning of this century, and this part of the landscape is now in use for industrial forestry. The only people to visit this land-scape are farmers who own the forest and professional firms that take out the timber. Finally, the contexts in which these legends were told have vanished.

According to the legends recorded by the sexton T. Lauvdal, the cairn fields of Vardal once were farms or even a group of farms that constituted a small hamlet. The clearance cairns are located in areas that were deserted from the late middle ages until the late 1800s, with the exception of a few, scattered summer farms. The farms associated with the cairn fields were said once to have been inhabited by *hakkebøndene* who tilled the soil with a hoe rather than a ridging plough, the traditional tool in the region. According to the legends these *hakkebøndene* died out in the Black Death, and their farm lands were abandoned. This epidemic hit Norway in 1349 and 1350. According to Norwegian historians up to 50 per cent of the population died as a result of this plague (Bjørkvik 1996). Many historical legends in Norway discuss the Black Death and the resulting desertion of farms. There are many local variants of the legend of hunters who, in the middle of the forest, come upon a deserted farm, where everything is left as it was when people lived there (Liestøl 1977).

In 1878, the first archaeologist to visit the district, Nicolay Nicolaysen from the Society for the Preservation of Ancient Monuments in Norway, mentions in his reports that the local population explained some cairns, which he considered to be grave cairns, as clearance cairns from the time of *hakkebøndene* (Nicolaysen 1879). This was their explanation when he did not find anything in the cairns he excavated. Nevertheless he continued to excavate this type of cairn, finding nothing that could prove them to be grave cairns (Pedersen 1990a).

A similar tradition about *hakkebøndene* is documented in Sweden by the Swedish folklorist, Olof Hylten-Cavallius, from the middle of the

1800s. When Swedish cultural geographers Clas Tollin and Leif Gren started research on the clearance cairns in southern Sweden in the 1980s, they referred to this tradition and to the work of Hylten-Cavallius (Gren 1989; Tollin 1989). According to Hylten-Cavallius the clearance cairns in southern Sweden were interpreted locally as agricultural fields from the 'hoe time'. The cairns were 'hoe cairns' from the time when giants cleared the land with hoes (Hylten-Cavallius 1863: 33).

It is difficult to establish the existence of an unqualified relationship between the traditions in eastern Norway and southern Sweden. It is possible that the existence of cairn fields in both regions is the source of the similar traditions.

Huldrefolket or the 'underground folk' who inhabited the abandoned and lost farms are an important part of many of these legends. *Huldrefolket* are said to live their lives parallel to humans. They have families, and live on farms with cattle and horses. They are very rich in silver and gold. They often live in houses that mortals have abandoned either permanently, such as at farms abandoned following the Black Death, or for short periods of time, like summer farms (Asbjørnsen and Moe 1888, 1993; Hodne 1995; Lauvdal 1930–41). *Huldrefolket* often inhabit summer farms during the winter (Kvideland and Sehmsdorf 1991).

There are similar traditions about beings living in the forest or under-ground in the other Nordic countries, in Germany and in Britain (Granberg 1935). According to Granberg in Germany these beings are called *Waldgeist*, *Waldfrau* or *Waldfräulein*. The female beings often try to seduce men working in the forest. *Huldrefolket* also have traits in common with the fairies of English folklore. Like the fairies, *huldrefolket* have a society of their own with families (ibid.: 12).

In Norwegian folklore *huldrefolket* are connected to the cultural land-scape, as opposed to trolls who live in the mountains. The forest where clearance cairns are found is that close to farms or summer farms and may be looked upon as a part of the cultural landscape.

Women among *huldrefolket*, often called *Huldra*, are extremely beautiful. Men could often see them out in the forest, with their large herds of handsome cattle. *Huldra* have cow's tails hidden under their skirts. Some men married these *Huldra*, and this marked their families for generations to come (Figure 14.3).

In my research area there are also tales of the men among the under-ground folk. On Saturday nights these men courted the dairy maids living on summer farms in the vicinity of the cairn fields. They behaved as normal Saturday night suitors and it was difficult for the dairy maids to know that they were dealing with *huldrefolket*. If a girl accepted a marriage proposal from such a man, she moved to his farm underground. According to most legends, the girls were seldom happy underground, separated as they were from their families.

Figure 14.3 Huldra, drawing by Hans Gude, 1878, for Asbjørnsen and Moe's collection of folk tales

Huldrefolket live, as mentioned earlier, a life parallel to ordinary people. They are even said to have their own churches. So if you heard church bells in the forest, it was *huldrefolket* having their Mass. One place in my research area is said to have been the location of such a church. The place is named Kjerkesvea, which means 'the church swidden'. Legends tell that prior to the Black Death there was an ordinary church here for *hakkebøndene* cultivating the cairn fields that surround Kjerkesvea. After the Black Death, the church was abandoned and left to decay, and then taken over by *huldrefolket*.

Huldrefolket are also associated with other prehistoric remains, such as standing stone circles. These are common prehistoric remains in the immediate vicinity of Oslo, but are rare in inland regions. According to Scandinavian archaeologists standing stone circles are graves from the Early Iron Age (Hyenstrand 1984; Resi 1986; Skjelsvik 1951). Local inhabitants refer to them as 'judgement stones' and believe that they were the locations for judicial assemblies, the old Norse institution *ting*.

Two of Norway's best-known folklorists, Peter Christian Asbjørnsen and Jørgen Moe, included legends of *huldrefolket* collected from the parish neighbouring my research area in their collection of Norwegian folk tales (Asbjørnsen and Moe 1993). One of these legends concerns a wife who was kidnapped by *huldrefolket* while she lay in childbed. Many years later a man from the same countryside was searching for his horse in a meadow where there was a stone circle. As he hunted for his horse near these 'judgement stones' he suddenly found himself in the kitchen of a prosperous farm. He recognised the woman in the kitchen as the wife who was kidnapped many years ago. These same *huldrefolket* have also traditionally been called *haugfolk* or 'gravemound folk', and are thought to live in grave mounds.

It is important to understand that *huldrefolket* were not regarded as the builders of the standing stone circles and the clearance cairns. *Huldrefolket* merely took these monuments into use after the original builders died out.

THE CAIRN FIELDS AND THEIR POPULAR INTERPRETATION

In the parish where I did my research, local people interpreted the clearance cairns as traces of farming pre-dating the Black Death. This is in sharp contrast to archaeologists who had interpreted the cairns either as groups of grave cairns or as hay fields from the 1800s. As mentioned earlier in this paper my research showed that the local people had made the correct interpretation (Holm 1995).

There are several possible reasons for the correct lay interpretation. It is possible that an unbroken oral tradition has existed concerning farming activity associated with the clearance cairns. My radiocarbon dates show that the cairn fields were in use after the Black Death, perhaps up to 1650 (Holm 1995). An unbroken oral tradition is therefore entirely credible. However I do not know of any data from Vardal or the nearby districts that confirm or deny this possibility.

Leif Gren refers to a section from the work of Saxo Grammaticus, a Danish historian, who during the thirteenth century described 'heaps of stone' in between the forest trees. Saxo considered this to be deserted farmland (Gren 1989: 74). The Swedish naturalist Carl von Linné also described cairn fields from his home in southern Sweden. He interpreted them as definitive indicators of agricultural activity (Linné [1741] 1960,

[1749] 1963). At the end of the eighteenth century J.N. Wilse, a Norwegian priest, describes 'heaps of stone' which he interprets as traces of farming related to 'our oldest forefathers' (Wilse [1779] 1991: 161). Wilse is describing the immediate Oslo fjord region, about 200 km south of Vardal. It is therefore difficult to take this as support for an unbroken oral tradition connected to the cairn fields in Vardal.

Another explanation for the correct lay interpretation is simply the fact that a farmer can recognise agricultural activity, even though many years have past and the farming methods were quite different from his own. Norwegian archaeologists have traditionally been recruited from the urban upper middle class. These archaeologists had little or no farming experience. I believe that it is highly probable that a farmer, rooted in a local tradition and familiar with his land, will be more likely correctly to interpret a clearance cairn as an indicator of agricultural activity, than an archaeologist with an urban background. My experience regarding farmers at cairn fields shows that they easily recognise clearance cairns as traces of agriculture. They see evidence of tillage on the ground and are able to distinguish fertile from infertile soil by looking at the vegetation. As an archaeologist you gain these skills only by long archaeological field practice and deliberate work with these types of ancient monuments.

It seems that only the archaeologists have failed to correctly interpret these prehistoric remains. As mentioned earlier only the cairn fields of south-western Norway were interpreted as traces of agricultural activity by archaeologists. The reason for this was that similar clearance cairns were found in the fields of deserted farms from the migration period, which are quite common in this part of Norway (Myhre 1972; Rønneseth 1975).

Farming has been a rather neglected theme in Norwegian archaeology, with the exception of discussions of the introduction of farming in the Neolithic (e.g. Mikkelsen 1989; Østmo 1988). Two major works based on extensive excavations discuss farming in the Iron Age. One is written by an archaeologist, Anders Hagen, and the other by a geographer, Ottar Rønneseth (Hagen 1953; Rønneseth 1975). Both authors have a farming background. Hagen has stated that it was his farming background that led him to study the whole farm, including the fields and pastures, and not just the houses (Holm 1993). He was the first person in Norwegian archaeology to conduct such studies, which were based upon excavations from a deserted farm from the migration period (Hagen 1953). Rønneseth has studied his own family farm from the Early Iron Age up to modern times. He interviewed his old aunts and uncles about prehistoric remains and the ancient farm structure (Rønneseth 1975: 22). He had in this way access to knowledge that urban archaeologists in most cases do not have.

On page 220, I referred to Kjerkesvea where, according to folk tradition, there should have been a church. This is a clearly marked locality with stone fences surrounding a cleared area with scattered clearance cairns. From an archaeological point of view there is nothing to indicate that there ever has been a church or a churchyard here. Archaeologically it appears that farming has resulted in a stone fence, fencing in a field, not a graveyard. Stone fences are quite rare in Vardal, the use of wooden fences predominating. But graveyards are often surrounded by stone fences. Local tradition concerning Kjerkesvea differs considerably from scholarly archaeological interpretation.

There may be several reasons why Kjerkesvea has been explained as the remains of a church. Kjerkesvea is surrounded by cairn fields. The local population has interpreted this as a hamlet, far away from the nearest church. It is possible that from this they have assumed that, when the cairn fields were tilled and probably inhabited by several families, this area must have had its own church. People wandering in the area have seen the stone fence and interpreted it as a fence surrounding an old churchyard.

It is also possible that Kjerkesvea is an authentic name derived from the land being owned by the church in the medieval period, when the church was Norway's most important landowner. After the reformation in 1537, church estates were confiscated by the throne and sold. It is therefore possible that Kjerkesvea has kept its old name after a sale, and the story behind the name has changed. There are no written sources concerning who owned Kjerkesvea in the middle ages. In the eighteenth century it was owned by a farmer (Lauvdal 1930–41).

It is common for places or antiquities to be associated with explanatory place names. There is another example of this from the parish of Vardal. A forest area is known as *domen*, which means cathedral. According to legends, there was once a church at this location. According to documents, the property changed ownership in 1694 as a result of a judgement, in Norwegian, *dom*. The area came to be called *dommen*, and later *domen*. As a part of this process the explanation of the history behind the place name also changed over time.

These popular etymological traditions are still an important part of the Norwegian landscape. This has been one way people have made their landscape closer and more understandable. The etymologies inspire people both to retell the old explanations and to create new ones, often as 'correction' to scholarly interpretations. In Norway the scholarly interpretations are mainly published in Oluf Rygh's work *Norske Gaardnavne* (Norwegian farm names) (Rygh 1897), the reference work for place-name studies in Norway. Popular etymological tradition has fallen between the research traditions of humanistic scholars (Burström *et al.* 1996).

I mentioned on page 221 the standing stone circles, called locally 'the judgement stones' and interpreted as the location for a judicial assembly, the old Norse *ting*. The same interpretation of these *domarringar* is found in Sweden (ibid.). As noted, the archaeological interpretation of these monuments is that they are graves from the Early Iron Age (Hyenstrand 1984). There was a debate concerning these monuments in Sweden in the first part of this century. The popular tradition interpreting them as locations for judicial assemblies was discussed by several authors. Almgren (1923) considered these monuments to be places for cult and rituals. Holmgren (1929) used written sources like the Swedish laws from the medieval period to support an interpretation of these monuments as locations for the *ting*. After several archaeological excavations, the Swedish archaeologist T.J. Arne interpreted the standing stone circles as graves (Arne 1938). This seemed to end the discussion about their use as locations for the *ting*. K.E. Sahlstrøm confirms their interpretation as graves in an article from 1942. But he also considers the possibility that these monuments have been in use for cultic purposes. He also discusses the German material and claims that these types of monuments originated in northern Germany (Sahlstrøm 1942). Archaeological excavation often found simple cremation burials from the Early Iron Age in the stone circles (Resi 1986; Skjelsvik 1951), confirming the interpretation as graves. The institution of the *ting* is deeply rooted in Norwegian folk tradition. The standing stone circles did not look like anything the early modern Norwegians were familiar with. They were then connected with the tradition of the local *ting*. However, there is no evidence that they were ever used for such a purpose.

THE ARCHAEOLOGIST, THE TRADITION AND THE LOCAL POPULATION

Oral tradition concerning ancient monuments is of great importance. It says something about the effective history of ancient monuments through the centuries. It also tells us as archaeologists what is considered important by the people to whom we present our interpretations. This might not be the exact dating of the monument or the result of the pollen analysis. It might be of greater importance that the son of a local farmer once hung himself at the actual grave mound or that a girl has been taken into the grave mound by *huldrefolket*.

It is also important that we as archaeologists do not kill local tradition through our 'expert statements'. We have traditionally had a monopoly over the interpretations of ancient monuments and prehistoric periods. We enter a local community as experts whom the population in many cases expects to have authoritative answers (Solli 1996). In this situation we have to find a way to partake in a dialogue and not only present a monologue where we have all the answers, or, even worse, provide answers to questions that the local population looks upon as more or less irrelevant. As Solli has shown (1996: 79, 251) this is not a dialogue on equal terms. We cannot escape our university background. The difference between me as an expert and the local population was there, even when I did my research in the same parish in which I grew up. It was quite clear to me that I was an honoured guest and not just another girl from Gjøvik when I was invited on trips to cairn fields by local amateur historians or interested farmers. They wanted my expert statement about the age of the cairns they showed me and my recognition of these cairns as important ancient monuments.

In spite of these problems it might be possible to have a dialogue meaningful for both the local population and the archaeologist. My experience through a series of conversations is that most often the dialogue consists of questions from the local population and answers from me. But very often questions are asked that I have not considered and do not have clear answers to. This leads to considerations that might have great importance for my own research process. As field archaeologists we come close to people. We are accessible in a quite different way from when we are in our university offices.

As I have shown, often there is a conflict between archaeological and popular interpretations of ancient monuments. We as archaeologists often react in a negative way when people do not accept our scholarly inter-pretations. For an archaeologist working in the district, it is a common situation to receive an inquiry from a devoted local amateur historian requesting an archaeological excavation of something he (it is always a man) believes are graves from a well-known battle, but you as an archae-ologist know are natural features. It is after the third or fourth telephone call that your open-mindedness, learned through long archaeological study and intensive theoretical debates, starts to shrink. It is important to accept a plurality of interpretations. But we as trained archaeologists also have to claim that not everything is possible inside an archaeological discourse (Solli 1996: 251).

My experience is that folk traditions have moved furthest away from what archaeologists accept as reasonable, when the subject is the more spectacular type of antiquity such as hill forts, church grounds, large burial mounds and standing stone circles. These monuments have encour-aged fantasy and given space for a rich oral tradition. Often kings, battles and similar dramatic occasions are associated with these monuments. The question is whether we as archaeologists have had too narrow a view of what is an acceptable interpretation. The folklorist Knut Liestøl refers to a story from the archaeologist Karl Rygh. In 1876 Rygh heard that, under a large boulder in a boulder field, there was a knight in armour with his horse, who had been overtaken by an avalanche (Liestøl 1977). Rygh excavated in the area and found remains of a man and a horse, a strike-a-light and two spear points from the Viking period. There were no forms of visible marking of a grave at the location. When local tradi-tions can give a complete description of the contents of a burial mound or of the knight who is buried under a boulder slope, is it the result of fantasy or do the legends have roots in a living, oral tradition?

Folk tradition is often closer to what archaeologists consider realistic when it comes to ancient monuments that have been a part of local industry, such as cairn fields and hunting pits. The local population most often recognise these monuments because they are situated where a farmer or a hunter would expect to find them. Cairn fields are situated on south-facing slopes with well-drained, but stony soil. Hunting pits are found in extensive systems where elk and reindeer have their seasonal migrations. The farmer and the hunter know something about farming and hunting which the professional archaeologist does not. This is why their knowledge is so useful. This is true both for the process of finding these types of monuments and for the process of interpreting them.

In my daily work I often employ surveys of ancient monuments. My experience is that the local population can make very useful contributions to this work. First they know their own surroundings, starting with natural resources, such as the migratory routes of the elk, bogs with iron ore and slopes with fertile soil. They also to a certain degree know the oral tradition still alive in the area. In many cases they know where ancient monuments to be surveyed are situated, either because they have learned to know them through local oral tradition or because they have recognised them as made by humans during their walks in the area.

Norwegian survey campaigns have a long tradition of using local informants and have been totally dependent on local knowledge in these surveys. There is a separate space for 'tradition about the monument' on the registration form. This information has been used in the work of identifying monuments, but aside from that, it is considered more or less anecdotal. Norwegian archaeologists have in this way used oral tradition, but just those pieces that suited their needs and interpretations. As shown on pp. 217–218 Norwegian archaeologists knew the tradition interpreting the cairn fields as clearance cairns from *hakkebøndene*. But as this interpretation did not fit with their archaeological world view, this knowledge was not taken seriously.

It is now possible in Norway, through heritage legislation, to protect locations with beliefs or tradition connected with them, even though there are no visible traces made by humans on the spot. This legislation has been enacted primarily in consideration of the Samii culture with its rich tradition of holy rocks and mountains (Hætta 1994). But it is also possible to protect other locations like holy St Olav springs, execution grounds, battle fields and rocks that tradition tells us the trolls have thrown. This new legal authority was established in 1993 when the law for protection of cultural heritage was changed. The paragraph defining cultural heritage was extended to include 'localities connected with historic events, belief or traditions'. Samii localities with belief or tradition older than a hundred years are subject to automatic legal protection. This is also the case for Norwegian localities where it is possible to prove the tradition to date to earlier than AD 1537, the date of the reformation, defined as the upper time limit for automatic legal protection of Norwegian cultural heritage. This protection may be possible for battle fields from the middle ages like Stiklestad where St Olav died or other places mentioned by Snorre or in the sagas (Sturluson 1990). As far as I know, this new legal authority has seldom been used by heritage management. It takes time to establish a new way of looking at the landscape and what it contains. Norwegian archaeologists are also very cautious in claiming traditions and beliefs recorded in modern times to be prior to AD 1537. However, as the example of Karl Rygh shows, there may be a long continuity also in oral tradition.

Archaeology claims to be a discipline that emphasises interdisciplinary approaches. Perhaps our interdisciplinary approaches should include listening to the local experts, those people who know every stone and mound on their farm and in the forest. My experience shows that this makes a useful and interesting contribution to the archaeological research process. The local experts can give answers to questions like 'where are the ancient monuments?', 'why are they just there?' and 'in what way have they been used?' This is important information and basic to the first part of a research process based on surveys or landscape analyses. But the local experts can also give information about the traditions connected with a landscape and the ancient monuments in it. They can tell something about their interpretation of the landscape, what features in this landscape are of significance and to what extent the ancient monuments are important in their understanding of their landscapes. These are kinds of information that Norwegian archaeologists have not collected or used to any degree. But this information would make valuable contributions to our research. It is a challenge to us to start working with these questions.

REFERENCES

Almgren, O. (1923) *Sveriges Fasta Fornlämningar från Hednatiden*, second edition. Föreningen Urds Skrifter vol. I. Uppsala: J.A. Lindblad.

Arne, T.J. (1938) 'Domarringarna äro gravar.' *Fornvännen*, 33: 165–177.

Asbjørnsen, P.C. and Moe, J. (eds) (1888) *Popular Tales from the Norse, by Georg Webbe Dasent. With an Introductory Essay on the Origin and Diffusion of Popular Tales*, third edition. Edinburgh: David Douglas.

Asbjørnsen, P.C. and Moe, J. (eds) (1993) *Samlede eventyr*, vols 1 and 2. Oslo: Den norske bokklubben.

Bjørkvik, H. (1996) 'Folketap og sammenbrudd.' In *Norges Historie*, vol. 4, edited by K. Helle. Oslo: Aschehoug forlag.

Burström, M., Winberg, B. and Zachrisson, T. (1996) *Fornlämningar och folkminnen*. Stockholm: Riksantikvarieämbetet.

Granberg, G. (1935) 'Skogsrået i yngre Nordisk folktradition.' In *Skrifter Utgivna av Gustav Adolfs Akademien för Folklivsforskning*, vol. 3, A–B. Uppsala: Lundenquistska bokhandeln.

Gren, L. (1989) 'Det småländska höglandets röjningsröseområden.' *Arkeologi i Sverige 1986*. Rapport RAÄ 1988(2): 73–95. Stockholm: Riksantikvarieämbetet och Statens historiska museum.

Hagen, A. (1953) *Studier i jernalderens gårdssamfunn*. Universitetets Oldsaksamlings skrifter, vol. IV. Oslo: Universitetets Oldsaksamling.

Hodne, Ø. (1995) *Vetter og skrømt i norsk folketro*. Oslo: Cappelen fakta, C.W. Cappelens.

Holm, I. (1993) 'Mellom fortid og framtid, et møte med Anders Hagen.' *Nicolay arkeologisk tidsskrift* 61: 16–28.

Holm, I. (1995) 'Trekk av Vardals agrare historie.' *Varia* 31, Universitetets Oldsaksamling, Oslo.

Holmgren, G. (1929) 'Ting och ring. Ett bidrag till diskussionen om de forntida tingplatserna.' *Rig, Föreningen för svensk kulturhistoria*, tidsskrift 12: 19–36.

Hyenstrand, Å. (1984) 'Fasta fornlämningar och arkeologiska regioner.' *Rapport Riksantikvarieämbetet och Statens historiska museer 1984*, p. 7. Stockholm: Riksantikvarieämbetet och Statens historiska museer.

Hylten-Cavallius, G.O. (1863) *Wärend och Wirdarne. Ett Försök i Svensk Ethnologi.* Stockholm: P.A. Norstedt & Söner.

Hætta, O.M. (1994) *Samene – Historie, Kultur, Samfunn*. Oslo: Grøndahl Dreyer.

Kvideland, R. and Sehmsdorf, H. K. (eds) (1991) *Scandinavian Folk Belief and Legend*. Oslo: Norwegian University Press.

Lauvdal, T. (1930–41) *Bygdebok for Vardal*, vol 1–4. Gjøvik.

Liestøl, K. (1977) 'Innleiing.' In Bø O. Segner (ed.) *Norsk Folkediktning III*. Oslo: Det norske samlaget.

Linné, C. von [1741] (1960) *Gotländska resa*. Reprint. Stockholm: Natur och kultur.

Linné, C. von [1749] (1963) *Skånska resa*. Reprint, Stockholm: Natur och kultur.

Mikkelsen, E. (1989) *Fra Jeger til Bonde: Utviklingen av Jordbrukssamfunn i Telemark i Steinalder og Bronsealder*. Universitetets Oldsaksamlings skrifter. Ny rekke 11. Oslo: Universitetets Oldsaksamling.

Myhre, B. (1972) 'Funn, fornminner og ødegårder. Jernalderens bosetning I Høyland Fjellbygd.' *Stavanger museum Skrifter* 7.

Møllerop, O. (1957) 'Gård og gårdsamfunn i eldre jernalder.' *Stavanger museums årbok 1957*, pp. 21–56. Stavanger: Stavanger museum.

Nicolaysen, N. (1879) 'Aarsberetning for 1878.' *Foreningen til Norske Fortidsmindesmerkers Bevaring*. Kristiania: Foreningen til Norske fortidsmindesmerkers bevaring.

Pedersen, E.A. (1990a) 'Rydningsrøysfelt og gravminner – spor av eldre bosetningsstruktur på Østlandet.' *Viking* 53: 50–56.

Pedersen, E.A. (1990b) 'Arkeologiske og paleobotaniske undersøkelser av rydningsrøyser. Eksempler fra Vestfold og Småland.' *Röjninsrösen i Skogsmark – En Nyckel til Sydsveriges Äldre Odlingshistoria*, pp. 20–31. Stockholm: Kungl. Skogs- och Lantbruksakademien.

Resi, H.G. (1986) 'Gravplassen Hunn i Østfold.' *Norske Oldfunn* 12. Oslo: Universitetets Oldsaksamling.

Rygh, O. (1897) *Norske Gaardnavne. Oplysninger Samlede til Brug ved Matrikelens Revisjon*. Kristiania: W.C. Fabritsius & Sønner.

Rønneseth, O. (1975) ' "Gard" und Einfriedigung.' *Geografiska Annaler, series B, Human Geography* 2.

Sahlström, K.E. (1942) 'Domarringarnas härkomst.' *Fornvännen*, 37: 115–136.

Skjelsvik, E. (1951) 'Steinringen på Hunn. Hunn i Borge. Gravningsresultater fra sommernen 1950.' *Viking* 15: 116–126.

Solli, B. (1996) *Narratives of Veøy. An Investigation into the Poetics and Scientifics of Archaeology.* Universitetets Oldsaksamlings skrifter, ny rekke, vol. 19. Oslo.

Sturluson, S. (1990) *Heimskringla, or The lives of the Norse kings by Snorre Sturlason,* edited with notes by Erling Monsen and translated into English with the assistance of A.H. Smith. New York: Dover.

Tollin, C. (1989) 'Röjningsrösen i södra Sverige.' *Arkeologi i Sverige 1986. Rapport RAÄ* 1988(2): 53–71. Stockholm: Riksantikvarieämbetet och Statens historiska museum.

Widgren, M. (1997) 'Fossila landskap. En forskningsöversikt över odlingslandskapets utveckling från yngre bronsålder till tidig medeltid.' *Kulturgeografiskt Seminarium 1/97.* Stockholm.

Wilse, J.N. [1779] (1991) *Beskrivelse over Spydeberg Præstegield og Egn.* Bibliofilutgave. Rakkestad: Valdisholm forlag.

Østmo, E. (1988) *Etableringen av Jordbrukskultur i Østfold i Steinalderen.* Universitetets oldsaksamlings skrifter, ny rekke vol. 10. Oslo.

CHAPTER FIFTEEN

COMING TO TERMS WITH LOCAL APPROACHES TO SARDINIA'S NURAGHI

EMMA BLAKE

ABSTRACT

Contemporary local discourses concerning sites put archaeologists in an uncomfortable position. Tutored in the notion of cultural diversity for some time now, they are used to insisting on the notions of multiculturalism and inclusion. However the local life of monuments would seem to have no place in the modern archaeological project. The result has been for archaeologists to acknowledge the abstract 'validity' of these perspectives but to ignore them entirely in practice. This is unfortunate, as how people of the present live through these monuments informs the structures' meaningful constitution in the past. Pragmatism is a strain of philosophical thought that supervenes the problem of cultural relativism without sacrificing open-mindedness and tolerance, thus permitting an incorporation of these non-archaeological approaches.

THE LOCAL LIFE OF THE NURAGHI

The local populations' perceptions of Sardinia's Bronze Age monuments (the towers known as nuraghi and their associated tombs) vary considerably from the archaeologists'. One experience brought home to me how great the differences between the approaches are. A forest ranger had taken me to a well-preserved nuraghe (Figure 15.1) adjacent to a farmhouse and outbuildings. From a distance, the conical tower rising above the modern rectangular structures was an impressive sight. On closer inspection, this nuraghe was indeed a key feature in the life of the farm, but not as I had expected. Stones had been removed from its external wall to provide steps up. On the upper level stood a mangy dog attached

Figure 15.1 Nuraghe Su Cobesciu (Chiaramonti, SS). This is the nuraghe I describe at the farm, but unfortunately when I took the photograph I was careful to do so from an angle that excluded the farm buildings! The dog is in the picture: his head is visible above the grassy bit on the far left

by a heavy chain wrapped around one of the tower's boulders, acting as a lookout. The ground-floor rooms were still intact and served as a shed, cluttered with farming equipment. Entering, we narrowly avoided tripping into a small trench just inside the doorway. The ranger scolded the farmer for this, a clear sign of clandestine digging, to which the man simply shrugged his shoulders and grinned sheepishly. It was obvious that the tower was far from being the pride and joy of the farmers. While by law the nuraghi are the property of the state and meant to be preserved, in practice, preservation is loosely defined. As long as the basic structure of the building is kept intact, the farmers are given free rein. For this reason, there was no question of legal action over the trench. Overall, the nuraghe was in relatively good condition, and that was considered enough. A tenuous balance between protecting the past and supporting the present is maintained in this way. Instead of trying to block out all the modern 'background noise' so as to focus on the structure itself, I see that right now the structure is a shed, and a dog house, and a lookout point, and a source of curiosity, inseparable from all it has been before. Archaeological knowledge of this nuraghe necessarily involves the evaluation of these identities, good and bad.

Such an incident as this makes it clear that whatever their age, origin or primary function, these monuments are features of today's spatio-temporal landscape as much as they were in the past, and are thus continually exposed to the constitutive gaze of the people around them. They have long inspired local stories, beliefs and customs, and feature in the experiences of those who live with them. The monuments are both visual landmarks and obstacles for tractors, shelter for flocks and a lure to outsiders, part of the island's patrimony and piles of reusable stones, magical places and sources of elicit antiquities. Their local significance clearly differs from their archaeological significance, which has resulted in a stand-off between these conflicting systems of knowledge. In the nineteenth and early twentieth centuries, when folklore was considered a tool for archaeologists, they observed the behaviour of the local shepherds and rural communities of Sardinia with regards to the nuraghi and giants' tombs for clues to their origins and function. The scholars were entertained by these quaint anachronisms and commented condescendingly on the apparent unstudied naïveté they demonstrated (see Mackenzie 1910, 1913). With the subsequent realisation that local traditions were as much tied to the present as to the past, folklore as a tool was discredited in favour of excavations only (Lilliu 1988: 13–20; cf. Gazin-Schwartz and Holtorf, chapter 1). The current approach by archaeologists to local views of the monuments is a blanket acceptance of their validity, yet no thorough examination of them is undertaken. Ignoring these local practices might be a short-term salve to our consciences but the price we pay is an incomplete picture of the material culture we study. Despite reticence on both sides, it is both possible and desirable for archaeologists to consider the local approaches to the material remains of the past. The local life of monuments as an alternative knowledge system has much to offer an archaeology that is prepared to consider it. Using Sardinia as my area of reference in order to address issues of wider bearing, this paper will consider how a Pragmatist philosophy permits us to engage actively with the local approaches to the material remains of the past, and then discusses what is to be gained from doing so.

THE ARCHAEOLOGICAL AND THE LOCAL: SEPARATE BUT EQUAL?

Though indeed other remnants of the past occupy significant roles in the present, architectural features, by their continuous presence in land-scapes, rather than being hidden underground or whisked off to museums, are particularly susceptible to immediate and everyday interpretation. The category of local approaches includes 'folklore', or oral traditions, as well as ungeneralisable behaviour by individuals. The latter refers to the many activities involving a monument which are case-specific choices of individuals based on the structuring elements of their environment and society, but not strictly explicable as a 'tradition'. This includes such activities as reusing a structure to house sheep, or naming the local bar 'Nuraghe Cafe'. While these latter activities may be informed by tradi-tion, they are nevertheless implicated in contingent circumstances of the present.

I insist on the term 'local' as habits and beliefs are mostly specific to the time and place and the people who use them, and are not accessible out of this context. For an English tourist to visit Sardinia briefly and adopt the notion that a certain nuraghe was inhabited by fairies would be ludicrous. The same is true of a tourist spontaneously deciding to dismantle a megalithic tomb in order to extend a nearby field wall. Such improbable scenarios highlight the fact that these traditions are made meaningful within the system of knowledge that is tied to the practices of individuals and their group solidarity.

Likewise, the archaeological community has its own customs and beliefs. We might encourage the dissemination of our ideas to a broader audience, but archaeological practice is habitually restricted to those in the profession, apart from a few opportunities for volunteers. Often the ideas produced by archaeology are incongruous outside the system of knowledge and lifestyle to which the archaeological community belongs.

Conflicts arise when local approaches interfere with archaeological ones, such as the farmers' reuse of the stones, or the long established practice of tomb robbing. An unfortunate consequence of the current climate of multicultural inclusion is the spurning of ethical debate, so that these conflicts are never adequately resolved. The old 'separate but equal' slogan has long since been exposed as innately discriminatory, subversive even, and yet the discipline's current stance is not unlike this approach. If, as Hilary Putnam (1995) for one has remarked, facts, theories, interpretation and values are all interconnected, then value judgements already are implicitly a part of our truth statements in archaeology. This is all the more reason to make our ethical stances explicit. And yet how do we evaluate other knowledge systems when we cannot transcend our own? Pragmatism is a strain of philosophical thought that may resolve this problem without sacrificing open-mindedness and tolerance, and has the potential to re-animate archaeological discourse.

INTRODUCING A PRAGMATIST ARCHAEOLOGY

For those who subscribe to anti-essentialism yet are repelled by the dehumanising tendencies and polemics of some of the continental philosophers, Pragmatism is a welcome alternative. Pragmatism maintains that abstract ideas are best understood through their practical results, and are best tested from the conditions of their existence. Further, objects and statements do not have intrinsic qualities, but are only understood in terms of their place in the world, their presence. These two ideas are interlinked: thus the concept 'truth' is only understandable in terms of the concrete situations and objects that we deem true and untrue, and following on from this, no statements or objects are true independent of the circumstances of their coming to be under consideration.

The Pragmatist philosopher Richard Rorty (1991) has most convincingly confronted the moral and intellectual scepticism brought on by pluralism by what he calls 'anti-anti-ethnocentrism': he asserts that we must acknowledge cultural diversity, accept that there are no independent objective criteria for judging between different cultural practices, but nevertheless recognise that we each participate in and feel an affinity for a particular culture, a solidarity.

Rather than being a separatist approach as it might first appear, on the contrary, this anti-anti-ethnocentrism accords more respect to cultures than the blindly inclusive approach, which denies holders of alternative viewpoints the right to struggle for recognition. As has been aptly pointed out, to say that we of the dominant group have a blanket respect for all other groups overlooks their individual differences and belies the actual power relations that are behind their continued marginalisation. By forfeiting the game in the conceptual arena, we take away other groups' primary opportunity for self-assertion. If we acknowledge theoretically what is evident de facto, that the act of belonging to one culture means that to some extent we buy into that culture more than another, then things become more interesting. Instead of walking on eggshells we can look at human behaviour (from our own perspective) situation by situation, culture by culture, and see what 'works', what is praiseworthy and what is not. It is only through these sorts of moral and intellectual dialogues that we can improve as a whole, that is, as Rorty would see it, we can minimise suffering in the world (Rorty 1991: 203–10).

Pragmatism incorporates a human element and a sort of empiricism which virtually demands case-specific applications. So to return for a moment to the scene at the farm: instead of trying to block out all the modern 'background noise' so as to focus on the structure itself, I see that right now the structure is a shed, and a dog house, and a lookout point, and a source of curiosity, inseparable from all it has been before. Now evaluating this, I find I do not mind its use as a shed; it appeals to me that this ancient structure is still of use to someone after so many centuries. I see the clandestine digging as a product of curiosity that is bound to occur as long as the government doesn't allocate enough money to archaeological research on the island, leaving the tower un-excavated. While it is a terrible shame that this occurs, to prosecute such offences without convincing reasons would encourage a resentment towards the monuments and towards the archaeological community that might result in more extensive damage. Finally, I do not approve of the treatment of the dog: while this might be well within the local bounds of decency, I feel secure in condemning this behaviour, though I am well aware that I do so based on my own cultural terms. The example above should demonstrate how Pragmatism is manifested rather than applied: my philosophical position comes out in my work rather than being put into it.

Though Pragmatism cannot be separated from the world-as-lived, it nevertheless has to be made relevant to specific projects. It lies on the high level of abstraction and as such it requires a theory of society to bridge the gap between it and archaeological theory and practice. As Dick Walker asserts, these middle-level abstractions are not a 'descent into empiricism' but an attempt to make the connection between the abstract and the concrete (Walker 1989: 144). Bourdieu's (1977) notion of habitus and Giddens' (1981) structuration lend themselves well to Pragmatism, with its emphasis on action. Similarly, time-geography's focus on particular places (locales) and particular lives (biographies) as informing the general social landscape (Pred 1986) falls within its scope. Any non-essentialist theoretical perspectives can be incorporated into Pragmatism.

LEARNING FROM THE LOCAL

So far I have tried to establish through a pragmatist approach how one may feel committed intellectually and ethically in a pluralist world. What is to be gained from doing so? Admitting value judgements permits the possibility of genuinely observing local habits and learning from them.

First and most obviously perhaps, the local perspective takes into account the sensory and aesthetic experience of the monuments. When a new building is constructed in a town, or on a campus, we readily make judgements about it: we may criticise it for being an ugly style, or shoddily built, or bemoan its placement on good park land. Or we may praise it for providing much-needed facilities, employing local labour and so on. In general, archaeological discourse withholds such comments. They are tacitly deemed irrelevant, even inappropriate to the archaeological project. This contrasts with my own experiences on Sardinia, where the local residents are quite candid about which monuments they feel are impressive and which are not. For them, a structure's age and scholarly significance do not exempt it from public opinion.

Second, local approaches emphasise individuality, the uniqueness of each structure, over categories of monuments. Those who live near a particular monument see it as a distinct entity, rather than merely an example of a 'type' of structure. While we must make a conscious effort to talk of 'context', and introduce a phenomenological element into descriptions of a site, they manage to blend individual sites and their landscapes seamlessly.

In addition to these first two factors there is a third way in which these local customs involving the material remains are important for archaeology, other than phenomenologically or aesthetically, because these still keep the approaches' relevance extremely marginal to most archaeological writing. These local approaches provide insight into the circumstances out of which new meanings are imposed on pre-existing objects. From their example one may reconceptualise the historical course of a site's attribution of meaning not solely as a cumulative trajectory but rather as a series of unrelated interludes involving continuities and disjunctures.

To illustrate what I mean by this, I will recount another experience, this time at a farm which contained both a nuraghe and a tomb. First of all the farmer led me to the tomb, then, realising that I was interested in 'old carved stones', he showed me a hollowed-out block of granite used as a water trough, which his father had made, with the year '1932' carved in the base. Apparently the farmer made an association between the trough and the tomb which was not an archaeological one, that is, not based on chronological or cultural points of contact between the objects. Around the nearby nuraghe, on a hill with signs of soil slippage, lay many sherds of pottery. My colleague and I recognised them from style and location as 'Nuragic' type. I brought some down for the man and his sister to see, saying they were several thousand years old, but they weren't having any of it. They said they were old bits of water pots from the days when their grandmother had to carry water over that hill balanced on her head, dropping them occasionally. They brought out a few of the old water carriers which they still had. Their jugs were glazed, while the sherds were not, the clay had many fewer inclusions and the shapes were different, but there was no convincing them they were not the same thing. So, instead of their personal histories being generated in part from these monuments, the pair had written the monuments into their own historical narratives. At the time I felt slightly frustrated that they did not appreciate the archaeological significance of the sites, but it struck me that this absence of any residual meaning need not be an exceptional case.

For some time now archaeologists have looked into the social role of material culture, focusing on the relationships between people and the objects they create and leave behind. The last part of this phrase is key, as these objects' producers only experienced them for a single lifetime: for a vast stretch of time their presence has been freed from the moorings of an original intentionality made explicit by their creators. For the archaeologist, the significance of an object cannot be separated from its origins or age or the circumstances of its creation – for this reason unprovenanced items are anathema. Yet I would argue that this is exactly what generations of people have experienced when confronted with these monuments, and they have managed to accommodate them into their own cultural context, in the absence of any historical baggage of meaning.

These days, there is much talk of how meaning is constructed, how material culture is meaningfully constituted, how structures operate as texts to be read and reread over time. There is a problem with this otherwise valid approach to material culture. An assumption underlies words such as 'rereading' and 'reinterpreting' that there are links between these interpretative readings over time. To reread a text would seem to imply a prior knowledge, a familiarity at least, derived from the first reading. However, such a familiarity in the later encounters with pre-existing objects cannot be presupposed. Archaeologists, habituated to linear time trajectories, interpret cultural change necessarily in light of what has gone before. Often in the case of the meanings of monuments, there is no before: ruptures occur that prevent any progressive evolution of meaning: the monuments are just there. Collective forgetting may be as significant as collective memory.

Practices generally build upon or react to former practices, rather than starting from scratch. As the old adage goes, 'There's no point in reinventing the wheel.' Not so with meanings. They do not necessarily progress cumulatively, or even emerge in opposition to prior meanings. They do not require previous meanings to go on at all, because they do not directly reflect knowledge accumulation.

To take issue with the prima facie claims to a genealogy of meaning is not to say that there are not numerous cases of continuities in cultural beliefs that carry on and evolve from one another, or emerge in reaction to earlier ones. Oral traditions may preserve meanings indefinitely. However, having observed a sharp disjuncture now with regards to interpretations of the prehistoric monuments, it seems likely that the slate would have been wiped clean at other times in the past too, since there is much evidence of periods of abandonment of structures. When people return to the structures it is with no prior interpretative links to renew, with only the object itself to go by.

The thought of material objects being the receptors of and inspirations for an unbroken chain of evolving meaning makes the past seem less remote. In terms of archaeology, the task of getting a grip on this slippery idea of meaning appears easier when thought of as a sequential process. However, while it is possible to conceive of a continuing narrative history of the practices surrounding a site, the history of that site's meaning is perhaps best described in terms of staccato periods often in no way linked together.

So the issue here is not one of seeking vestiges of past meanings in current ones: it is about understanding how people confront what already exists, how they reuse and recycle the material around them, often without any prior knowledge or memory to build from. We know that meanings are constructed by people from various factors: personal character and values, knowledge base, economic circumstances, legislative policies, outside opinion. Along with these factors one should consider to what degree folklore about the monuments is influenced by their material presence. Since we now recognise that folklore may be a recent innovation of a community, we can consider how the architectural anachronisms have been negotiated in a later period to produce these 'traditions'. We need not see oral traditions as alternative explanations of the past: such beliefs are not currently viable within the archaeological community, nor need they be, for the reasons stated earlier. What is interesting is to look at the circumstances that lead to their development.

To conclude, through engaged observations of situated practices, in other words the subjective empiricism that is the Pragmatist ethos, one can turn to the contemporary local life of prehistoric monuments not as an anomalous modern phenomenon, nor as a pristine relic of past thoughts, but as an insight into earlier people's unregulated responses to the continuity of form and presence of ancient material objects.

ACKNOWLEDGEMENTS

I am grateful to Ian Hodder and Stuart Reevell for reading early drafts of the talk from which this paper comes. Thanks to Amy Gazin-Schwartz and Cornelius Holtorf for extremely useful comments on my paper, and for organising both the TAG session and the book. Thanks also to Victor Buchli, Carol McDavid and Lynn Meskell for subsequent discussions that broadened my understanding of Pragmatism.

REFERENCES

Bourdieu, P. (1977) *Outline of a Theory of Practice*. Cambridge: Cambridge University Press.
Giddens, A. (1981) *A Contemporary Critique of Historical Materialism, Vol. 1: Power, Property and the State*. London: Macmillan.

Lilliu, G. (1988) *La civiltà dei Sardi dal Paleolitico all'età dei nuraghi.* Torino: Ed. Nuova ERI.

Mackenzie, D. (1910) 'The dolmens, tombs of the giants, and nuraghi of Sardinia.' *Papers of the British School at Rome* 3: 87–137.

Mackenzie, D. (1913) 'Dolmens and nuraghi of Sardinia.' *Papers of the British School at Rome* 6(2): 127–170.

Pred, A. (1986) *Place, Practice and Structure: Social and Spatial Transformation in Southern Sweden: 1750–1850.* Cambridge: Polity Press.

Putnam, H. (1995) *Pragmatism: An Open Question.* Oxford: Blackwell.

Rorty, R. (1991) *Objectivity, Relativism, and Truth.* Cambridge: Cambridge University Press.

Walker, D. (1989) 'What's left to do?' *Antipode* 21(2): 133–165.

CHAPTER SIXTEEN

ARCHAEOLOGY AS FOLKLORE

The literary construction of the megalith Pentre Ifan in west Wales

JULIA MURPHY

ABSTRACT

This paper is a textual journey, the destination being the literary construction of the megalithic monument Pentre Ifan in Pembrokeshire, Wales. By tracing the roots of the discourses which are so familiar to us today, I show how the label 'burial chamber' is a misnomer, which has implications for present-day theories about megalithic monuments and the Neolithic burial tradition. I also demonstrate how archaeological interpretation can grow from the same roots as folklore, but how it gains a different status because of the reiteration of theories by authoritative voices, and how this leads to the privileging of archaeological interpretation over folklore.

Once upon a time there was a giant, a sad and lonely fellow whose only comfort was to sit at his large stone dining table feasting on his daily meal of raw meat and young saplings and watch the sun set over the sea to the west . . .

Once upon a time there was a great king, a legend in his own time, whose loyal knights convened at a round table and followed him on his ventures across lands to the west, leaving structures in the landscape where he had deigned to stop and rest, or fight a heroic battle, or play quoits . . .

Once upon a time there was a mighty chieftain, so honoured that upon his death a huge structure was erected in a prominent place by his one remaining son, in which his body and those of his sons were laid to rest . . .

Once upon a now there is a stone structure of the portal dolmen classification, built in the Neolithic . . .

Figure 16.1   Pentre Ifan
Source: Photograph by Cornelius Holtorf

These stories refer to Pentre Ifan, a megalith in Pembrokeshire, Wales (Figure 16.1). Would you, as an archaeologist, choose the last story, dismissing the others as flights of fancy, folklore, nonsense?

Let me take you on a textual journey, one that constructs a monument through words from the pages of archaeological journals. The destination is the structure that stands in the sight of Carn Ingli, called Pentre Ifan Burial Chamber (Figure 16.1). It has been known by this name since the archaeologist W.F. Grimes wrote reports of his excavations there in the earlier part of the twentieth century. I will show you how the current interpretation of this monument is a literary construction. This has implications for contemporary theories about megalithic monuments, because I will show that the interpretation of these monuments as burial chambers has been chosen above many other valid discourses which can be traced from the earliest writings about megaliths.

EARLY INTERPRETATIONS

The earliest recorded account of Pentre Ifan dates to 1603, when the historian George Owen (1552–1613) wrote his *Description of Pembrokeshire* ([1603] 1994). He is first impressed by the size of the monument and writes that 'a man on horseback may well ride under it without stooping' (ibid.: 195), a description which to most readers gives a better idea of the size than dry lists of measurements. He feels able to interpret the reason for the size of the stone: 'Doubtless this stone was mounted long time since in memory of some great victory or the burial of some notable person', referring to this as an 'ancient rite', and saying that it is 'mounted high to be seen afar off' (ibid.: 195). Owen is aware of how Pentre Ifan dominates the landscape, and he believes that it was put there for some particular reason, as a reminder or commemorative stone. For him, it is a monument true to the meaning of the word, like a statue or memorial today.

Owen sets up a method of description which others then follow in their work. The significant motifs are a detached empirical description of measurements, a sense of awe at the size of the structure, and also the notion of being able to ride a horse under the monument. Two interpretations are mentioned: that the place could be associated with a burial, but equally that it may be a marker of 'some great victory' (Owen [1603] 1994: 195). This idea comes from the Bible (1 Maccabees 13: 27–29). Written in Latin, the passage describes a character called Simon building a tomb for his father and his brothers. The translation reads that 'he made it high that it might be seen, with polished stone front and back'. Simon's tomb is visible to those sailing at sea, and from this comparison, Owen believes that Pentre Ifan, too, is a prominent marker probably associated with burial. This is an important point! For in this very first piece of writing, not only do we have a description of the monument, but also the idea, drawn from a biblical analogy, that this monument is associated with burial and death.

During the seventeenth century, the monument is described but not mentioned by name in some correspondence addressed to a Welsh Oxford scholar Edward Lhuyd. The correspondent Sanders reports his observation of a cavity he had been asked to look for, which was said to be associated with sacrifices and offerings. Finding a cavity, he concludes that the monument was used as an altar. From 1695 onwards Pentre Ifan is described in Camden's *Britannia* using terms established by the previous authors. A dominant adjective used to describe the stones is 'rude', so that whilst the monument appears to be impressive it is also regarded as a primitive structure.

The next author to write about Pentre Ifan is Richard Fenton in his *Historical Tour through Pembrokeshire* in 1796 ([1903] 1994). He writes of this cromlech: 'taking its height and its other dimensions into account, unquestionably the largest Druidical relic in Wales', and also that it is a 'scene of Druidical mysteries'. He describes the stones as 'coarse', 'immense' and 'rude', and goes on to mention that 'you have a singular view of Carn Englyn through, and it admits a person on horseback riding under' (ibid.: 307–308; Figure 16.2). Fenton quotes Owen's description of how massive the structure is, and states that it surpasses the size of other monuments across a large area. Already, in this example of how

CROMLECH. PENTRE IFAN, PEMBROKESHIRE.

Figure 16.2   Riders under Pentre Ifan
Source: *Archaeologia Cambrensis*, 3rd Series, XLII (July 1865), after p. 284

elements of the original description were reiterated in writings two hundred years later, we can demonstrate how a first description shapes not only subsequent writings on the same subject, but also the way in which a place is approached and viewed. Fenton introduces new elements with his references to the Druids, although there were previous references to the place being some kind of altar. There is already a certain recognition that it was a place of either burial or sacrifice.

The monument is mentioned throughout the nineteenth century in the journal *Archaeologia Cambrensis*, which was distributed to members of the Cambrian Archaeological Association, particularly because Pentre Ifan was a place that the Association would visit as part of its annual week-long meeting, about which reports were published in the journal afterwards. More people were visiting the monument and it became part of an established circuit of field trips.

In 1859 a report of the Cardigan meeting by an anonymous author describes Pentre Ifan as 'probably the finest monument of the kind existing in the kingdom, certainly the highest – a tall man mounted easily riding under the single covering stone now remaining' (Anonymous 1859: 336). During their visit that year, 'six ladies and gentlemen, on horseback, stood together under it at the same time', and so we see a fulfilment of Owen's estimation at last! The anonymous author writes that 'It is curious that Arthur's name is associated with it; but that it was the burial-place of some distinguished chieftain or warrior is most likely' (ibid.). The association with King Arthur seems to have first occurred in the previously mentioned letter written by Sanders to Edward Lhuyd, where he calls the main structure of the monument 'Coetan Arthur', a name commonly given to such 'altars'. Indeed there is a monument in nearby Newport which bears this name today. At that place King Arthur is said to have stopped on his travels to play quoits using the large capstone of the tomb. However, the author of the report believes it is the burial place of someone important, which seems to be a common belief about such structures.

In 1865 H. Longueville-Jones' article about 'Pembrokeshire Antiquities' in *Archaeologia Cambrensis* included an illustration of five mounted riders underneath the capstone, representing the visit of 1859 – between these two dates they lost a person! This illustration also gives some human perspective to a monument which is normally depicted alone in the bleak landscape. Without any human perspective, the monument looks larger and more imposing than it would otherwise do (cf. Figure 16.2). The author mentions that what is left of the

> great cromlech of Pentre Ifan . . . seems to have formed one of several other sepulchral chambers, covered by a common mound, traces of these others, and of the carnedd of stones, being visible in the immediate vicinity, but the enclosures of the land have been brought close to the south side of the monument, or have cut through it; and hence the disappearance of its contents and materials is easily accounted for.
>
> (Longueville-Jones 1865: 284–285)

Jones is the first to mention the remains of a cairn of stones, and he also believes that there was more than one chamber. Additionally he suggests the possibility that more evidence and remains might be found 'if the soil all around were carefully probed and examined' (ibid.: 285) which of course is what happens later when Grimes excavates there. However Jones does not report finding anything there himself, and he blames the lack of a covering mound for the absence of remains that he expects would be associated with the monument. This does not stop him from attempting to explain the purpose of the monument, and he writes:

> Here the cromlech stands some five or six miles away from the sea; and it probably served as a resting-place to a chieftain and his family dwelling in comparative security, though at what point in the period of the history of Wales it would be vain to conjecture. The adjacent district offers a tempting field of operations for any one interested in the early antiquities of Pembrokeshire; and it would not be surprising if other remains, now not known, were brought to light by sufficient research.
>
> (Longueville-Jones 1865: 285)

It is noteworthy that there are so many articles in this journal over a relatively short period that basically reiterate what has been said before and add nothing new to the debate. This is also surprising because it happens within a comparatively closed community of amateur scholars who subscribe to a journal and belong to an association that dedicates its time to visiting and describing local antiquities. They are writing for each other, but presumably they are also writing in the hope that their words will be preserved for future generations of scholars. The authors are already aware of how the monument is deteriorating over time and feel the need to establish a definitive account of its physical presence, which is why their measurements are so precise. It seems that, apart from remarking on its size and the amazing arrangement of stones, there is a general reluctance to take interpretations any further than passing comments on the 'sacred area' or stating with authority that it must have been a burial chamber. The dominant idea is that it must have been built by or for some kind of chieftain. Any further discussions of the social uses of the monument are non-existent.

TWENTIETH-CENTURY WRITINGS

Writings in the twentieth century are more diversified than the procession of reports in *Archaeologia Cambrensis*, although this journal still figures strongly as the place in which to publish articles about Pentre Ifan.

W.F. Grimes' excavation of Pentre Ifan in the 1930s was fully reported in *Archaeologia Cambrensis* in 1949. I am aware that I seem to be referring to his work as an authority on the subject, but in this case I am noting that his excavation and subsequent report represent a turning point in the way that Pentre Ifan could be written about, particularly after all the calls in the nineteenth century for further investigation of the site. Moreover, Grimes formulated his theories over a period that was crucial in the history of archaeology, as he was writing at least until the mid-1960s, when, with the introduction of radiocarbon dating and other scientific methods, previous theories were dramatically disproved. The new dating of monuments dispelled some of the speculations about migrating peoples building the monuments as a copy of their own Mediterranean structures. These traditional notions predominate, and are included without question, in the literature of the first half of the twentieth century.

W.F. Grimes starts to write about Pentre Ifan in the 1930s. In 'The megalithic monuments of Wales' published in the *Proceedings of the Prehistoric Society* for 1936 he starts by saying:

> Time after time, in the pages of *Archaeologia Cambrensis* and other journals will be found scattered papers in which the same familiar tombs present themselves; they have formed very inadequate foundations upon which to build, and none of the writers has attempted to place matters upon the only really sound basis, which is that of the study of each and every individual site in the field.
>
> (Grimes 1936: 106)

By 1937 Grimes is reporting on his current excavation work at Pentre Ifan in the *Bulletin of the Board of Celtic Studies.* He finishes the piece by writing:

> The finds included a few flint flakes of nondescript character, and several fragments of pottery of Neolithic A type. These came from a black layer of limited extent (about 2 ft. square) directly behind the portal stone. The layer (which did not appear to have a funerary origin) also yielded some charcoal. There was no bone in it, and elsewhere in the chamber only very few minute fragments of bone were observed. Pieces of white quartz were fairly common.
> (Grimes 1937: 271)

Grimes makes no further commentary, but I would like to emphasise that Grimes had found nothing to suggest that funerary rituals took place at the monument.

Grimes' excavation report was published as 'Pentre Ifan burial chamber' in *Archaeologia Cambrensis* for 1949 and I wish to look at the conclusions he draws. (Grimes carried out a later excavation but this was never written up.) He starts by reporting its location and the nature of the environment of Pentre Ifan, but the tone he uses is particularly telling, as in this sentence: 'I am not competent then to do more than point out the fact (which will be obvious to the most casual observer) that here once again is a Welsh chambered tomb below the tree-line in its area' (Grimes 1949: 3). Grimes slips in the word 'tomb' which he believes is an obvious statement to the reader. Before we venture very far at all into the report, an interpretation has already been applied to the monument; there is nothing neutral and objective about this. Grimes even calls a section 'The burial chamber before excavation' (p. 4). He acknowledges the debt owed to previous archaeologists though, and states that based on their work and the recent work he himself has carried out: 'Pentre-Ifan can therefore be recognised from knowledge accumulated in recent years as an example, rare for Wales, of the rectangular type of chamber . . .' (ibid.: 5). Grimes manages to categorise the monument, with all the associated assumptions that categorisation brings, before he even excavates there.

In later publications, Grimes reaffirms the claim that Pentre Ifan was a 'burial monument' and 'communal tomb' without ever arguing his case (Grimes 1960, 1965). He does not consider that there may not have been any burials at Pentre Ifan. Because burials and evidence of cremation have been found at other megaliths, Grimes approached his excavation and writes with the conviction that the primary purpose of megalithic monuments was funerary.

The point I wish to emphasise here is that a particular discourse has been constructed and sustained not by examining the evidence found at one particular site, but by consulting writings about this site and others. At what percentage of megaliths has such evidence been found? Of course, over the centuries this evidence may have been lost or plundered. Nevertheless, none of the authors up to and including Grimes consider that megaliths may have held symbolism which was far greater than this one functional purpose. Other theories are not considered by Grimes, because he writes with the intention of categorising the monument within established modes of thinking rather than making an original contribution to its interpretation.

From this study of the literature, we can see that a discourse of death is common to the study of megaliths, so that 'megalith' is synonymous with 'tomb', giving what may be a misleading interpretation of the monuments. This discourse continues in the later twentieth century. It can be found in *Regional Archaeologies: South Wales* by C. Houlder and W.H. Manning in 1967, where although the authors talk of 'tomb-builders' (p. 27), their description of Pentre Ifan presents no interpretation until they write: 'It is fair to say that such a monument as this must have been constructed and used with great ritualistic ceremony, for the mysteries of life and death are usually prominent in the religion of primitive farmers' (Houlder and Manning 1967: 26).

In Frances Lynch's 1972 article 'Portal dolmens in the Nevern Valley, Pembrokeshire', the word 'tomb' is used throughout to signify 'megalithic monument', and by using the language in this way, further discussions and interpretations are restricted. In describing the physical layout of the stones, Lynch writes:

> The later adaptation involved the addition of the high façade stones and the lengthening and regularisation of the cairn. No further burial chambers were added, so presumably these changes were simply designed to up-date the appearance of the original tomb which may still have been in use or, more probably, was still the venue for regular ceremonies
>
> (Lynch 1972: 71)

Lynch goes on to compare Pentre Ifan to a similar monument at Dyffryn Ardudwy. The literature has changed from an insular study of Pentre Ifan, as written by the antiquarians of the nineteenth century, to a comparative study of the type that Lynch is making. Is this furthering the debate about the monument? Lynch is still writing with the notion that this is a tomb, an idea that was suggested by the earliest of writers, and is continuing this discourse by looking for points of similarity in other monuments, or even suggesting that other monuments can show what Pentre Ifan is missing. Lynch looks for trends and patterns in tombs as a whole.

In 'Towards a chronology of megalithic tombs in Wales' (1976), Lynch suggests again that Pentre Ifan is the result of two periods of building. Lynch writes:

> Whatever the reasons for the emphasis on south-west Wales, the chronological implications of the history of Pentre Ifan are clear; the Portal Dolmen was already established as the dominant tomb-building tradition in the area before the renewed periods of contact with Ireland brought in the idea of the monumental façade.
>
> (Lynch 1976: 69)

Lynch is relying on classification for answers about the so-called 'tomb', but recognises that other factors in society indicate a period of change in the middle Neolithic.

As a contrast to the repetitive descriptions outlined above, below is a poem written in 1989, which encapsulates the themes of the dominant discourse, that of death.

Cromlech Pentre Ifan

Phil Carradice

> Just here, at dusk,
> the light may move
> so many, varied ways
> that huddled, staring,
> by the capstones' lintel buttress
> we shudder in the silence.
> The still, oppressive presence
> of the place serves now
> to bend the mind,
> transcend long years
> to when the dark men
> phantomed through the cromlech's
> legs of stone.
> Their eyes black charcoal
> with the fervour of the dance,
> some pagan incantation
> to their gods still ringing
> pulsing centuries of pain.
>
> No flight of fantasy –
> the dark ones still remain,
> their white, blanched bones
> still churning with the richness
> of the soil; sleeping gods
> still watching in the night fire's
> ravenous glow.
>
> Like some prehistoric phoenix
> their ashes move, grow solid
> as flint-edged eyes
> conspire.

The whole tone of this poem is threatening and ghostly, as the author demonstrates a fear of what he does not know or comprehend. The monument itself is described twice, as 'the capstones' lintel buttress', and then as 'the cromlech's legs of stone'. The author visualises men walking in and out of the 'legs' of the monument; he has no recognition that the monument was covered in soil or turf. He sees their eyes as 'black charcoal', referring to the remnants of a fire, a light gone out, or the black of evil, and the 'fervour of the dance' suggests something out of control, reinforced by the notion of 'some pagan incantation' in the next line. Their gods are not those we know, and the author believes that this is a place of religion and wild ceremonies.

The images of prehistory that appear in this poem are of stone, bone and flint, and also predominantly of fire, throwing up images of something primeval, and of religious activity and self-abandonment. The ghosts of the past Carradice imagines are not real and he makes no attempts to reconstruct past life, and yet the reader is left with a very strong impression of some presence and there is room for the reader's imagination to fill in the gaps that the author seems to have deliberately created. Interpretations of this monument as a tomb have seeped through even to the poetical conscience, so that it is a fearful place of wandering ghosts. The equation of death with fear is reinforced, and does not consider alternative approaches to death, for example the possibility that in the Neolithic it may have been a time for celebration and joy, and nothing to do with fear.

BREAKING WITH TRADITION

In his 1994 book, *A Phenomenology of Landscape*, Christopher Tilley strives to see the monuments of his case studies not in isolation, but as part of patterns in the landscape that would have been experienced by prehistoric inhabitants of the Nevern area in south-west Wales. His thesis is that Neolithic stone monuments focused attention on natural features of the landscape, and that meaning was created in the landscape by this socialisation of it. Tilley draws attention to the fact that Pentre Ifan is located in such a way that those approaching the entrance of the monument could not avoid the view of Carn Ingli, and that: 'Here important architectural features of the monument appear to duplicate the incline of the mountain outcrop' (1994: 105). This approach leads him to draw the conclusion that:

> Their primary purpose, in fact, seems to have been neither for burial nor deposition. It is difficult to make out a case that they acted as central territorial markers. There is no evidence to suggest that they were marking the centres of areas of land with a high arable component. They rather seemed to have acted primarily as symbolic reference and ritually important ceremonial meeting-points on paths of movement, drawing attention to the relationship between local groups and the landscape – itself already a constructed symbolic form of named places, pathways and significant locales from the Mesolithic onwards.
>
> (Tilley 1994: 109)

Interestingly, the work that Tilley carries out on the connections between monuments in the landscape has more in common with alternative interpretations, some of which are connected with ideas about the 'New Age', than it has with the volumes of antiquarian writing or other archaeological interpretations and approaches. This may be because earlier archaeologists considered their discipline as a subject requiring objectivity rather than the personal intervention that recent approaches such as phenomenology invite. The basis of 'New Age' interpretations often involves the relationships between natural features and monuments in the landscape, something which was only considered in archaeological studies relatively recently and is a result of the rediscovery of paganism. Authors writing under these auspices do not consider their works to be part of what they see as a scientific, objective discipline of archaeology. Instead, writers such as Philip Heselton, who co-founded the journal *The Ley Hunter* in 1965, prefer to see stone circles and other prehistoric monuments as 'Earth Mysteries' and cloud such phenomena with secrecy (Heselton 1991). An example of this 'New Age' approach is *Walks in Mysterious Wales* by Laurence Main (1995), in which the author writes, 'Pentre Ifan burial chamber is another magical place, connected to the spot where St Brynach had his visions and where the current dreamwork takes place at the summit of Carningli by a lay or spirit path' (Main 1995: 103). Main has carried out experiments on these ley paths, and believes that Carningli is the focus of spiritual activity, linked as it is to various threads of folklore and spiritual beliefs. Although it is easy to dismiss the ideas of someone who sincerely writes: 'Carningli is also the gateway to hell, or, rather, the Annwn of the Celts. This Underworld includes the realm of the fairies and there's no better place to go looking for them than on the slopes of Frenni Fawr' (ibid.: 103), this kind of work does remind us that there are a multitude of possibilities when attempting to understand the psyche of prehistoric (as well as modern!) people, and their motivations and beliefs.

Antiquarians writing in the nineteenth century and earlier did not include much of the folklore in their works, although these tales are reported elsewhere. As I have already indicated, there are references to Druids using the stones as an altar, and to the associations between such monuments and King Arthur. Folklore associated with Pentre Ifan does not offer an explanation for the monument itself, but rather it tells stories of superstition with both religious and fairy-world bases. Strongly connected with the area is Saint Brynach, whose church is at nearby Nevern. When he returned from his pilgrimages to Rome and Brittany he lived as a hermit on Carn Ingli, where angels administered to him, and Carn Ingli means 'The Mount of Angels' (Gwyndaf 1989: 79). Pentre Ifan features as a point of reference in many tales, as a marker in the landscape, as in the tale of Einon the shepherd lad who is led to the Otherworld of fairies by way of a flight of stairs underneath a standing stone near Pentre Ifan. He marries a fairy called Olwen and together they have a son who is Taliesin, the mythic poet who chronicled the exploits of Merlin (John 1991: 72). Of course, here is another link to King Arthur.

Another tale is of an incident that is supposed to have occurred in the 1830s. It is the story of the golden idol of Trewern, which tells of an ancient manor house about a mile from Pentre Ifan, where the new owner was directed by ghosts to a hidden recess. Inside he found a solid gold pagan idol, and he sold bits of this and became incredibly rich. The statue was rumoured to have been stolen hundreds of years before from an ancient Druid site amongst the oak groves of Pentre Ifan (John 1991: 63).

Although the founders of the Folk-Lore Society, in 1878, believed that 'it would be possible to fill out some of the details of the life of prehistoric man from the lore of the contemporary peasant' (Grinsell 1980: 213), these tales do not enlighten our understanding of the original uses of the monument, but instead demonstrate more recent theories about the place. However, folklore does not just refer to the collections of super-natural tales, but also to the stories which are passed from one generation to the next:

The grey old man in the corner	Yr hen wr llwyd o'r cornel
Of his father heard a story,	Gan ei dad a glywodd chwedel,
Which from his father he had heard,	A chan ei dad fe glywodd yntau,
And after them I have remembered.	Ac ar ei ôl mi gofiais innau.

(Parry-Jones 1953: 13)

I refer here not only to quaint notions of families sitting around an open fire on a winter's night exchanging tales, but to more pedagogical actions such as the teaching of such tales in school, and the inclusion of these stories in guide-books and histories.

We can view the labelling of Pentre Ifan as a tomb as a phenomenon which has occurred in a similar manner. One interpretation of this arrangement of large stones was that it had something to do with burial. I have shown how this discourse originated, when the first documentation of the monument by George Owen uses biblical analogy to explain why such a structure could have been built, and we are presented with a comparison to a large tomb built by a character for his family. This notion that Pentre Ifan was associated with death, and particularly burial, was then seized upon by subsequent authors, until the origin of this idea was omitted from the literature and forgotten, but the impression that was left was that this structure had been a tomb of some sort, and a piece of common knowledge had been created. Even when the structure was excavated and Grimes searched unsuccessfully for evidence of burials, Pentre Ifan was still to be known as a tomb, and treated as such in the literature. The story of the stone tomb, the discourse of death, was passed down from antiquarian to archaeologist by their dominant form of communication, the written word, and is still being propagated in this manner.

The grey old men of archaeology have passed down to us certain narra-tives which are accepted, sometimes without questioning their origins.

Look what happens when we do wonder where the discourses originate from. We find their beginnings in the shaky source of a biblical comparison. It is interesting to note that the early Welsh word for storyteller is *y cyfarwydd*, meaning 'the familiar one', who was 'a leader and inspirer of his people – the one who helped them to "see"; to visualize the invisible; to give meaning to the meaningless' (Gwyndaf 1989: 26). The prehistorian is constantly trying to visualise the invisible, and give meaning to what, at first glance, would appear to be the meaningless. To give meaning, stories are created, and handed down.

CONCLUSION

The ease with which archaeologists categorise Pentre Ifan as a 'tomb' and readily associate the monument with spooky feelings of death and awe is really not much less far-fetched than dreaming of fairies at the site. I say this because the evidence unearthed does not suggest funerary practices occurring there, let alone burial, and yet this is the dominant narrative about the monument. Pentre Ifan has been assigned features and meanings which the canon of archaeological writing has perpetuated along the years: the awe at its size, its rural location, its designation as a tomb, the horseback motif, druidical associations, and associations with Arthur. I have shown how a body of writing almost four hundred years old has dominated our thinking about megalithic monuments, so that the narratives passed down to us still shade our understanding of such structures. The interpretation of Pentre Ifan as a burial chamber, when no evidence of this has been found, is more closely related to the third option in the multiple choice with which I opened this paper. Yet this discourse can trace its origin back to the biblical quotation.

Whether archaeologists have agreed or disagreed with previous writings, or built on the collection of work, the idea that Pentre Ifan was a tomb has always been at the forefront of the interpretative writings, so much so that other interpretations are overshadowed by this. Pentre Ifan, the monument, now a bare and yet still impressive collection of stones, has been constructed and reconstructed by the literature, so that it resembles something quite different from its original meanings, the reality of which we can never truly know. The power of the written word can be seen to be stronger than the stones themselves, and the continuity of the discourse has evolved into the backbone around which the body of archaeological writings has grown.

The realisation that funerary practices may have been marginal or absent at many megaliths is finally being discussed, for example by Tilley (1994) and Barrett (1994). This new discussion releases us from the narrow focus of the scholarship of the past four hundred years. Barrett points out the implications these generalisations have had on the study of the Neolithic, based as they are on 'the fragmentary remains of a variety of different monuments' which has led to 'the synthesized totality which is known as the "Neolithic burial tradition"' (1994: 49).

Archaeology has grown alongside folklore, from the moment of conception when people wanted to explain and understand the long-forgotten reasons and meanings of these monuments; the pair only went their separate ways when archaeology met something that seemed then to be more desirable, namely science. Yet the apparent objectivity of counting and measuring and reporting was no more detached from personal experience of the site than other ways of encountering and seeing and experiencing the place. These methods of describing Pentre Ifan have persisted down the years, as have the interpretations which have their roots in the first years of the seventeenth century. Is the archaeologist so far removed from *y cyfarwydd*, the storyteller, the familiar one who tells us familiar tales? We should break with tradition, challenge the grey old man in the corner, and discover where our narratives have their origins before embracing them so freely, merely because of their familiarity.

REFERENCES

Anonymous (1859) 'Report of Cardigan meeting.' *Archaeologia Cambrensis*, 3rd Series, 5: 336–337.

Barrett, J. (1994) *Fragments from Antiquity*. Oxford: Blackwell.

Carradice, P. (1989) 'Cromlech Pentre Ifan.' In T. Curtis (ed.) *The Poetry of Pembrokeshire*, p. 21. Bridgend: Seren Books.

Fenton, R. [1903] (1994) *A Historical Tour Through Pembrokeshire*. Reprint of the 2nd edition [1st edition 1796] for Dyfed County Council, Haverfordwest.

Grimes, W.F. (1936) 'The megalithic monuments of Wales.' *Proceedings of the Prehistoric Society* 2: 106–139.

Grimes, W.F. (1937) 'Current work in Welsh archaeology.' *Bulletin of the Board of Celtic Studies* 8(3): 270–271.

Grimes, W.F. (1949) 'Pentre Ifan burial chamber, Pembrokeshire.' *Archaeologia Cambrensis* 100: 3–23.

Grimes, W.F. (1960) *Pentre-ifan Burial Chamber*. London: HMSO.

Grimes, W.F. (1965) Neolithic Wales. In I.L.L. Foster and G. Daniel (eds) *Prehistoric and Early Wales*, pp. 35–71. London: Routledge.

Grinsell, L.V. (1980) 'A century of the study of folklore of archaeological sites, and prospects for the future.' In V.J. Newall (ed.) *Folklore Studies in the Twentieth Century*, pp. 213–218. Suffolk: DS Brewer.

Gwyndaf, R. (1989) *Welsh Folk Tales*. Cardiff: National Museum of Wales.

Heselton, P. (1991) *The Elements of Earth Mysteries*. Shaftesbury: Element.

Houlder, C. and W.H. Manning (1967) *Regional Archaeologies: South Wales* London: Heinemann Educational Books.

John, B.S. (1991) *Pembrokeshire Folk Tales*. Newport: Greencroft Books.

Jones, J. (1847) 'Correspondence.' *Archaeologia Cambrensis*, 1st Series, 2: 373–374.

Longueville-Jones, H. (1865) 'Pembrokeshire antiquities.' *Archaeologia Cambrensis*, 3rd Series, 2: 284–285.

Lynch, F. (1972) 'Portal dolmens in the Nevern Valley, Pembrokeshire.' In F. Lynch and C. Burgess (eds) *Prehistoric Man in Wales and the West*, pp. 67–84. Bath: Adams and Dart.

Lynch, F. (1976) 'Towards a chronology of megalithic tombs in Wales.' In G.C. Boon and J.M. Lewis (eds) *Welsh Antiquity*, pp. 63–79. Cardiff: National Museum of Wales.

Main, L. (1995) *Walks in Mysterious Wales*. Cheshire: Sigma.

Owen, G. [1603] (1994) *The Description of Pembrokeshire*, edited with introduction and notes by D. Miles. Welsh Classics Vol. 6. Llandysul: Gomer.

Parry-Jones, D. (1953) *Welsh Legends and Fairy Lore*. London: Batsford.

Tilley, C. (1994) *A Phenomenology of Landscape*. Oxford: Berg.

CHAPTER SEVENTEEN

THE LAST REFUGE OF THE FAERIES

Archaeology and folklore in East Sussex

MARTIN BROWN AND PAT BOWEN

ABSTRACT

As mysterious landscape features archaeological monuments have probably attracted folk stories for more years than they have attracted scholarship and the tales and songs are important factors in the monuments' continuing histories. However, the development of modern archaeology, with its emphasis on fact and evidence, can all too easily dispel the past which makes up the present of a monument. Indeed, it could be argued that scientific archaeology should dispel the shadows of unreason. This paper will contend that folklore is an important factor in the historic environment. It will consider some of the folklore-rich sites of East Sussex in the context of an initiative to bring archaeology and folklore together to create complementary landscape histories.

To walk attentively through any landscape is to drink at the river of time.

J. Elder, quoted in Greeves 1992

SETTING THE GROUND

The last refuge of the fairies is said to be Burlough Castle, a natural rise above the Cuckmere river in East Sussex (Figure 17.1). The site is also a Scheduled Ancient Monument and has featured in one of a series of guided walks organised and led by the authors.

Our work is to take people on walks. Each walk is different, even when we follow the same route: there are seasonal changes, our on-the-spot decisions about material used and put aside and group dynamics. In bad weather there may only be six of us, with an intimate family feeling to the group (some of the people may have been on other walks with

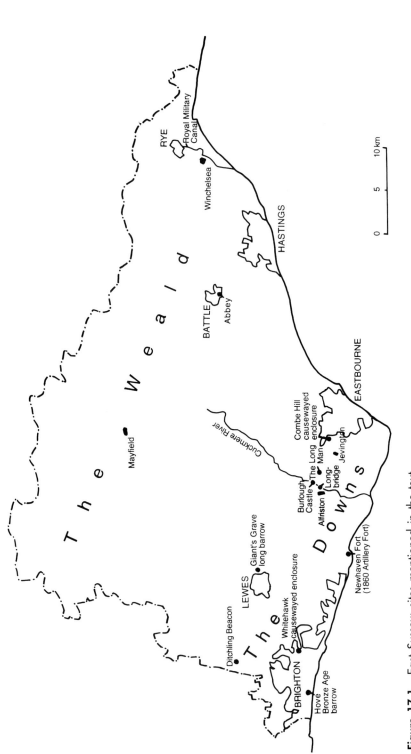

Figure 17.1 East Sussex: sites mentioned in the text

us); on other occasions there are thirty or more adults, plus children and dogs and the event becomes something more of a production!

Rather than give a 'blow-by-blow' account of a particular outing, here are some 'snapshots'. Imagine Pat (Figure 17.2a), by the Longbridge over the River Cuckmere, warning folk that it is May Day, when the gates between the worlds are traditionally believed to be open and inhabitants of one world may encounter those of another. See Martin (Figure 17.2b), in the same place, with a sweep of his arm, taking in the barrows on the sky-line and the reed beds before us – evidence of continuous human occupation of the land over thousands of years.

On the mound that is Burlough Castle, watch us sit and wonder about the reliability of the resistivity meter used on a chalk hill in a hot dry summer and consider the mysteries of the hill left unsolved by modern archaeology. Hear the story of Chol's and Harry's encounter with the little people, said to have occurred on the same site. Listen to us surmising the possibilities of just what it may have been that we are sitting on, and consider the meanings of the field named Mag Mire which we can see at the bottom of the hill.

Picture a field corner, hay nearly fully grown, a view of the Downs and Ditchling Beacon hillfort dominating, Black Dog Lane to the west of us and Pat telling the traditional tale of the origin of the Wild Hunt that's been known to make its howling midnight way along the top of the ridge (and woe betide any who fall in its path). At the climax of the story, see the one dog on the walk go completely crazy, chasing its tail round and round in the hay and distracting all our attention to laughter so overwhelming that the story must have a break and start again in a minute.

On that same Midsummer Day listen as a woman from south-east Asia tells us that people also lament the passing of the fairies in her country, but say that if any of the last few hear someone telling a story they will be sure to gather to listen.

Share Pat's disappointment when she chose the theme of birds for her stories on a walk at Winchelsea because every time she visited the locale while preparing the walk she saw herons, lapwings, terns, swifts, reed bunting . . . only to find that on the day itself, the wind was so strong that there was not a bird to be seen or heard. Then on the very last section of the route, observe a group of swallows give a breathtaking and extended display of high-speed, low-level aerobatics over a field of ripening barley.

See Martin's face as he realises no one is listening to his careful description of the shifting coastline that made the port of Winchelsea rich and then abandoned it far inland, because right behind him a fox, with a rabbit dangling from its jaws, is walking nonchalantly along the field's edge as if we were not there.

And then there is the fetid scent of the stinkhorn calling us off the path to admire its phallic magnificence in the woods and reminding us

Figure 17.2 Pat and Martin in action. Photographs by Julian Howell

that it is the season of the Green Man; but isn't that his head carved into the ancient timbers of the inn which was once a watering hole for medieval pilgrims and will soon fulfil the same role for us?

Or be astonished beside the Royal Military Canal, built as a defence against Napoleon, at the combined cacophony of the rookery above us and the mating frogs below, their song presaging soaking rain.

Stand, or try to, in the middle of a causewayed enclosure, leaning into the wind, experiencing the same elements our ancestors knew and looking over the land they worked and walked. Or shiver as the mist swirls around the bowl barrows above Jevington as we walk on All Souls' Eve . . .

So we explore the different layers which make up the landscape. Our intention is, in part, to interpret that land to the group but – as you have noticed – it is wider too.

We believe that we are enacting theory in our walks, addressing issues including perceptions of landscape and sense of place. What follows is, in part, an interim report on our work in Sussex, but it is perhaps also a manifesto, describing our own feelings and proposing our reasons for working together.

THE LANDSCAPE

Our broad intention is to explore the connections between the landscape, the journey, the person and the place, the past and the present. We are concerned with the outer world in which we walk and the inner journey each person on the walk also undertakes: the stories and the historical and archaeological information about the landscape contribute to the individual's understanding and to their responses.

At the time of writing all the walks under discussion have been in a rural setting. We acknowledge that landscape is a creation, a myth even (Cosgrove 1993), and that the rural landscape does not reflect the lives of the majority of the population of England. However, we believe that it is important to seek to reconnect an urban population with the country-side which surrounds the dwellings and towns where the majority of the population of Britain live. It is important to restore this connection with the land: our food does not grow in supermarkets and 'green-field' devel-opment happens in the landscape affecting our wider environment. In addition, there are other reasons that will be explored later. We have not, to date, led walks in an urban context because there are practical difficulties with town walks, including traffic noise, narrow pavements and urban bustle. However, at least one urban walk is at the planning stage, as are two walks around individual large monuments, including a nineteenth-century artillery fort.

Our starting point for any walk is the landscape: the ground which we inhabit, traverse and explore. We perceive this ground as a many-layered phenomenon with constituents including the geological, ecological, archaeological, historic, economic and cultural (Chorlton 1993): much of what makes up the landscape is the product of human activity and management, creativity and imagination (Clifford and King 1993). As Chris Tilley has written, the landscape is constantly fashioned by human action. It is changing and so is the relationship between the people and the land (Tilley 1994). It may be said that the land has a great cultural depth built up by responses to it and, in turn, to the previous artistic concepts and conventions (Schama 1995; Trant 1997). These responses may be either the 'high' art of the ruling elite or folk culture coming from below. They should be seen as distinct manifestations even though they may share characters, imagery and iconography demonstrating cross–fertilisation and a blurring of boundaries. Nevertheless there are tensions apparent between these class-based strands of creativity and activity which may reflect wider tensions in society (Bender 1993). This process can be seen at work in contemporary British environmental protest, where storytelling, folk art and a man claiming to be King Arthur, supported by a Round Table, have appeared reflecting attitudes of opposition to an establishment which builds roads and airports, significantly altering the landscape. That same establishment commodifies Stonehenge – a symbol of an older, different Albion[1] (McKay 1996) – and denies access to many who place contemporary sacred values on the monument (Bender 1993). The landscape is abundant of meaning (Morris [1884] 1996).

If we accept that the landscape is a cultural product then we acknowledge, however tacitly, that it is an archaeological monument or artefact. Like all monuments, it is a dynamic thing, not frozen in time: any archaeological site has been colonised, developed, declined and endured decay, damage and reuse. Many have gathered stories, including the stories based on evidence found by antiquarians and archaeologists. If we consider a prominent example such as Avebury we see a Neolithic site which developed over many years and which has, since that time, been hated, loved, shunned, visited, attacked and preserved (Burl 1979). In addition, it has gathered to it an immense cultural baggage of legends, theories and artwork, and the story continues over time. Our past is ever-present and constantly changing as our own attitudes and interpretations alter.

However, there is a danger that archaeological science may drive off the cultural aspects of a monument; once we know a barrow is a prehistoric burial mound is there still a place for the barrow wight? Terry Pratchett's exchange between Nanny Ogg, a witch, and the barrow-dwelling King of the Fairies illustrates this point perfectly:

> I'll get em to dig into the Long Man with iron shovels, y'see, and they'll say, why its just an old earthworks, and pensioned-off wizards and priests with nuthin' better to do will pick over the heaps and write dull old books about burial traditions and suchlike, and that'll be another iron nail in your coffin.
>
> (Pratchett 1993: 311–2)

While it can be argued that archaeology is about the scientific testing of theories about earthworks and burial tradition we diminish the monument, and ourselves as part of creative humanity, if we ignore the factors that make one monument distinct from another of the same age and type. These include the folk tales as much as the individual arrangements of burials, flints and pots. Indeed, the way in which our forebears thought about monuments and places can only add to our understanding of them as landmarks, of the place in which they are to be found and, ultimately, ourselves. In addition, on an emotional level, one should ask whether the sense of wonder felt at ancient places is something which we ought to preserve. It is all too easy to diminish the non-factual in the archaeological classification of sites. While we should know that such-and-such a site is a 5,000-year-old burial mound, give it a number, record and interpret it, should we not also remember that generations of locals have called it the Giant's Grave or that it was a place to go on May Eve?

Archaeology and folk tales and songs can also be seen as different ways of coming to terms with the unknown or the little understood. Until the development of history and antiquarianism the naming of features such as 'Giant's Grave' and the accretion of stories to the Long Man of Wilmington (Figure 17.3; Sidgwick 1939) may be seen as a response to the unknown – an attempt to understand features which are clearly not natural but which lay outside the experience of the viewer. In a world where the Devil was a real character it is not unnatural to suppose that he might really have thrown stones at a church, as at Boroughbridge, North Yorkshire, or shaken clods of earth from his boots to form the Isle of Wight.

Archaeology cannot be carried out without a recognition of place, geography, environment or landscape (Tilley 1994). Why, for instance, do barrows cluster on the edge of the Downs and how does Flag Fen's Bronze Age site relate to the nearby marshes (Pryor 1991)? To understand place one needs a knowledge of the archaeology and to gain a fuller understanding of the monuments their context must be considered. By recognising the human hand in the environment one gains a greater understanding of the world around; for example, the knowledge that the ripples on the Downs are 2,000-year-old field boundaries gives insight into a place over many centuries and binds people and place together. A graphic illustration of this was the Milton Keynes Archaeology Unit, which existed to dig sites before the development of the new town. In so doing the Unit provided a history for a place which superficially had no past before a Whitehall planning meeting. Elsewhere, locally distinct monument types, landscape boundaries and features, such as the remains of Wealden iron industry in Kent and Sussex, have produced landscape features which are peculiar to a specific area and which contribute to a very localised understanding of place.

Archaeology is inextricably tied up with place, in the position of the monuments, in the role of people in the development of the landscape,

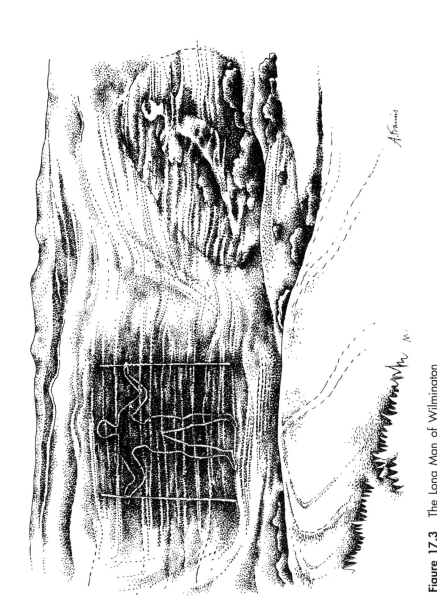

Figure 17.3 The Long Man of Wilmington

Source: Drawn by Alexi Francis

in the cultural prompts they have provided and in the evidence they offer of other people and other cultures in Britain.

The archaeological layers give a time depth to the landscape, complementing its other cultural components. The present past – surviving relics – in the landscape includes historical aspects – the places where events took place but where there is little or no physical trace – and the archaeological remains, either visible built structures and earthworks, or the less obvious stratigraphies and crop or soil marks which may be invisible or only seasonally perceived by the naked eye. These features express the continuity of human activity and experience in a place over time, often thousands of years, where succeeding generations have contributed to the shape of the landscape we have inherited and on which we, as humans, will leave our own traces. These features do demonstrate a human continuity in the past and in the British landscape but it is important to remember that we are not surveying a rural idyll and a vision of social continuity cannot be supported. The landscape is a space wherein tensions and resultant actions are played out between both individuals and groups within society. Those actions may be short-lived, such as a nineteenth-century 'Swing' riot which necessitates the rebuilding of a now old barn, or part of a longer process, such as enclosure or fen drainage, which has changed the land and the lives of its inhabitants. It is important that these challenging layers are uncovered, as well as the more palatable aspects of the countryside. This consideration presents questions about how history is presented.

PRESENTING PASTS

Our walks are concerned, amongst other things, with the presentation of ancient landscapes and the archaeological components of the ground we walk. This inevitably brings us up against issues relating to the interpretation of the heritage. We must decide whether we are revealing hidden aspects of the place or moving in a group and discovering together.

There is a body of opinion which has developed concerning archaeological interpretation which seeks to make the non-archaeologist a participant in the process of interpreting and understanding the past. It has been argued that archaeological interpretation should be encouraging people to think for themselves, engendering a sense of discovery, while retaining the sense of wonder about a past that is remote and different (Parker Pearson, 1993; Shanks and Tilley 1987). It is clear that to achieve these aims in any form anyone involved in public archaeology (the practice of archaeology with the public) is going to have to use their imagination to develop ways to engage public interest. In addition three useful 'golden rules' have been suggested for archaeological interpretation (Pryor 1989). First, the past should never be mystified, cheapened or trivialised by those interpreting it. Second, always remember that any interpretation is only a construct based on the available evidence. Third, make sure that the public is aware that any interpretation can be questioned, challenged and changed. Another useful golden rule has been expressed thus: 'The green archaeologist's challenge is to honour both science and the reader' (Pitts 1992: 203). The past can be manipulated and commodified in an attempt to make it readily attractive to the public at large, but this would be an abdication of responsibility by the archaeological practitioner, especially one who is concerned with the wider environmental and social issues springing from the discipline.

It is our belief that by taking people out into the historic environment and examining the layers which comprise the landscape with them we are encouraging that spirit of discovery and interaction which those authors cited above advocate; we are exploring together rather than revealing information. In addition, by being out in the landscape we have become active participants rather than detached passive viewers of objects. We seek to abide by the golden rules cited and do this by knowing the ground we walk well, by being well briefed with current knowledge about the sites and about the wider issues raised by aspects of the walk, be they the ploughing of ancient monuments, development in the countryside or the role species of trees play in the countryside. Where there is a difference of opinion about a particular site, the interpretation of a story or an aspect of the landscape, we attempt to provide people on the walk with a flavour of the arguments.

We are aware that the past and the manipulation and exploitation of land and identity raise difficult issues for archaeologists in general and for us specifically as we deal with issues of place. We do not seek to sanitise either land or its history. Rather we try to present, discuss and confront some of the uncomfortable aspects of our work, be they individual acts of inhumanity or the fact that our vocabulary includes words such as identity, place, tradition and land which can be hijacked and used to further an extreme right-wing agenda. We openly acknowledge this danger and challenge it, seeking to reclaim and use these potentially charged words to present the diversity of the land and its inhabitants over time to anyone who wishes to hear.

It is the nature of stories to use metaphor and symbol, so to listen to a story is itself a process of interpretation. When Pat tells a tale such as the traditional version of the building of Alfriston Church, there is plenty of room for individual understanding of the significance of the events. A site had been chosen for the new church, but every night the stones were dismantled and scattered. One day, a frustrated builder saw four oxen lying on a mound by the river, their rumps making the shape of the cross, so it was agreed that this was the proper site for the church. There was no further unaccountable disruption of the building. Was the mound the site of pre-Christian ritual activity (the cross was a potent pagan symbol)? Who exactly was throwing the stones around? Why are all the churches in the area built on mounds? Why are there other stories from different regions about supernatural interference in the siting of churches? There are many possible answers to these questions – we invite each listener to find their own meanings.

In 1988 English Heritage published *Visitors Welcome,* a manual for on-site interpretation (Binks *et al.* 1988). While this document is primarily aimed at those seeking to open up a large excavation to the public, many of the principles set out by the authors are generally applicable inter-pretive methods based on actual examples and still in general use by British archaeologists. Like Parker Pearson we have reservations about the concept of 'visitors'; the term implies a passivity in the public (Parker Pearson 1993). The very act of walking means that there are no spectators on our expeditions; each individual connects with the land by walking it and with the seasons and weather by experiencing them, and all, like us, become participants. Nevertheless the book contains some useful suggestions concerning methods of interpretation which we have employed.

Visitors Welcome includes the following approaches to interpretation in a wider list of suggested methods: identifying key themes and stories; focusing on the human angle; 'having a go'; seeing sites in the context of the historic environment; explaining features rather than merely iden-tifying them; and stressing the remains as clues in a 'detective story'. Each guided walk has fulfilled most of these aspects as each walk has distinct themes, such as that from Mayfield in the High Weald which focused on the medieval and post-medieval iron industry and its impact on the remote and beautiful Sussex Weald. The human angle emerges strongly both from the stories and from the archaeological and historical information which focuses on how people have lived in and shaped their landscape; particular sites we visit are explained as individual places but are also related to the land around them and to the people who lived and worked on them. The technique of reading archaeological 'clues' to the land's story is explained to those accompanying us. However, the criminal analogy is not overplayed; we do not intend to hand down an authoritative verdict on all that we have seen in the course of an after-noon (Shanks 1992). The party will have been given data and theory and our own interpretation of evidence – it cannot be otherwise since we give so much of ourselves – but our intention is to encourage people to look at the landscape in a new way and to revisit, look again and retell the stories, as well as exploring other places. If they also read some-thing on historic geography, landscape archaeology or local history and folklore then so much the better (we do sometimes suggest titles). We are supplying the tools and inspiration for further explorations, adventures even, by our walkers.

In seeking to interpret the historic environment through these walks we hope to open up the landscape, both by exploring new ground and by investigating its components. We want to share our pleasure in the land and in our knowledge of, feelings about and theories concerning the places we visit. We feel that the land was shaped by people who have left us fields, forests, monuments, villages, stories and other cultural legacies we employ. Like the land the archaeology and folklore belong to all of humanity for all time: it is our heritage and we are working to assist others in enjoying the inheritance which is theirs also.

INNER JOURNEYS, INNER VALUES

The walk is more than an exploration of the history of a place and of the stories which pertain to it. It becomes a journey, even on a circular walk, and may even be termed a pilgrimage. Like archaeologists and folk-lore collectors, like pilgrims or adventurers in stories, we are exploring a place and seeking those discoveries which will help us understand the place, people and even ourselves. The journeys we undertake as a group are outer physical journeys, but we can also embark upon an inner journey.

The act of pilgrimage is time-honoured in many diverse cultures. Pilgrims often don't take a direct route, rather an *auspicious* one, sometimes with ceremonies enacted at appropriate places as they travel. Tilley, quoting Relph, refers to placelessness as a problem in our culture due to what Tilley refers to as 'the systematic erosion of locality as meaningful' (Tilley 1994: 20). In the past meanings accrued to the land from our living in and working with it on a daily basis – so that people felt, in a close, physical way, their connections with it and its support, both material and spiritual, for them. In the modern world we may know that the earth supports us, but it can be hard to feel it.

Also, in the past, ritual and magic gave power to the land: a ceremony for the success of the crops or the fertility of the cattle may have always taken place at a certain spot; or a landmark tree may 'always' have been the home of a deity or dryad. Most of us no longer believe in the power of dance or song to make the rain fall or the winter turn to spring (although we believe that a butterfly's wings in New York can have astonishing effects with no apparent intentionality at all!). We cannot enact the walking of songlines in the Australian aboriginal way and the process of pilgrimage is no longer widespread in our increasingly secular society, but love of the land is common to many of us. It has been claimed that people in our culture now find it hard to bear the past – it reminds us too closely of our frailty and mortality (Moore 1994). But without it our souls are under-nourished. Finding the vestiges and stories of the past in the land provides some of the nourishment we need and gives us a way of talking about who we are and how we perceive ourselves. Our inability (as a culture) to do this and the consequent alienation is called a 'new malady of the soul' by Julia Kristeva (Kristeva 1995). The stories and the walks are an attempt to recreate the connection with the land and to introduce people to the past which is all around them. Making a meaningful journey seems to be of value and benefit to our companions, in that many come back for more. Exercise, companionship, entertainment and education are all factors that have built our audience. Sharing the archaeology, history and stories that seem to belong there allows us to experience a long view of our past and our place. Jacquetta Hawkes has a memorable image for the sense of connection that comes from such a long view in her comments on the qualities of Purbeck marble: 'So Jurassic water snails, in their individual lives commemorated by murky scribblings on the surface of the marble, helped medieval Christians to praise their God' (Hawkes 1951: 116). On our walks our consciousness of ourselves is stretched to include the Neolithic barrow makers, generations of shepherds, the folk who struggled against invaders, landlord or squire and who made stories honouring the wit and resourcefulness that enabled them to survive. We walk a while in other people's shoes and grow in awareness of how strange yet how familiar it feels.

Roger Abrahams, writing on the differences between seasonal celebrations enacted now and those of pre-Industrial times, calls what we do now 'serious play' (Abrahams 1982: 162). We can no longer feel the lived-in power of the land from daily survival contact with it. The certainties expressed in the Apache belief that the land stalks the people and, in so doing, makes them live in a sustainable manner are not for us but neither are we happy with an objectified landscape for 'contemplation, depiction, representation and aestheticisation' (Tilley 1994: 26). Sentimentalising the land may be as likely to lead us to abuse of it as will disregard – a complaint often made by countryside dwellers when discussing their relationship with townsfolk.[2]

Our intention in our work is to avoid objectification. It may be a new way of honouring the particularity of a locale. The place takes us into it, close to it, it invites us to explore and discover some of its past and its secrets. It stimulates our enjoyment and imagination and invites us to absorb and contemplate its beauty. This beauty may not be 'country calendar' style, but beauty in the sense of that which arrests our attention and demands our consideration. We long to be arrested by beauty, to be intrigued by mystery and to reawaken a sense of wonder. We seek to offer people an experience of these things in their own familiar land. While this may sound fey and is spiritual, it is also a deeply elemental – particularly earthy – business involving mud and clambering, picnics and hedgerow pee-breaks. There is rain and sweat and laughter too – the body is fully engaged.

In preparing for a walk we explore the route, making the circle this way and that, trying out different stopping places and alternative vistas. We consider whether a sun-wise or widdershins circuit would be more appropriate for the season. We look at how features emerge into view as we move around them. The people are gathered into a notional space by imagining Pat's outstretched arms to be part of the circumference of a circle (a useful device learned from Malcolm Green of Rising Sun Country Park, Newcastle). Lightweight individual mats are also carried for people to sit on, allowing longer opportunities to stop and look. In winter, the group may huddle in the shelter of a barn or hedge and Pat tells her stories in instalments.

By telling the history and stories of the folk, the unnamed who lived and died in this land on which we walk and sit, we try to affect people. We also try to commemorate and celebrate our forebears, their place in the land, their traces, their imaginations and memories.

Hearing stories moves our consciousness to feeling places: we laugh at the absurdities and impossibilities of old folk stories, the exaggeration of character and action, such as St Anselm so absorbed in the song of the lark and his praise for its maker that a century passes without his noticing and when he returns to his abbey he is not recognised. We know it is not true yet we are still touched by the truth of it. Similarly we recognise the superstition of tales that warn us to treat the fairies with respect or bad luck come of it, but we may then think of the notion of the *genius loci* and the need to see the land as other, with its own integrity and life rather than as a tool for our own inconsiderate use or fanciful projection.

So, by walking and talking, sitting still and sharing information and stories from the past, by just being there for a while in the land, we acknowledge its individuality, astounding longevity, its irreducible 'that-ness'. It affects our sense of ourselves. Perhaps we can place ourselves a little more realistically in the world with more awareness of the levels of meaning in the familiar, a little more in tune with our own imaginations and those of our ancestors. However, it may not be possible to sum up that inner journey – each one of us makes our own pilgrimage.

We are consciously involved in the quest for a sense of belonging or place. Our walks are primarily aimed at local Sussex people, though others do come with us and are very welcome. Our intention is to explore the local, seek out the significant places close to home and to enhance the landscape at hand. There have, one suspects, always been the 'honey pots' – the sites which everyone sought to visit: in the middle ages it was Canterbury and today, perhaps, it is Shakespeare's Stratford-upon-Avon or Goa, on India's west coast, where young Westerners seek gurus by day and party all night. Increased mobility has led us to travel further afield in search of spiritual refreshment and experience, and connections with special places nearby and with their symbolic language have been broken. It is possible to become too close to one's immediate environment and a wider vision is necessary, but equally one should have firm roots in a place and value its own local qualities (Common Ground 1993; Trant 1997).

While we acknowledge that it may be easier to experience these feelings near the great sites with well-documented histories and mythologies, we believe that it is equally important in the local landscapes which are available to us all the time and which are less well visited. How many people travel miles by car to visit well-known sites without ever exploring the landscape immediate to their own homes? Surely we should seek to value the more ordinary places. By encouraging individuals to explore their environment and see other layers in it we are encouraging a sense of belonging. Some may simply react to places as a pleasant spot, others may see them as special and it may even be that *genii loci* are evoked and, over time, local sacred places with meaning for a community or group come into being. In this sense we are on common ground with environmentalists, New Age pagans and established religion (WWF 1997). Whether ground becomes 'sacred' or not it is our understanding that knowledge of one's locality and connections with its features can foster a sense of belonging and community and give context to life and inspiration for the future (Department of the Environment 1990; Morris [1884] 1996).

EXPERIENCING SPACE

Sense of place is hard to define but is much discussed and sought after, probably, in part, because of that loss of connection with the land. It includes within it local distinctiveness. Our own definitions of and feelings about sense of place underpin this paper, but they include the elements which follow. There is a dynamic created in the relationship between the physical place and our awareness of it. This has been created by a willingness to spend time reaching and being in that place, exploring it and trying to understand some of the factors which go to create it. It is also based on a sense of being open to how it feels to be there, rather than anywhere else.

Every person brings to the place their own knowledge of the archaeology, legends, history, folklore, ecology and associations with features or place names. Each one of these will affect the individual's experience of the place. For this reason it is unlikely that we could ever agree on a detailed description of the spirit of any one place with which all visitors could concur. However, there is much that may be shared based on our senses and the lie of the land. We acknowledge that each person listening will hear the stories slightly differently and will probably put their own biases onto the archaeological information and interpretation, depending on their own associations and the nature of their imaginations, background, even politics. So being in a place, and relating to it, will evoke both shared and private associations.

Pat's contribution often includes accounts of her own experiences in discovering the locality of a planned walk. These include finding out just how many churches in East Sussex claim to be the resting place of St Lewinna (only her finger bones, of course, since the rest of her bones were stolen by the unprincipled relic thief Balgerus of Flanders): the answer is currently four. Another similar case is the discovery that one of the accepted stories in guide books of the origin of the hill figure known as the Long Man of Wilmington (Figure 17.3) is the result of a summer afternoon's reverie. Arthur Beckett walked over and wrote about his beloved Sussex countryside in the early years of the twentieth century (Beckett 1909). His vision of victorious Saxons celebrating Woden with sacrifice, feasting and the cutting of the figure is a delight – but it is clearly signalled as a reverie in his writings. However, it is subsequently quoted as fact in a number of guide books (Sidgwick 1939). Including such accounts draws attention to the nature of local legend and story. There are no original versions, no possibilities of authentication. The pleasure is in the hearing and telling of the stories themselves, aware of their dubious background, enjoying wondering whether and how they belong in this land we are exploring. And then there are the truly local stories that arise from our activity – such as the occasion when Pat got lost while reconnoitring a walk near Mayfield. A man approached, so she asked for help. She proffered her map so he could point out their location. He told her he could help but not with the map as he was completely blind. He explained how his blindness had come on slowly, allowing him time to learn his much-loved walks so that he can now, with his dog, follow many different routes and even direct lost strangers.

The experience of being part of a group, in the landscape, listening to stories and to archaeological and historical information can create a sense of shared culture and community. This is a very different experience from reading a book, watching the television or engaging with virtual reality, however sophisticated the computer program. There is an undeniable presence of weather, the seasonal effects of landscape, flora, fauna and the companionship and interaction of the group. There is a special connection made between speakers and listeners by the voicing of the stories and ideas. We have found that people engage more fully as a result of this process, asking questions, contributing their own ideas and experiences and relating to one another within the group. They want to linger at the end of the walk in order to prolong that interaction. Furthermore, we hope that they will return to the places, take others with them and re-tell the stories and pass on the information.

The processes at work in our walks are very personal. They rely on our own ideas and personalities as leaders/co-ordinators, but also depend on the perceptions of the land and receptions of the stories which each individual experiences. In turn, these experiences depend very much on the individual and what they bring in terms of personal knowledge, interest, initial perceptions and their desires. Our walks are in the craft tradition. We work at the individual pieces; each is shaped using the same skills used in a different way to create something special. The finished product can enhance the life of the person to whom it passes, it can alter perceptions and create new possibilities of experience (Shanks 1992). As with a crafted artefact each individual response to it will be different.

In conclusion we extend an invitation to experience our work. We believe that we are forging connections, making journeys and exploring our place in time, space and identity. Our investigations of these connections will continue. These links are, perhaps, best expressed in the unpublished poem 'On the Bridge at Caistor' by storyteller Hugh Lupton (reproduced here by kind permission of the author).

On the Bridge at Caistor

All that a place is
Holds immanent all of its becoming.
All that a place has been
Is still within all that it is.
And I, being there, have been part of all that,
Caught and thrown
Like sun on water
Have entered into all around me.

NOTES

1   According to legend, Albion was the pre-Roman land of Britain. The idea has a pedigree from William Blake to the New Age and is used to embody an English Utopia. The term encompasses proto-communism, New Age ideology, libertarian ideas, back-to-the-land self-sufficiency, some aspects of English anarchism and anti-technological thought and action. Albion is the alternative Britain to that of industrialism, privilege and over-mighty government (McKay 1996).

2   This complaint was made many times by members of a crowd of up to 100,000 countryside dwellers who rallied in London's Hyde Park in July 1997 in support of their traditional sports and in defence of their rural way of life. This rally was called because the new government was regarded by many countryfolk as a threat to traditional practices and rights, through restrictions of gun ownership to bans on hunting and proposals to allow greater public access to private land.

REFERENCES

Abrahams, R.D. (1982) 'The language of festivals.' In V. Turner (ed.) *Celebration: Studies in Festivity and Ritual*, pp. 161–177 Washington, DC: Smithsonian Institution Press.

Beckett, A. (1909) *The Spirit of the Downs*. London: Methuen.

Bender, B. (1993) 'Stonehenge – contested landscapes (medieval to present).' In B. Bender (ed.) *Landscape, Politics and Perspectives*, pp. 1–17. Oxford: Berg.

Binks, G., Dyke, J., Dagnall, P., Morgan Evans, D. and Wainwright, G. (1988) *Visitors Welcome: A Manual on the Presentation and Interpretation of Archaeological Excavations.* London: HMSO.

Burl, A. (1979) *Prehistoric Avebury.* Newhaven and London: Yale University Press.

Chorlton, E. (1993) 'Devon is!' In S. Clifford and A. King (eds) *Local Distinctiveness*, pp. 55–63. London: Common Ground.

Clifford, S. and King, A. (1993) 'Losing your place.' In S. Clifford and A. King (eds) *Local Distinctiveness*, pp. 7–20. London: Common Ground.

Common Ground (1993) 'Rules for local distinctiveness.' In S. Clifford and A. King (eds) *Local Distinctiveness*, pp. 82–83. London: Common Ground.

Cosgrove, D. (1993) 'Landscapes and myths, gods and humans.' In B. Bender (ed.) *Landscape, Politics and Perspectives*, pp. 281–305. Oxford: Berg.

Department of the Environment (1990) *This Common Inheritance.* London: HMSO.

Greeves, T. (1992) 'Reclaiming the land: why archaeology is green.' In L. Macinnes and C.R. Wickham-Jones (eds) *All Natural Things: Archaeology and the Green Debate*, pp. 14–21. Oxbow Monograph 21. Oxford: Oxbow.

Grinsell, L.V. (1976) *Folklore of Prehistoric Sites in Britain.* Newton Abbot: David and Charles.

Hawkes, J. (1951) *A Land.* London: Cresset.

Hills, C. (1993) 'The dissemination of information.' In J. Hunter and I. Ralston (eds) *Archaeological Resource Management in the UK*, pp. 215–224. Stroud: Alan Sutton/IFA.

Kristeva, J. (1995) *New Maladies of the Soul.* New York: Columbia University Press.

McKay, G. (1996) *Senseless Acts of Beauty.* London: Verso.

Moore, T. (1994) *Care of the Soul.* London: Piatkus.

Morris, W. [1877] (1915) 'The lesser arts.' In M. Morris (ed.) *The Collected Works of William Morris, Vol. XIII*, pp. 3–27. London: Longmans, Green & Co.

Morris, W. [1884] (1996) 'Architecture and history.' In C. Miele (ed.) *William Morris on Architecture*, pp. 99–121. Sheffield: Sheffield Academic Press.

Parker Pearson, M. (1993) 'Visitors welcome?' In J. Hunter and I. Ralston (eds) *Archaeological Resource Management in the UK*, pp. 225–231. Stroud: Alan Sutton/IFA.

Pitts, M. (1992) Manifesto for a green archaeology. In L. Macinnes and C.R. Wickham-Jones (eds) *All Natural Things: Archaeology and the Green Debate*, pp. 203–213. Oxbow Monograph 21. Oxford: Oxbow.

Pratchett, T. (1993) *Lords and Ladies.* London: Corgi.

Pryor, F. (1989) ' "Look what we've found" – a case study in public archaeology.' *Antiquity* 63: 61–63.

Pryor, F. (1991) *Flag Fen, Prehistoric Fenland Centre.* London: Batsford.

Schama, S. (1995) *Landscape and Memory.* London: HarperCollins.

Shanks, M. (1992) *Experiencing the Past. On the Character of Archaeology.* London: Routledge.

Shanks, M. and Tilley, C. (1987) *Re-Constructing Archaeology.* London: Routledge.

Sidgwick, J.B. (1939) 'The mystery of the Long Man.' *Sussex County Magazine* 13: 408–420.

Simpson, J. (1973) *The Folklore of Sussex*. London: Batsford.

Tilley, C. (1994) *A Phenomenology of Landscape. Places, Paths and Monuments*. Oxford: Berg.

Trant, C. (1997) 'Art, landscape and the past.' In B.L. Molyneaux (ed.) *The Cultural Life of Images*, pp. 11–21. London: Routledge.

WWF (Worldwide Fund for Nature) (1997) 'The Sacred Land Project', press release.

INDEX